Modern Japan

Modern Japan

An Interpretive Anthology

IRWIN SCHEINER
University of California, Berkeley

MACMILLAN PUBLISHING CO., INC.
NEW YORK

Collier Macmillan Publishers
LONDON

MACMILLAN PUBLISHING CO., INC.
866 Third Avenue, New York, New York 10022

COLLIER-MACMILLAN CANADA, LTD.

Library of Congress Cataloging in Publication Data

Scheiner, Irwin, comp.
    Modern Japan.

    1. Japan—History—1868–   —Addresses, essays,
lectures. 2. Japan—Civilization—1868–
—Addresses, essays, lectures. I. Title.
DS881:9.S3   915.2'03'308   73-8582
ISBN 0-02-406770-9

Printing: 2 3 4 5 6 7 8   Year: 4 5 6 7 8 9 0

To explain to my parents and sisters

Preface

This anthology (like its companion volumes, *Modern China: An Interpretive Anthology,* by Joseph R. Levenson, and *Modern India: An Interpretive Anthology,* by Thomas R. Metcalf) has four parts. The first asks, How does one define Japan—how have the Japanese defined themselves—as a vessel of history in modern times? The next, What was the role of the past, and of Japanese feelings for the past, in establishing definitions? Third, What made the old order seem threatened, what made men feel the urgent need to threaten it? Lastly, What were the goals (and why were they goals) of the bearers of the threat? The selections that follow do not comprise a flowing narrative. They offer, instead, connecting links of interpretations of the evidence of the senses.

I. S.

Contents

PART THREE
The Sense of Urgency

PART FOUR
The Sense of the Future

PART ONE
The Sense of Identity

1

In this essay, Robert N. Bellah presents a summary view of the various theories, subtheories, and conflicting theories the Japanese have had about themselves. He takes particular notice of the contrast between Japanese particularistic and universalistic concepts derived from both the West and East. As we will see, the conflict between cultural uniqueness and universalism pervades almost every discussion of Japan's modernization.

Japan's Cultural Identity: Some Reflections on the Work of Watsuji Tetsurō

ROBERT N. BELLAH

IT has become customary among many Western scholars to consider Japan as part of an East Asian cultural area, or as a participant in Chinese or Sinic civilization. In a general conception of Asian culture viewed as consisting of East Asian, South Asian, and Middle Eastern cultural areas dominated by Chinese, Indian, and Islamic civilizations respectively, it seems obvious that Japan belongs in the first category. Yet most Japanese scholars use another classification which would divide Asian culture into four areas: Islamic, Indian, Chinese, and—as a separate category on the same level as the other three—Japanese. Without denying the close relation to China, the Japanese scholar is apt to emphasize the unique configuration of Japanese culture which makes it in some sense *sui generis*. This is only one among many manifestations of the widespread feeling in Japan that Japanese culture is "unique," and "different." This sense of Japan's uniqueness may give rise to pride, sorrow, or a feeling of loneliness; but that it is shared by Japanese with otherwise quite varying views is itself a fact of significance.

Correlative with the sense of uniqueness is a strong feeling of personal identification which Japanese feel with their culture. A Japanese abroad seldom forgets that he is Japanese, just as a foreigner in Japan is seldom allowed to forget that he is not Japanese. (The overtones of the Japanese

Robert N. Bellah, "Japan's Cultural Identity," *Journal of Asian Studies*, Vol. 4 (August 1965), pp. 573–578. Reprinted with permission of the Association for Asian Studies, Inc. Footnotes omitted.

word *"gaijin"* are scarcely captured in the translation "foreigner.") Perhaps it would even be possible to stretch the concept of role narcissism, which George DeVos has developed, to apply to the representative role of being Japanese. Such a "national narcissism" is of course found to some degree in any country. To apply the term especially to Japan is not to say that Japan is in this respect pathological, but to emphasize that Japan is, comparatively speaking, extreme.

Given the salience of Japanese self-consciousness, it follows that Japanese would be likely to show great concern about the national self-image or cultural identity. This in fact seems to be the case. Not only has there been a long and continuing concern with what is Japanese, but often studies of other societies seem more interested in placing Japan relative to them than in understanding them for their own sake. Again, the Japanese are not alone in this, but the preoccupation seems greater than elsewhere. Some effort will be made to explain this special Japanese preoccupation in the final section of this paper after illustrative material on particular Japanese self-conceptions has been presented. The main body of evidence will come from the work of Watsuji Tetsurō, one of the leading interpreters of Japanese culture in this century. But first I will turn to a brief sketch of some of the conceptions of Japan's cultural identity which have appeared in the last century.

Few Japanese in late Tokugawa times had any very sophisticated conception of the world and Japan's place in it. Hirata Atsutane (1776–1843) knew more than most about the West, but he was capable of bizarre views as to the physiological peculiarities of Westerners and seems to have believed that Japan's superiority over other nations is proved by the fact that the sun first shines on it each morning. As an example of the sort of thing which was current in early nineteenth century Japan, we may cite a passage from the influential thinker of the Mito School, Aizawa Seishisai:

> The earth in the firmament appears to be perfectly round, without edges or corners. However, everything exists in its natural bodily form, and our Divine Land is situated at the top of the earth. Thus, although it is not an extensive country spatially, it reigns over all quarters of the world, for it has never once changed its dynasty or its form of sovereignty. The various countries of the West correspond to the feet and legs of the body. That is why their ships come from afar to visit Japan. As for the land amidst the seas which the Western barbarians call America, it occupies the hindmost region of the earth; thus, its people are stupid and simple, and are incapable of doing things.

The cruder aspects of these comfortable assumptions were soon to be exploded, but the habits of thought which lay behind them were not so easily dispelled. A tacit assumption that Japan itself provides a standard for all values goes far back in Japanese history. This cannot be called nationalism as there was no concept of nation, certainly no notion of a sovereign people so indestructibly bound up with modern nationalism. If there was any structural reference at all, it was not to the nation but rather, as in the case of Aizawa, to the imperial dynasty. Shinto, on the whole lacking an explicit theological structure, gave ritual expression to the largely inarticulate union of land and people. It is true that Buddhism in the case of Shinran and Dōgen and Confucianism in the case of Ogyū Sorai produced thinkers oriented to transcendent or universalistic values for whom Japan itself had no ultimate meaning; but it was generally the fate of Buddhism and Confucianism to become subsumed in and subordinated to Japanese particularism. Since loyalty was primarily to what Nakamura Hajime speaks of as a "social nexus," however broadly or narrowly defined, and not to a set of abstract ideas, there was not, in the Japanese tradition, a strong philosophical or religious orthodoxy such as existed in China, the Islamic world, or the West.

The opening of the country in the early Meiji period gave a severe blow to Japanese cultural particularism and provided the possibility for the growth of certain tendencies counter to it. But from middle and late Meiji times Japanese particularism, never seriously menaced as an unconscious assumption, was able vigorously to reassert itself. As examples of the counter-trends, two of the most important thinkers of the Meiji period may be mentioned, Fukuzawa Yukichi (1834–1901) and Uchimura Kanzō (1861–1930). Both of them were Japanese nationalists, but neither of them was a Japanese particularist. Both of them based themselves on values which could not be derived from or reduced to the Japanese social nexus.

Fukuzawa, who seemed to embody the rather untheoretical pragmatism of Tokugawa culture, found theoretical expression for it in English individualism and utilitarianism. For him personal independence and national independence were inseparably related. But the independent nation made sense for him only as a framework for the independent individual, not subordinate to any ultimate social nexus. As a tactical measure Fukuzawa could support the suppression of political freedoms for the sake of national unity in the dangerous international climate of the late nineteenth century, for loss of national independence would destroy any hope of independence for the individual. But it was to liberal individualism that he gave his ultimate loyalty.

Uchimura was linked more to the idealistic current in Japanese tradition, to the great religious thinkers and the men of action who died happily for lost causes. He found in Christianity an absolute religious reference for his idealism. Japan would become great to the extent that it embodied the commands of Jesus. The individual, because he is ultimately a citizen of the kingdom of heaven, can never find final meaning in an earthly social nexus.

Both liberalism and Christianity were important currents in Meiji

thought, but they by no means went unchallenged. Rather, Japanese particularism found a new degree of theoretical explicitness in the thought
of what the Japanese call the "emperor system" which began to crystallize
from about 1890. The problem was raised sharply by the beginning of
constitutionalism in Japan. Western constitutionalism rests ultimately on
a natural law basis with strongly theistic presuppositions. If the Japanese
constitution was not to rest on a notion of God which was neither indigenous nor well understood, what would be the locus of ultimate authority
and value? The answer as embodied in the imperial rescript on education
and the constitution itself is: the imperial line, unbroken for ages eternal.
No clearer assertion of Japanese particularism was possible.

Though sometimes referred to as an "orthodoxy," it should be evident
that emperor-system thought was not an abstract philosophical or religious
system. It was rather an assertion about ultimate authority and value
which for many proximate purposes need not be invoked at all. A wide
variety of types of thoughts could operate under its mandate, rousing no
strong objections unless certain sensitive areas were touched upon. The
difficulty was that what was considered sensitive could not be predicted
but varied in accord with the general state of Japanese society. What
might be said with hardly a mutter of protest in 1914 could be condemned as un-Japanese and treasonable in 1935. What had changed was
not the idea expressed but the sensitivity of Japanese society, or rather of
its established guardians.

Though emperor-system thought was securely established from the
eighteen nineties, anti-particularistic tendencies were also present in Taishō
and early Shōwa times. Chief among these were liberalism and socialism.
It is true that liberalism, or at least populism, and some aspects of Marxism, could be harmonized with the emperor system and indeed did provide
strands in the "emperor-system fascism" which developed in the nineteen
thirties and early nineteen forties. But to the degree that liberals or Marxists maintained a loyalty to universalistic principles which transcended
Japan there was always the possibility of direct confrontation. The liberal
Kawai Eijirō (1891–1944) and the Marxist Kawakami Hajime (1879–
1946) provide cases where the confrontation became irreconcilable.

Having briefly outlined the development of Japanese particularism and
its counter-tendencies in modern Japan, we now turn to the conceptions of
Japanese history and culture developed in association with these various
trends. The old praise and blame historiography of largely Confucian
inspiration which took loyalty to the emperor as its highest criterion was
seriously undercut in the rush of new learning which entered early Meiji
Japan. Both Christians and liberals taught a conception of history dominated by the idea of progress in terms of which Japanese history could be
understood but which endowed it with no special meaning. While social
Darwinism could be appropriated, like almost everything else, by the

emperor system, and indeed was as a justification for imperialism (as else-where), nineteenth century positivistic history could not solve all the needs of revivified Japanese particularism.

Inoue Tetsujiro (1856–1944), author of the official commentary on the imperial rescript on education, was perhaps the closest approximation to an "official" philosopher of the emperor system. Inoue, whose chief claim to scholarly standing rested on surveys of Tokugawa Confucianism, ran-sacked the Japanese tradition for suitable materials. He came to focus on three concepts which became the heart of Japanese ethics as taught by the Ministry of Education: *kokutai, chū,* and *kō. Kokutai* is the almost un-translatable terms for the quintessence of Japanese particularity; *chū* and *kō* are loyalty and filial piety. Inoue and others like him asserted the ulti-mate value of the harmony of Japanese emperor and people (*kokutai*) and the obligations to emperor and ancestors which flow from it (*chū* and *kō*).

But even as Inoue was arguing with the liberals and Christians, other sensitive and educated Japanese were finding commitment to simple minded "national ethics" or to doctrinaire Western ideologies unaccept-able. The writer Natsume Sōseki (1867–1916) and the philosopher Nishida Kitaro (1870–1945) were representative of this latter group. Feeling a deep nostalgia for Japanese culture and values, yet unable to turn away from the intellectual achievements of the West, they hoped for a reconciling position to which they could devote themselves. It was Nishida, more than anyone else, who, with the help of Zen Buddhism and German idealism, contributed to the formation of the new position which strongly influenced all Japanese literature, thought and culture from the period of the First World War.

The new basis which Nishida found rested on aesthetic experience and mystical insight, neatly skirting the issue of ultimate value and authority, for the personal experience which he valued so highly had no immediate relevance to social and ethical reality. Nonetheless from his positions there were certain social implications. Though never engaging in vulgar na-tionalistic propaganda, he nonetheless spoke of the individual and the whole mutually negating themselves with the imperial household as the center. Absolute negativity which was so central to his philosophy pro-vided in actuality no alternative to the human nexus as a locus of author-ity and value. It is not surprising then that though Nishida himself withdrew into obscure privacy as the Second World War approached, some of his leading disciples were ardent, though sophisticated, propa-gandists for Greater East Asia.

Finally, before turning to Watsuji, we must mention several cultural historians who took positions in varying degrees outside the established view and who produced conceptions of Japanese culture quite different from that of the Nishida school. Tsuda Sōkichi, a great scholar of China

as well as of Japan, represents the liberal and pragmatic position applied
to the history of Japanese culture. For example, he interpreted the Taika
Reform in terms of power politics rather than lofty ethical idealism, and
he viewed Bushidō as a cover for the essentially self-interested land-grab-
bing of the feudal warriors. In a book published in 1939 and suppressed
during the war Tsuda argued that Japan is essentially modern and has
little in common with "oriental" culture as found in China. He held that
the old Japanese pattern of an emperor who reigns but does not rule is
appropriate in modern society. In all these respects Tsuda's work tended
to explain Japanese cultural history with the categories of liberal utilitarian
social thought leaving little basis for a mystical Japanese particularism.

Hani Gorō is one of the best known of the Marxist writers who from
the late nineteen twenties began to give their version of Japanese cultural
history. Hani interpreted certain Tokugawa thinkers such as Arai Hakuseki
and especially the Kokugaku movement as representing middle class
thought in opposition to feudal thinking. The Marxists interpreted Japanese culture in terms of general categories rather than particularism.

Still another anti-particularist interpretation was that of Ienaga Saburo
who, in his pre-war writing, developed a view of Japanese culture which
might be seen as consonant with the position of Uchimura Kanzō. In
Ienega's view the greatness of Japanese thought rests in those few men
who were able to transcend Japanese particularity and attain to universal
value, especially Shōtoku Taishi (in his rather special interpretation of
him), Shinran and in the modern period Uchimura.

It should be remembered that these men, who were either persecuted
or led very retired lives during the war, were representative of a small
minority. Most writing during the nineteen thirties and early nineteen
forties dealt with the Japanese spirit in mystical and absolute terms, based
either on fairly straightforward translations of classical Confucian and
Shinto texts or utilizing more or less elaborate theoretical structures like
those of the Nishida school. A few, of whom Muraoka Tsunetsugu is
perhaps the outstanding example, were neither particularist nor anti-particularist, but devoted themselves to the highest standards of scholarly
research.

2   *In this short paper the young Japanese historian Seizaburō Sato explores the changing images Japanese have had of the world since the Tokugawa period. Sato skillfully shows how the Japanese developed a national identity that would allow them to face both the cultural tyranny of China and the technological might of the West.*

Japan's World Order

SEIZABURŌ SATO

I

JAPAN's image of the world is greatly different from that characteristic of China and different as well from views held in the West. It has profoundly affected Japan's approach to modernization. Japan's view of the world has developed and changed throughout the course of history. The Restoration period, however, was a critical turning point. Tokugawa bureaucrat-intellectuals had developed their own complex of ideas about the outside world. Under pressure of Western encroachments these changed and a new framework was moulded, certain common elements of which span the Restoration period and continue in some form up to the present.

The main purpose of this paper is to analyze the basic framework through which Japanese perceived international relations in this critical Restoration period. A very rough examination of the historical background will be done in section 2. Before discussing the subject I would like to make some reservations. First very few materials are available on the opinions and attitudes of the mass of people who were politically and intellectually inarticulate at that time. Therefore when I speak of "Japanese" views, I mean only the views of the educated few.

Secondly even among the relatively small group of the vocal people there existed a vast variation. Especially in the time of change and confusion such as the Meiji Restoration, you can point out some contrary phenomena in almost any general propositions about the society in question. All I can do is to indicate the modal points in a very crude way. Thirdly I feel rather hesitant to use the phrase "Japan's World Order."

Seizaburō Sato, "Japan's World Order." Reprinted with permission of the author. Footnotes omitted.

As discussed later, in marked contrast with traditional China, in Japan there existed no clear, consistent, stable and self-contained image of the World. In this sense there was no "Japan's World Order." It seems to me that one can at best find out several frames to which the Japanese referred most frequently when they tried to understand the outside world.

II

Tokugawa Japan was by no means a subordinate tributary country to the Chinese Empire, though China still regarded her as one of the "barbarian states on the eastern periphery." In this sense Japan did not accept the Chinese world order, which was based on her long-standing superior position in East Asia and on the Confucian cosmology. At the same time, however, after Hideyoshi's unsuccessful attempt to conquer the whole known world (1592–98), Tokugawa Japan never challeneged the Chinese order. Japan did not try to invade the Chinese Empire, nor build up another empire. No countries brought tribute to Japan, except the Ryukyu Kingdom to Satsuma, and no congratulatory missions were sent to Edo, except from Ryukyu and Korea.

It is true that the Ryukyu island kingdom was a vassal state of Satsuma-*han* in Kyushu. Satsuma, however, never claimed its cultural superiority over the Ryukyus. The Satsuma daimyō actually encouraged the Ryukyus to continue their tributary relationship with China because of the economic benefits which accrued. Korea did send missions to Japan to congratulate each new shogun on assuming his title. But these envoys were treated as "national guests," not tribute bearers.

Moreover, because of the seclusion policy which the Tokugawa government enforced since the early seventeenth century, Tokugawa Japan had small experience in interstate relationships. Japan's relations with her closest neighbor, Korea, amounted to no more than an occasional greeting. With China there was no official contacts. Her contact with the Dutch in Nagasaki was rigidly restricted. The foreign trade (with Holland, China and Korea) had been gradually declining to a very low level by the end of the eighteenth century.

Despite the lack of direct intercourse with foreigners, Tokugawa samurai bureaucrat-intellectuals had developed a strong sense of national "cohesion and distinctiveness." While Japan was divided into many semi-feudal fiefs, by the mid-Tokugawa period the sophisticated Shogunate rule had welded the already homogeneous Japanese into much more of a "nation." A Dutchman who visited Japan in the 1820's remarked that many Japanese said emphatically and proudly to him "I am a Japanese!"

The other side of this emerging national consciousness was a deeper realization that Japan was small and backward, and that she had been indebted to China for much of her culture. Thus a sense of national consciousness was accompanied by a sense of national inferiority. In the early wake of "nationalistic" sentiment stirred by the Mongol invasions in the thirteenth century, the Buddhist prophet Nichiren called Japan "a small group of islands scattered like millet seeds far away from the center of civilization." Many Tokugawa intellectuals shared this point of view.

This sense of inferiority was further sharpened by the Sino-centric connotations of Confucian ideas which became orthodox during the Tokugawa period. Yamaga Sokō (1622–85), a famous Confucian scholar, said, "When I was young I believed that little Japan was inferior to China in every respect. Therefore I never did study Japanese books, but Chinese books instead." Ogyū Sorai (1666–1728), another leading figure in the Confucian scholarship, considered that the stability of Tokugawa rule was itself a result of Japanese "backwardness." "Japan is small and uncivilized; that is why it is so easy to govern," he said. There existed a great gap between natural or emotional identification with Japan and intellectual estimates of the country.

This gap naturally produced uneasiness, discomfort and an "identity crisis." Tokugawa intellectuals tried to resolve this tension in various ways. Some, like the young Sokō identified themselves at least intellectually with the Chinese. More people tended to suppress their consciousness of inferiority. Many scholars sought to transform the notion of the "Middle Kingdom" into a state of mind or state of soul, by removing it away from the Chinese way of life and the geographic Chinese Empire. Thus the notion of the "Middle Kingdom" became more abstract and transcendental in Japan than in China. As Dazai Shundai (1680–1747) said, "Chinese who don't observe moral principles are no better than barbarians; men in peripheral countries who do observe moral principles belong to the Middle Kingdom." If the "Middle Kingdom" meant the achievement of moral excellence, even Westerners as well as Japanese could aspire to it, Yokoi Shōnan (1809–69) came to feel.

Such a "functional" approach could be more aggressive. Nationalistic Confucian scholars such as Yamazaki Ansai and those associated with the Mito School argued that the true Confucian virtues were already lost in China (it was dominated by the "barbarian" Ch'ing dynasty); these virtues were best preserved in Japan. It was not China but Japan, they continued, that should be called as the "Middle Kingdom." Anti-Confucian Kokugaku scholars (Nationalist School) carried this idea of Japanese moral superiority even further. They believed that since the Japanese emperor was descended from the Sun Goddess, Japan was not only the Divine Land (Shinkoku) but the Father County (oyaguni) of all the nations on earth.

Those who said that Japan was superior to other nations, however, had many difficult questions to answer: How could Japan be the "Middle Kingdom" or the Father Country when it clearly was so small? Why had

Japan not given birth to a great cultural tradition like Confucianism or Buddhism? The answer of Aizawa Yasushi (1782–1863), a leading figure of the Mito school, to the first question was that "Japan is the head of the world community. Therefore it is smaller than the other countries which comprise the body." To the second question Okuni Takamasa (1792–1871), an eminent Kokugaku scholar, answered that "Confucianism, Buddhism, and western learning all originated in Japan, but emanated away from Japan in antiquity." Only true believers could be convinced by such far-fetched arguments.

To sum up: Tokugawa Japan's attitude towards China was ambiguous. It did not accept the Chinese world order, but could neither challenge or ignore it. A clear feeling of national cohesion and distinctiveness was already widely shared when Japan was still culturally dependent on China. Tokugawa intellectuals could never successfully resolve the tension between their emotional identification with Japan and their consciousness of Japan's backwardness and cultural debts. Thus a consistent, stable, and coherent image of the world order could not be developed.

III

When Western expansion in East Asia intensified in the early nineteenth century, samurai bureaucrat-intellectuals were highly sensitive to the new development in East Asia. The lack of a self-contained image of the world, a strong sense of national consciousness, a deep-rooted feeling of inferiority, all made Japanese extremely uneasy about Western expansion.

In addition, by the mid-nineteenth century Japanese were relatively well informed about the West. From the mid-eighteenth century more and more people became interested in advanced Western science and technology. In the early nineteenth century there were more than one hundred so called "Dutch Scholars" in Japan. Considering the strictly limited cultural exchange with the West, this number is fairly impressive. Many of those interested in the Western technology might be motivated primarily by curiosity and exoticism. But the threat of the Western Powers turned many bureaucrat-intellectuals to the serious study of recent developments in the West. When Commodore Perry arrived in Japan, he was astonished at Japanese knowledge about the West. His report observed, "The higher classes of the Japanese with whom the Americans were brought into communication were not only thoroughly acquainted with their own country, but knew something of the geography, the material progress, and contemporary history of the rest of the world. Questions were frequently asked by the Japanese which proved [sic] an information that, considering their isolated situation, was quite remarkable. . . . . Thus they were enabled to speak somewhat knowingly about our railroads, telegraphs, daguerreotypes, Paixhan guns, and steam-ships, none of which had they ever seen before Commodore Perry's visit. Thus, too they could converse intelligently about the European War, about the American revolution, Washington, and Buonaparte."

The intellectual framework that the Japanese used to explain and deal with the Western encroachment had four main aspects: (a) parallels with the Japanese and Chinese "Warring States" periods; (b) a utopian belief that eventually a "great unity" would emerge; (c) a belief in a hierarchy of nations; and (d) a belief in a confrontation between East and West.

Several reservations are again necessary. First these ideas were naturally given different weight and emphasis by individual thinkers. Second there existed not a few other ideas which played some roles in the Japanese perception of the Western expansion. The ideas pointed out above were nothing but the four most frequently referred to. Third these beliefs are not necessarily consistent. As in the previous period, the Japanese image of the world in the Restoration period contained contrary elements. Fourth a wide range of attitudes and policies could emerge from a similar idea. From a belief in East-West confrontation, one could either identify oneself with the West or become an ardent advocate of Asianism.

(A) PARALLELS WITH THE "WARRING STATES" PERIOD:

The Japanese had no experience in competitive international relations among sovereign states, when they were confronted with the new situation in which the Western Powers were carrying on strenuous competition with each other for global expansion. The only analogous situation they knew was the Warring States Period in ancient China and pre-Tokugawa Japan. Despite the two hundred years' peace, Confucian indoctrination and their highly bureaucratized way of life, the samurai rulers still maintained their military orientation. The military presence of the West, added to the proclivity of the samurai intellectuals to view interstate and inter-personal relations in military terms, made the analogy with the "Warring States" seem very convincing to them.

From this analogy they drew the conclusion that all foreign countries were potential enemies. Iwakura Tomomi, one of the central figures in the new Meiji government, said "All foreign countries are our national enemies (kōteki) because each of them is trying to surpass and overcome the others. While we should observe etiquette, we should never forget that they are enemies."

The Japanese thus, unlike the Chinese, saw the Western intruders not as barbarians to be despised, but as enemies on the same moral plane. Their first attitude toward the Westerners was strong hostility, not ar-rogant contempt. As in a battle-field the valor of brave soldiers command the admiration of their friends and enemies, the brave Westerners won the respect of the Japanese samurai. Kawaji Toshiakira, who negotiated with Admiral Putiatin in the 1850's said of the Russian "Putiatin is a

real hero (gōketsu) and devoted to his lord and country. When I compare myself with him, I feel ashamed."

To the extent that the Western countries were regarded as military
enemies, the cultural and racial prejudices against them were thrown
away. This "soldier's candidness," combined with the traditional weakness
of ethnocentrism, made the Japanese attitude toward the West fairly
open-minded. Official Tokugawa documents, again unlike the Chinese,
never refer to foreigners as "iteki" (barbarians), but rather as "ikoku"
(foreign countries) or "seiyō shokoku" (Western countries).

The "Warring States" image of international relations implies that the
strong will prosper and the weak will perish. And it seemed only too
clear that the Western Powers were more powerful than Japan. Thus
the situation was critical. This deep sense of crisis aroused an ardent
passion for national defense. The Sonnō Jōi (Honor the Emperor, expel
the barbarians) movement was one political expression of this passion.

To be a victor of the war, one should have an accurate understanding
of the situation and should be well prepared. Hence the Japanese were on
the one hand very eager to get information on the latest developments in
the world as discussed earlier, on the other hand they were quite cautious
not to enter a hopeless war. In 1825 the Tokugawa government issued
an order that Western ships in Japanese waters should be repelled. But in
1842 when they heard of China's fate in the Opium War they revoked the
order and enjoined their agents not to provoke the Westerners. Even the
Sonnō Jōi fanatics changed their former stand when they understood the
military supremacy of the Western Powers.

(B) UTOPIAN PROSPECT FOR A UNIFIED WORLD:

The Japanese thought that highly competitive international relations
were too unstable to continue for long. The historical parallel with the
Warring States periods also implied that eventually one of the con-
tenders for power would vanquish his rivals and attain the unification
of the world as had Ch'in Shih Huang Ti in China and Tokugawa
Ieyasu in Japan. Viewed from this perspective, the Western expansion
into Asia was nothing but one phase of the long process of world-wide
unification. This rather "eschatological" prospect for the future of the
world is already found in Satō Nobuhiro's "Strategy for the conquest of
the world" (Udai Kondō Hisaku) which was written in 1823. Closely
connected with the image of the "Warring States," and supported by the
traditional ethnocentric ideas such as "the Father Land" of the world,
such future prospects became widely held by the mid-nineteenth century.

If Japan did not come out on top, she would, according to this reasoning, be subjected to a lowly position for an indefinite period. Japan's poor
prospects made some deeply pessimistic. "Russia and Britain are the two

most powerful countries," observed Hashimoto Sanai in 1857. "Either one will rule the world. Japan cannot compete with them. Therefore our best strategy is to ally with the most likely winner." His choice was Russia.

Some, however, thought Japan's chances were not so bad. After all, Tokugawa Ieyasu had risen from lordship over a tiny han to become ruler of all Japan. In the same year as Hashimoto had despaired of Japan's hopes, Hotta Masatoshi, a chief Tokugawa councillor, said "We should conduct trade throughout the world and adopt every merit of other countries. Then Japan will become wealthier and stronger and Japan's prestige will increase. Then Japan should become the leader of the right-thinking countries, helping the poor countries and conquering the vicious countries. Through this process the world will be unified under Japan's hegemony and justice and peace will prevail forever." Such a dream was, of course, an inverted expression of a deep-rooted sense of inferiority. But it was such a utopian (or "eschatological") dream that spurred Japanese into the revolutionary effort to build the Japanese Empire.

(c) SENSE OF HIERARCHY:

The image of international relations are often constructed after the predominant pattern of interpersonal relations in society. Tokugawa society was a rigidly regimented "vertical society." Here interpersonal relations were almost always viewed hierarchically, in terms of "high" and "low." This image of hierarchical relations was naturally applied to the international scene. Military power and national wealth were the most popular criteria for rank on the international ladder. We can easily find a clear sense of hierarchy measured by these criteria both in the image of "the Warring States" and in a utopian dream of the future world. The slogan "Wealthy Nation; Strong Military" which was adopted by the Meiji Government and became the national goal showed how predominant these criteria were. When many Japanese admitted the general supremacy of Western civilization, the level of Westernization was also adopted as a standard for rank in the world hierarchy. Fukuzawa Yukichi graded each country into three ranks: civilized countries, half-civilized countries, and uncivilized countries, in which Japan came out in the middle.

By any of the above-mentioned criteria Japan's grade could not be so high. Japanese were extremely sensitive about their relatively low position. Their desire to redress Japan's position on the world ladder was a major spur to Japan's modernization.

What value could so-called "Eastern morality" have if international ranks were determined on the basis of westernization? Obviously only Eastern nations can possess Eastern morality. And once this was adopted as a criterion, the image of the world hierarchy turned into the image of confrontation between East and West.

All of the above discussed factors—historical parallels, a coming utopia, a sense of hierarchy—were not directly connected with differences between East and West.

But just as Tokugawa intellectuals were ambivalent towards China, so leaders of the Restoration period were ambivalent towards the West. Their determined effort to introduce the achievements of Western civilization was primarily motivated by their ardent desire to beat the Western Powers at their own game. Like their Tokugawa counterparts they felt a tremendous tension between their national pride and their sense of debt. In some ways the tension was much greater because Westerners, unlike the Chinese, were racially different. Further, unlike Ch'ing China, the Westerners posed a military threat to Japan. Neither total acceptance nor total rejection of the West was possible.

Combining the good points of both East and West seemed like the obvious solution. "Tōyō no dōtoku, seiyō no gijutsu" (Eastern morality, Western technology) and "Wakon yōsai" (Japanese spirit, Western expertise) symbolized this syncretic attitude. But was this synthesis? Could Eastern morality and Western technology be fused? No clear answer was given.

Furthermore, the arrogance of the Westerners deeply injured Japanese pride, which was already tender enough. They justified the Western invasion into Asia as a crusade by the civilized West against the uncivilized East. "Westerners who think highly of the Japanese think we are some kind of human being next to the monkey; those who think ill of us think we are some kind of monkey next to human beings," wrote Tokutomi Sohō.

All of these factors confirmed the image of the East-West confrontation and bred various kinds of Asianism: from the alliance with China to the liberation and unification of Asian countries under Japan's leadership.

Despite tremendous changes since the Restoration period, these ways of thought have more or less persisted, until World War II, and even to the present. In the 1930's Ishiwara Kanji anticipated that the final round of the struggle for world hegemony would soon be fought between the United States and Japan. The cold war conflict has often been regarded as the last confrontation before the emergence of a unified world.

After the Meiji Restoration, Japan climbed to the upper ranks of the international hierarchy only to plummit to the bottom. Since the war she has started over again to climb the new international hierarchy in which ranks are established by economic power measured by Gross National Product, and Japan has reached the number three position. Today the Japanese are, it seems to me, the most GNP conscious people in the world.

Until World War II, Japan oscillated between East and West, between

Asianism and westernization. When, after the war, the "East" came to mean the communist camp, Japan chose the West. Nevertheless Japan's attitude towards communist China is greatly different from her attitude towards communist Russia. The China problem is not simply a transitory political issue but a deeply moral and emotional one to the Japanese people.

Thus the basic elements of the framework through which Japanese perceived international relations in the Restoration period have persisted in various forms. To analyze their forms and functions even in brief, however, is beyond the scope of this paper.

3   *In this selection from his pre-war study of a Japanese village,
the anthropologist John Embree takes us through the rituals
surrounding the life of a typical villager. We see that every
villager became aware of himself and his place in society by a
constant cycle of rites, and that through these rites he learned
who he was and what roles he must play within his society.*

FROM

Suye Mura: A Japanese Village

JOHN F. EMBREE

THE LIFE-HISTORY OF THE INDIVIDUAL

I N the life of each individual in Suye there is a series of important events
marking his various changes of status in the community. After birth,
the chief events of a man's life are entering school, entering the barracks, entering married life, becoming a house head, reaching old age, and
dying. For a woman the list varies somewhat from this: she does not go
to the barracks nor does she usually become a house head, and she has
one experience not shared by her husband, that of giving birth to a child.
Practically all these events call for a gathering of the *buraku* and also of
the relatives to drink and to celebrate, thus recognizing the individual's
change of status in his *buraku* and in his kin group. The parties follow
the pattern already outlined, and the different occasions call for various
types of gift exchange as described below.

BIRTH

When delivery is easy,
Childbearing is easy too.
—*Rokuchōshi hayashi*

Two things are always done as secretly as possible in Suye—sexual
intercourse and its consequence, child delivery. Sexual intercourse, leading
as it usually does to conception, is called "making a baby" (*kodomo
tsukuru*). Childbirth being so secret, a woman never cries out, for, if she
did, the neighbors would know what she was doing, and she would be
ashamed.

Births follow one another pretty regularly. Farmers have heard of birth control but do not know how to obtain it or are afraid of the police. It is believed in the *mura* that schoolteachers use birth control, proof of which might be the fact that most of them have few or no children. However, one amusing incident occurred in the *mura* when a girl who had gone away to work in a factory sent home to her mother a condom, telling her to give it to father. This incident caused considerable laughter and broad humor among the neighbors.

There is practically no infanticide in the *mura*. The only known case in recent years occurred in a family, both poor and nonnative, in which the mother was regarded by the villagers as insane.

A baby boy just born is often called *taiho* (cannon) or *rikugun* (army); a baby girl *gunkan* (warship) or *kaigun* (navy). These terms are used among friends in a jocular sense.

Soon after the neighbors have heard that a woman has had a baby, they call on her with a gift of *ame* candy, which is considered to be good for her. There are no real food taboos after childbirth, but certain foods are recommended such as soft rice, *tai* fish, *iwashi* fish, tuna fish, soups, and a few vegetables, while others such as pumpkin, meat, certain kinds of fish, and sweets except *ame* are avoided. The reasons given for these preferences and avoidances are that they are good or bad for the health of the new mother.

For two or three days after birth the child eats nothing. On the third day the midwife, a few relatives, and close friends are invited to a naming ceremony (*kamitate* or *natsuke*). Among those invited is usually the man who was go-between for the wedding of the baby's parents. The midwife usually arrives first and bathes the baby. When most of the guests have arrived and had tea in the *daidokoro,* they are invited into the *zashiki* where the midwife is seated in the place of honor next the *tokonoma*. A tray of food, chiefly fish soups, and a tray of formal congratulatory cake are served. The cake has been purchased from the local cakemaker if the family is poor, from a caterer in a near-by town if more well to do. It is made of dry rice flour pressed into shapes of *tai* fish, pine, plum, and bushy-tailed tortoise, the traditional Japanese symbols of good fortune and long life, and into the shape of Momotaro coming out of a peach. The peach is a female sex symbol in Japan, and Momotaro is a legendary hero in a famous Japanese fairy tale where he brings wealth and happiness to his foster-parents. A *shōchū* cup is on each person's tray, and he is expected to begin drinking immediately. The father exchanges drinks with the midwife, then with other guests.

When everyone is served, the selection of the name is performed. Sometimes the father selects a name. The customary way, however, is for all present to suggest names and write them on paper. These papers are rolled up into small wads and put in a paper basket made from a square piece of writing paper. Then the midwife takes a Buddhist rosary from the *butsudan* and dips the tassel in *omiki* that has been offered at the *tokonoma*, then into the paper basket. After a few attempts one of the wads clings to the tassel. It is opened, and the name on it read by the midwife. The name is discussed, and, if everyone seems to approve, it is accepted; but if for some reason it is not liked, the midwife may try for another. Even so, if the father has his heart set on some name, he is likely to insist on it regardless of wads and rosaries.

To such a naming party, as with almost every ceremony and party except weddings and funerals, only one person from each house invited is expected to come—either the head or his wife, son or daughter, but not a servant.

The exchanges of goods at a birth are: (1) a relative or close friend sends some materials for baby *kimono* and, if he attends the naming-ceremony, brings rice and *shōchū;* (2) the guests receive feast food and *shōchū* in return.

The midwife, having given her services for which she is paid, does not send any *kimono* material but does bring rice and *shōchū* in exchange for the feast food. The parents feel themselves under an obligation to the midwife, and it is considered proper, although not always done, to call on her a month later, at *hiaki* (see below) with *sekihan* (festive rice mixed with red beans).

This naming ceremony and party is the first introduction of a child into society. The local group now recognizes the child as a new member, with a name and a real, if limited, personality. This celebration is the first party of one's life and one of the lesser ones. As with subsequent **rites de passage** it is not the individual concerned who counts but the event. The parents gain status through adding another member of their family to the community, the community takes the opportunity to welcome a new individual into their society and, incidentally, to get together for good fellowship cemented by plenty to drink and by indulging in the old familiar folk songs and folk dances.

The birth of a child is a much more certain sign of a permanent marriage than is a wedding ceremony. Indeed, a marriage is often not put in the village office records until after a child is on its way. The birth of a child also gives the new wife a definite standing among her new neighbors. She is now truly a married woman and may indulge in the privileges of smoking, drinking, and sexual jokes. An unmarried woman may laugh at a broad joke, but it is unseemly for her to make one herself.

A few days after the naming ceremony the father goes to the village office and records the birth of the child, giving sex, name, and parents' names. If the child is a bastard, the birth is recorded, but there is no naming party. The child in this case takes the family name of the mother and is brought up in her house.

At thirty-one days if a boy, thirty-three if a girl, a child is taken to visit the shrine of the village patron god (*ujigami*). On this day the mother with the child and often one or two other female relatives, such as an aunt, dress in their finest and also dress the child in his best silk. At the shrine a candle is lit, the mother claps her hands for the god's attention, and a copper and some *shōchū* are offered. The child, by this ceremony, is introduced to the deity whose good will allowed him to be born and to survive his first thirty-odd most dangerous days. Then the party walks back home. If not taken to the *ujigami*, the child is taken to some local *buraku* Shinto shrine and is also sometimes taken to the Kwannon *dō*. Kwannon is regarded as a deity of mothers and so is often prayed to for children or to make child delivery easy. Sometimes a man on his way to call the midwife will stop at a Kwannon *dō* to light a candle. The mother sometimes takes the child to her native home to visit the *ujigami* there. *Sekihan* is cooked to be distributed to all those who came to the naming ceremony and who gave gifts. This is often replaced by some wheat or rice cakes (*dango*) and completes the reciprocal obligations incurred by the family at the time of the child's birth.

This day and event are called *hiaki*. Before this time the child has not been carried across rivers or on the back, and the mother, theoretically, has had no sexual intercourse with her husband. During the first thirty days or so of a child's life his soul is not very well fixed in his body—it is a period of danger and uncertainty. *Hiaki*, therefore, represents the end of the birth period and is, significantly, the same term as that used for the end of the forty-nine-day period of mourning for the dead.

The child has now passed another stage. From now on he may be carried on the back and may cross water safely, for he is now recognized by the gods as well as by the people of his world.

The child is nursed for several years by the mother, or until the next child is born. Many people can remember when they suckled their mothers. Then comes a critical period of weaning at which stage children frequently die. If a mother's milk goes dry and a child must be weaned early, he is fed on rice water, i.e., water in which raw rice has been cooked.

EDUCATION AND SCHOOL

During the first year a child is the favored one in the family. At any time he may drink milk from his mother's breast, and whatever he cries for will be given to him. He is cuddled and fondled and rocked to sleep. He learns by imitation as his mother repeats unendingly baby talk for this and that.

But almost inevitably his mother bears another baby, and the child faces his first hard knocks. While the mother devotes her attention to the newcomer, the child is turned over to an older sibling or nursemaid who carries him about on her back or sits him down somewhere to play. When he cries, he may not be listened to, for his mother no longer gives him first attention. This rapid weaning from milk and maternal attention results in several weeks of temper tantrums. Occasionally, the tantrums are effective, especially if they last long enough, but eventually the child readjusts himself; he gets acquainted with other children also put out to play, and he is soon a member of a new age group of the two- and three-year-olds of the neighborhood. He learns to get along with his contemporaries.

Even in these early years a boy receives a few special educational influences different from those of his sister. On a walk to some shrine festival the mother may tell the sister to walk behind because she is the lady and he the gentleman. And, if a first son, the boy will always have preferred treatment over his younger brothers.

He learns about sex early because older children frequently engage in sex play, his mother often draws attention to his genitals when playing with him, and he sleeps in the same room as his parents.

In general, children are very much spoiled. They can and do strike their mothers in a rage and call them the favorite Japanese epithet of *baka!* (fool). Anything a child asks for or cries for long enough he gets. He learns the ways of society not through discipline but through example and instruction patiently and endlessly repeated by his mother. The father, softhearted to the younger children, becomes more strict as they grow older. As a child grows older and finds other people not so inclined to do his bidding, he develops a strong sentimental love for his mother.

At full six years the child goes with all the other little six-year-olds and their fathers or mothers in April to the village shrine of Suwa-san. Here, with teachers and other older school children, a short Shinto ritual is performed. The priest gives the young a little talk on the virtues and greatness of Japan, the Emperor, and the gods and then hands to each of the neophytes a copy of the first-year book of ethics published by the department of education. This is a child's first introduction to a world beyond his *buraku* and *mura*. After the shrine service he attends school for the first time as a student, dressed up in a new black uniform and cap. (He has been here often before with his mother when she came to some meeting or party held in the school auditorium, or with his nurse to play in the schoolyard.) The trip to the shrine did not mean much to him, but it was significant of the close association of official Shinto and the public-school system.

At school he meets for the first time children from all over the village. His constant association with them for the next six years in an important one both for him and for the unity of the village. The ties of men who were classmates in school are very close.

The school building, a long one- or two-storied wooden structure, is partly paid for by village taxes, partly by prefectural and central government funds. As there are no heating facilities, children shiver and sniffle their way through the winter months. There is a confirmed belief that cold and discomfort are good for learning and mental discipline. If any child complains of the cold, the teacher tells him to think of the brave soldiers in Manchukuo, where it is *really* cold. Every day after school hours pupils clean up the yard with straw brooms, while girls get on their hands and knees to wipe up the floors. A school servant exists but chiefly for the purpose of running errands and making tea for the teachers to drink between classes.

Every morning now the child gets up about five and washes; he need not dress as he probably slept in his school uniform. After bowing to the household gods, he has a breakfast of bean soup and rice and runs out of the house and off to school. If he lives far from school, this trip by foot may be as long as two or three miles; if close by, it may be only a few yards. On the way he plays games, chiefly a kind of cops and robbers. These games are played with boys and girls alike amid shouts and shrieks as someone is captured. On entering the school grounds, he bows toward the closet in the main auditorium where the Emperor's portrait is housed. (More well-to-do schools have a special concrete house costing a thousand yen or more to house the sacred photograph.)

At school shortly before eight all the children from first grade to sixth line up in the schoolyard for radio exercises. From 7:50 to 8:00 the entire youth of the nation under the leadership of hundreds of teachers goes through the same daily dozen to the shrill directions of the same government radio announcer.

After this, the school children break ranks and file into their various classrooms. Here the boys or girls find their places, small fixed cramped wooden benches and desks, each sex on a different side of the room. The teacher in black uniform comes in—all children rise and bow to him, receiving a slight bow in return—and class begins, with singing perhaps. Many of the songs are simple little nursery rhymes about birds and insects, but the first one the children learn describes the "beautiful national flag with the red sun on it" and the next one is called "The Soldier" ("With the gun over his shoulder the soldier marches, to the sound of the bugle he marches; the beautiful soldier, I love the soldier"). Then they learn to read and write. In their first-year reader they again read of the soldier and the flag.

The older children are expected to help the newcomers find their way around school. From now on for six years the child goes to school from April to July and from August to April again. School is from nine to twelve noon for first-year children, eight-thirty to three-thirty after that. Most of the time is taken up with singing, reading, and athletics—all three with a leaven of nationalism. No attempt is made to teach children to think critically either in primary school or in high school. The schoolmaster of the primary school sets as his aim the rules for primary-school education of the department of education in Tokyo, the schoolmaster of the middle school sets as his aim the rules of middle-school education of the department of education, and so also for the agricultural school, girls' high school, etc. The schoolmasters vary from the sacred word of the department only on the side of greater nationalism. In the agricultural school in Menda, for instance, boys are given many lectures on Japanese spirit, and second sons are encouraged to emigrate to Manchukuo.

The great difficulty of learning two or three thousand characters in the first six years, in addition to two sets of fifty-syllable characters, gives but little chance for a student to do much original composition. Geography, arithmetic, and drawing are taught. The drawing is European style, but in arithmetic emphasis is on the use of the *soroban* (abacus)—so much so that many a man can scarcely add two and three without the aid of this device. In Suye boys and girls are also given some practical lessons in farming on a few *chō* of paddy and upland fields belonging to the school.

In higher grades some geography, history, and general science find their way into the curriculum, but the major part of the child's time is still taken up with reading and writing, singing, and ethics. The reading lessons are performed by the deafening method of the whole class reading aloud at once.

In rural schools practically all children are promoted every year, the emphasis in teaching being more moral than intellectual. Teachers feel that, if they left some child behind his class, he would feel very badly about it and that the resulting psychological effect and family chagrin would not be compensated for by any good the child might receive mentally by repeating a school grade. Similarly, at school athletic contests all entrants, not only first, second, and third, receive prizes. By giving prizes thus generously, no one feels unduly slighted. While occasionally people are shown the virtues of initiative and leadership, they are more often shown the virtues of co-operation, and the good but mediocre child is held out to be superior to the bad but brilliant one.

Unquestioning acceptance of everything the teacher says at school is the rule. Occasionally, this causes trouble at home when the father says something to the boy and he replies that the teacher did not say so. The more a child is educated, the wider becomes the gap between the old people's folkways and the young people's ideas. By the time they reach university the gap is too wide to bridge, hence college graduates from villages almost never return to their homes.

To solve this and other behavior problems that arise, there is an annual parents' day on which old people, many of whom went to no school at all or to only a four-year elementary course, come to the school, see classes in action, and later have discussions with the teachers. With a touching faith in the rightness of their children's teachers, the parents discuss their parental troubles.

At frequent intervals during the school year there are other special days. Some are national holidays, such as the Emperor Meiji's death day, when there is a general assembly with a solemn reading of the Imperial rescript on education while all present bow their heads, followed by an uplifting lecture by the schoolmaster and by the singing of the national anthem. On other occasions the students have more fun; for instance, at the annual athletic meet, for which they train for weeks ahead. This is attended by practically everyone in the village, the families coming with lunch baskets to stay all day. People of a *buraku* sit together. Another big day is the old students' day, when the graduates come to watch the present students perform skits and dances.

After six years a boy or girl has learned enough to read simple things. He has also imbibed a good deal of nationalism and martial Japanese spirit by means of games of war and the watching of young men drilling in the schoolyard four times a month. If he leaves school at this point, he will probably forget much of his reading ability and his nationalism will lie dormant in a life whose primary object is to raise good rice and get along amicably with his neighbors.

At school the children, especially boys, form close friendships with their own classmates, children mostly of the same age. Classmates are called *dōkyosei*; people of the same age, *dōnen*. It is the *dōnen* tie which is more important. All through life male *dōnen* remain close. When two men meet for the first time, if they turn out to be of the same age, they are well on the way toward being friends. The ties of *dōnen* increase with age. As a man grows old and the sexual desires die down, parties of *dōnen* are the only true pleasures left in life, and the farmers of Suye say that a *dōnen* then becomes closer than a wife.

The primary school came to Suye about sixty years ago. It was then a four-year course. Most of the older generation have attended this. Thirty years later a six-year course was begun, and more recently have come the continuation classes called *seinen gakkō* and *kōtō shōgakkō*. The *seinen gakkō* is young people's school that meets at night and on *mura* rest days. The *kōtō shōgakkō* is fulltime regular school for two or three years after the sixth grade. The *seinen gakkō* instructs girls in sewing and cooking and boys in fencing, wrestling, some general knowledge, and a lot of military drill.

All young men in the *mura,* including young servants from outside, are expected to attend *seinen gakkō.* The women's participation is much more limited; some do not go at all, and those who do go, go only on *mura* holidays, there being no night school for them.

Before leaving the classroom all pupils stand and bow to the teacher, and before leaving the schoolyard at the end of the school day all classes line up for dismissal by the schoolmaster, and every child bows in the direction of the Emperor's portrait. If not going home right away, a boy may while away the afternoon with other little boys playing war games. The girls will play at juggling, beanbags or bouncing a ball, as often as not with a baby sibling bouncing in rhythm on their backs. Parents like to have their children come home first, say, "I have returned," and then go off to play.

There are many songs to go with ball-bouncing and other games, also many lullabies sung by older children to soothe a baby carried on the back. An example of each is given below.

HAND-CLAPPING GAME SONG

Arutoki Hanako no	At one time Hanako's
Namida ga hori hori	Tears poured down
Hori hori	Poured down.
Ammari deta no de	Too many tears
Tamoto de nugūimasho	With the sleeve let us wipe
Nugūimasho	Let us wipe
Nugūta kimono wa	The wet *kimono*
Araimasho	Let us wash
Araimasho	Let us wash.
Aratta kimono wa	The washed *kimono*
Shiburimasho	Let us wring
Shiburimasho	Let us wring.
Shibutta kimono wa	The wrung *kimono*
Hoshimasho	Let us hang out
Hoshimasho	Let us hang out.
Hosh'ta kimono wa	The hung *kimono*
Tatamimasho	Let us fold
Tatamimasho	Let us fold.
Tatanda kimono wa	The folded *kimono*
Naoshimasho	Let us put away
Naoshimasho	Let us put away.
Naoshita kimono wa	The put-away *kimono*
Nezumi ga poki poki	The mice (ate), *poki poki*
Poki poki	*Poki poki*
On puku pon—na—pon	*On puku pon na pon.*

LULLABY (KOMORI-UTA)

Nenne ko Torahachi baba no mago
Baba oraren jī no mago
Jī wa doke ikaita
Jī wa machi fune kai ni
Fune wa naka tokya uma kōte
Uma wa doke tsunagaita
Uma wa sendan no ki tsunagaita
Nan kwasete tsunagaita
Hami kwasete tsunagaita

Go to sleep Torahachi, granma's grandchild.
Granma is not here, granpa's grandchild.
Granpa, where did he go?
Granpa went to town to buy a boat;
There was no boat, he bought a horse.
The horse, where did he tie (it)?
The horse he tied to a *sendan* tree.
What did he feed (it) tethered?
The bit he fed (it), tethered.

If a child's family is rich, he will probably be sent to high school. A girl will go to the girls' high school (*jogakkō*) in Taragi or, more exceptionally, in Hitoyoshi. A boy will be sent to the agricultural school (*nōgakkō*) in Menda or, more exceptionally, to the middle school in Hitoyoshi. A high-school education helps a girl's family to make a good marriage for her.

More boys than girls receive education outside Suye. In the last ten years nine boys and no girls went from Suye families to some college or university. Of these, one became a government official in Tokyo; two, doctors in Hitoyoshi; one, an army doctor; one, a newspaper man in Tokyo; three are still in college. Only one has come back to Suye. He came back because of illness while working at an office job in Kumamoto and because his father died, forcing him to come home and take care of his household consisting of his mother and three unmarried younger sisters. He has made a virtue of his necessity by deploring the fact that educated citizens of Suye leave the place and saying he must now stay here as a duty to his native village.

At fourteen or fifteen a young person begins taking his full share of farm work. At twenty about one boy in four goes off to the barracks; girls continue helping their mothers or perhaps work as maids for some richer families. Young men of poor families also work out as menservants.

ADOLESCENCE

Young men and women work together a great deal, often a son of the house and a maidservant or a daughter of the house and a manservant.

As they work side by side in the mud of a paddy field or go to the forest to cut firewood in February, there is little chance for romance as each is too busy. Work clothes are always ragged, and no self-respecting farmer tries to look pretty at work; but there is opportunity for talk and jokes. In the evening, sitting by the fire pit, there is leisure for romantic thoughts.

In the old days when there was no electricity it was easy for a young man to enter a maid's room unobserved by the family and unseen by the girl until he actually lay down beside her. In such a case she could accept or refuse him as she pleased. Since his face was covered with a towel, he could not be recognized unless the girl happened to know him well already. Even so, if refused, the towel saved his face. The next day as they saw each other they could appear to know nothing of the night's attempt.

Today every house with electricity leaves its lights on all night, and this makes clandestine affairs much more difficult. They still go on, however, though not so frequently as formerly. It is said that girls have become more "moral" now. One reason for this is school education. All young girls are encouraged to attend *shojokai* (Young Ladies' Society, which is part-time school for girls who have not gone beyond the sixth grade). These school meetings occurring on *mura* rest days take up most of the girls' leisure time, and it gives them something to do at home in the evening, for there is always some sewing assignment. They are told by the teacher about the value of virtue, so, as one man put it, "even a servant girl now has enough education to know that she must keep her virginity."

A girl never admits publicly that she likes a certain young man, but of an evening girls still go out for a walk occasionally. This is especially true of maidservants who, not living at home, have less strict parental supervision.

In the village there is little dressing up among older women with a view toward attracting male attention. Young unmarried women, however, dress up in their finest on big festival days, often with some young man in mind.

Love letters are much written and much denied. About the only use a young farm girl ever gets out of her grammar-school education is the ability to write a misspelled love letter. This letter-writing is a "fling" that all young girls must take before they are married. Nothing ever comes of it. It is mostly an innocent occupation which furnishes much excitement and gives the girls something to talk about when they meet and tease one another. There is a poem:

> Hana tsubomi no jogakusei
> Eigo de fumi kaku oya no mae

Fumi to wa futaoya shirazu shite
Erai benkyō to homete aru

High-school girl, beautiful as a flower bud,
Before her parents writes a love letter in English.
The two parents, not knowing it to be a love letter,
Praise her for studying so much.

Even though a young woman is made pregnant by some secret lover, she rarely marries him. The love affairs are secret and individual, but marriages are arranged by the families and, after secret preliminaries, public. Usually an affair does not get beyond the love-letter and joking stage.

If a girl becomes pregnant, the parents try to arrange a marriage for her before the child is born. This usually results in her marrying into a class below her as it is difficult to arrange a quick marriage for a pregnant daughter in one's own social class, especially among the lower upper and upper upper. Such girls often marry widowers.

While the actual sex act is very private, jokes about it and imitations of it in dances are both free and frequent. Young children, especially boys, often play at sex games, jokingly chasing girls and exposing themselves.

When puberty is reached, boys and girls, especially girls, become shy and reserved in their relations with one another. Girls tend to go in groups together and boys to do the same. With this separation begins the sharp social division of the sexes that lasts until old age. From now on a couple, married or single, is a rare sight on the public streets. Even when going to the same place a man and wife will go separately.

CONSCRIPTION

Every year the army holds physical and mental examinations for men twenty years old. The so-called mental test is largely a civics and patriotic attitude test. In Kuma the examinations are held in Hitoyoshi about June. Fifteen or twenty young men of Suye are called each year for this. As one must report from the village in which one's *koseki* is kept, this often means a return home from some other region where one is working as a servant at the time examination comes up. From Suye in 1936 about half the boys examined were working in other villages as menservants.

The examination is a routine medical one accompanied by a long talk on patriotism and the duties of a soldier. That some boys do not care to be conscripted can be seen from the warning given by the colonel in charge not to tell lies.

Even before this official medical examination all men to come up in a given year are first examined in the village by a doctor hired by the village office. This preliminary examination is chiefly concerned with trachoma and venereal diseases.

About a third of the young men pass the examination. Families of boys who do not pass, while somewhat sorry to miss the honor and glory of sending a son to serve the country, actually are rather glad to keep him at home. When an able-bodied young man is suddenly taken away from a farming family, its productivity is reduced. Often a family must hire a manservant to replace the conscripted son, and farmers always complain that such a hired man is not so good as their own son. For a poor family there is nothing to be done but grin and bear it.

Though it is actually only to the training barracks that a young man goes, the whole attitude on his departure and return is as if he had been in active service in defense of the country. It is probable that much of this attitude has been instilled into the people by the authorities. The conscript army only began under Meiji with the dissolving of the old hereditary soldier class (*samurai*). The very allowing of a common man to be a defender of the godly Emperor and his country is made to appear a great honor. When the times comes for the soldier to leave, usually in January, preparations are made by the family for a big send-off party.

When a boy has been chosen to serve in the barracks, someone from his household goes to the woods and cuts a tall bamboo, trimming off all but a topknot of branches. Just below the top spray of leaves a national flag is fastened, and this flag pole is erected in the house yard. The front entrance of the house is decorated with an evergreen arch, two national flags crossed, and a sign reading: "Congratulations on Entering the Service" (*Shuku nyu dan*).

Whenever anyone goes on a long journey to be away from home a long time, he holds a going-away (*wakare*, "separation") party for the *buraku* a few days before leaving; then the *buraku* in return sees him off to the edge of the village and returns to his house to sing, drink, and dance for several hours to "lighten the feet of the traveler."

For a departing soldier this going-away party is a tremendous one—one of the largest parties his family will give for years. All the *buraku* is invited, as well as the village headman and all village officials, schoolmaster, and all schoolteachers, and the head of the village Reservists' Association. Besides these, several of the boys' paternal relatives may come, or, if not, they will send gifts for the occasion.

To these soldier send-off affairs only male guests come, usually house heads. They come dressed in silk *montsuki* (formal *kimono*), the first ones arriving about the middle of the afternoon. Each guest brings an envelope with fifty sen or one yen in it as *sembetsu* (farewell gift money). While having tea in the *daidokoro,* one puts this envelope on the tray and gives it to the master or mistress of the house.

By the *tokonoma* is a small cut willow tree. Guests are given paper on which to write poems for the soldier, and these poems, after having been read aloud, are tied to the willow tree.

When everyone is present, the master of the house makes a speech thanking the guests for coming, apologizing for the poor food served. Then the headman responds for the company. He gives words of praise to the house head that his son is thus honored and words of advice to the son to be patriotic. Then perhaps the head of the Reservists will say a few words. The son who is to leave answers the speeches of the guests. During the speeches everyone kneels in formal manner, with eyes downcast out of respect for the speakers.

Meanwhile the serving girls have brought out trays of food to each guest. The food served includes *kazunoko* (fish eggs), a dish also characterizing wedding and other banquets on happy occasions. At present the feast food of soldier parties is rather meager. Formerly it was quite lavish, with the result that families sending off soldier sons would be fifty or a hundred yen the poorer after a party; but now, by advice of the village office and agreement among themselves, villagers limit the amount spent on fish to twenty-five sen a head. There is no limit on *shōchū*, however.

By the time of the last speech, several drinks have already been consumed between readings of poems. The host and his son now go around the room and exchange cups with each guest. Then guests also make the rounds, and it is not long before everyone is feeling gay. This follows a pattern often met in village functions. At first all is very stiff and formal, then an hour later, after the drinks have circulated, all is easy and informal, often verging on the hilarious. In fact, the more formal the beginning of such a function, the more riotous the end.

Guests stay until after dark. A few days later the hero of all this leaves on the 10:21 A.M. train from Menda to go to the barracks in Kumamoto. Early in the morning all the *buraku* people, women as well as men, come to his house with *shōchū*-filled *gara* to exchange drinks with him. Someone will bring a *samisen,* and songs will be sung. Soldiers of several *buraku* often leave the same day. All the school children gather at school to march with the soldiers to the bridge across the river in the next *mura* of Fukada. After the early-morning party of *buraku* neighbors in each soldier's home has given everyone lively spirits, they start off. Both men and women join in this party and procession. Someone carries the willow poem tree. Some young woman plays the *samisen,* while others carry *gara* and give drinks to anyone they pass. One woman makes a point of pouring drinks for exchanges with the departing soldier. As the procession goes by, people come out of their houses with *gara* and exchange drinks with the soldiers.

It is cold weather, and everyone wears heavy clothes and felt hats. The *shochū* warms their vitals. All the soldiers, their accompanying *buraku,* and the school children merge in Kakui, and from here a long procession winds to the end of the *mura,* where the party halts. The schoolmaster makes a parting speech to the soldiers, and they make replies. Then three *banzai* are given for them, and most of the people return home. Only close friends, relatives, and village officials go on. At the station the soldiers take a branch from the willow tree, and more *banzai* are given as the train pulls out.

The event rather than the individual person concerned is what counts in this send-off. There is no crowding about a soldier to give him a last-minute message. Rather one shouts *Banzai!* for the departure of a soldier.

After the train pulls out, the party slowly returns home. Most people —men, women, and their suckling babes—go back to the soldiers' homes. Here everybody has more *shōchū*—this "lightening of the footsteps of the traveler" may last all through the afternoon. Only the people of the *buraku* attend these post-departure parties, each soldier's home holding a separate one.

The ceremonial evergreen gate by the soldier's house comes down a few weeks after he leaves, but the flag is left up rain or shine the whole time the son is away. By looking around in a *buraku* one can tell just which houses have soldiers in training or overseas by the location of these flags.

The willow tree on which the poems are hung is planted as soon as the party returns from the station. If it takes root, the omen is good, and the parents may expect their son to return home safely. The willow has symbolic meaning, it being said that, as the branches of this tree grow toward its roots, so the wanderer will come back to the place of his birth. In towns this planting of the willow is not observed, and it is merely thrown away after the boy leaves on the train.

A year or more is spent in the barracks. Here are hundreds of similar boys living under the same conditions of military training. Fathers sometimes visit sons in the barracks, and sons occasionally come home on leave but in such an event there is no special party.

At the end of the barracks term the young man makes a triumphal return. He is met at the train by his father and friends. School children, the Young Men's Association, and Reservists all come to meet him at the train. His father and his age group will often go to Hitoyoshi to meet him. The women of his *buraku* dress up in outlandish costumes, often as soldiers or tramps, and meet the returning procession by the bridge in the next *mura.* The women make obscene jokes as if they were men, try to rape the young school girls, and in general cause bursts of laughter and gaiety. They are always well disguised, and it is not always possible to tell the identity of a given masquerader.

At the soldier's home the front gate now, as at his departure, is specially decorated with branches of evergreen and flags. A welcome party is held there. Again the guests are all men; but, after the party is begun, older *buraku* women come to drink and to dance, one or two younger ones to play the *samisen*. The party ends in song and dance many hours later.

The soldier, like any returned traveler, brings back with him some small gift for everyone who attended his farewell party and brought him money as *sembetsu*.

When a young man comes back from the barracks, he is no longer a rustic farmer but a chauvinistic Japanese subject. He finds it difficult to readjust himself to the unexciting routine of farm work and local custom. The occasional soldier who has been sent to Tokyo as an Imperial guard or to Manchukuo to fight what he really believes to be bandits feels the ennui more strongly than others. After a few months, however, he drops back into village patterns, and it is not long before he is married to some girl selected by his parents.

Sometime before going to the barracks, or on any long and important first trip from Suye, and upon his return, a man makes a trip to Mount Ichifusa. Mount Ichifusa is a great imposing mountain standing out above the rest of the range surrounding Kuma County. It is at the head of the valley, i.e., the eastern end. This mountain has a shrine on it and is considered sacred, its celebration being on the sixteenth of the third month (lunar). People from all over the region make pilgrimages to it on that day.

On this day or some other, the traveler makes a trip to the mountain shrine, pays respects to the god, offers some *shōchū,* and takes some earth of Ichifusa done up in a paper to act as a charm or talisman (*omamora*). The trip is made on foot; the scenery is impressive with immense crypto-meria, the largest trees to be seen anywhere in the region. If one goes in the spring, the mountain is a profusion of beautiful azalea; if in autumn, of brilliant maple leaves. To approach this mountain, visible from all Kuma east of Hitoyoshi, and find it as impressive as it seems from a distance, to gain from it a perfect view of all Kuma Valley below one— these are soul-satisfying things. Taking some earth from this mountain gives a man a feeling of security when away from home. One young man who had served in Manchukuo and who was wounded there said that in the morning of the unlucky day he had had to leave camp in a hurry and thus forgot his *omamori* of Ichifusa earth. As soon as he realized it—on a sledge miles from camp—he felt uneasy. Before the day was over he was wounded in the leg by a "bandit." Some time after returning home, often on the next Ichifusa Day, the returned soldier takes the earth back to the sacred mountain.

MARRIAGE

A year or two after returning from the barracks, i.e., at twenty-three or twenty-four, a young man marries. His wife will be seventeen or eighteen years old. Long before the village as a whole realizes that any marriage is afoot, secret negotiations have begun. Of the three big events —birth, marriage, and death—only marriage can be controlled by a villager, and it is controlled to the greatest possible degree.

Marriage is primarily a social and economic arrangement between two families. When a boy's family feels that it is time he was married, they tell some close friend of the family to keep a look out for a likely girl. Sometime later this friend reports that he has found someone who might be suitable. This friend is called *naishōkiki* (secret finderout) and is often a woman. A semisecret meeting of the two people concerned is arranged. Perhaps the boy and one of his parents go over to see how so-and-so's silk worms are getting along, so-and-so's daughter who is tending them being the girl in question. Or perhaps by seeming chance they may both appear at a healing spring the same afternoon, the girl being with the *naishōkiki*. This preliminary meeting is supposed to be by sheer chance and to have no significance, but actually it is prearranged in a round-about noncommittal way. Afterward the opinions of the boy and girl are sounded, and, if either voices violent disapproval, the matter is likely to be dropped—with no embarrassment to anyone, since nothing has been openly or admittedly started. If, however, this first meeting is satisfactory, matters will proceed. If the girl's family is of another *mura,* they will secretly investigate the boy's family to see that there is nothing wrong with it such as madness or leprosy, and to determine its social and economic condition as far as possible. The boy's family also does this of the girl's family. If both families are of the same *mura* and are well known to each other, such investigation is unnecessary as it is impossible to keep family skeletons hidden from fellow-villagers. Similarly, one need not do this if the boy and girl concerned are first cousins. Some people prefer cousin marriages as they reduce the cost of a marriage, it being all within the family; also, probably because each family feels sure of the other family, and has no fear of acquiring some unexpected disease to affect descendants, or some queer family as relatives.

When all these preliminary and secret moves have been made, an official go-between (*nakaudo*) is selected. The selection of a *nakaudo* is important as he performs the marriage ceremony and is responsible for the future welfare of the marriage. Usually some outstanding person in the community is chosen as *nakaudo* such as a headman, village councilor, or a rich landowner. The groom's family usually selects him.

If the man chosen as *nakaudo* accepts, he will take charge of the negotiations between the two families. From the time the two families have decided on a marriage between their children, they begin to keep at a distance. That is so that, if anything goes wrong from now on, or a divorce takes place after the marriage, it will not be so embarrassing as if they had been on very close personal terms.

Well-to-do families hold a formal betrothal or *yuinō*. This is not true of the majority of families. At *yuinō* a banquet is given only for the members of the two families concerned, and the bride is presented with a formal *kimono* (*montsuki*) bearing the groom's crest which she will wear at the wedding.

From now on the bride and her family are busy working on wedding clothes and trousseau. The groom's family fix up their house, putting in new paper on the paper doors (*shōji*) and new mats (*tatami*) on the floor if they can afford it. Often a kitchen is renovated for the bride to work in. The groom's family prepare to receive the bride, and the bride's family prepare for her reception. A good day for the marriage is decided upon. Certain unlucky days are avoided. Nearly all the marriages in Suye occur in the tenth, eleventh, and twelfth months (lunar); a few in the third and fourth months.

On the day before the wedding the womenfolk of both houses are very busy with banquet preparations, and on the day of the wedding there is even more ado and excitement in the bride's house. A hairdresser comes early in the morning to arrange the hair of all the women of the family and of all women relatives present into a special formal hairdress. The bride's hair is done last as it needs most attention.

Relatives come in the morning, bringing their formal clothes to change into later and bringing gifts of various clothes, fish, and *sake*. The *sake* comes in special red-lacquer buckets. Those sent by the groom have attached to them conventionalized male and female butterflies of paper. Some bring money in lieu of goods. All gifts are wrapped in a special wedding manner and presented on trays with many bows.

While men relatives arrive later and act as guests, the women help around the house and only come out to greet guests, not partaking of the banquet food. Preparation of the banquet food is done by the fishman, who also arrives early with beautifully decorated gift boxes (*orizume*) and much fish.

Her hair done up and decorated with a special set of pins, the bride has her bath and is finally dressed in her very formal wedding *kimono*, her elaborate coiffure covered with a white piece of silk (*tsunokakushi*, the "horn concealer"), a traditional purse containing a mirror, pin, and crystal ball, and a fan tucked in her very wide and very tight belt.

All is now ready to receive the groom's party, usually consisting of the groom, one or both of his parents, and the go-between (*nakaudo*) and his wife (who more or less takes charge of the bride). They bring gifts of fish, *sake*, tea, and rice cakes (*mochi*) for the bride. After drinking the first cup of tea, they bring in the gifts done up in special wrappers. The gifts are received by the bride's mother, who puts them in the corner where the trousseau and other gifts are displayed. (The wrapper she will later return; the basket containing fish she will use to take back her return gift of fish.)

The bride's male relatives come, and the banquet is begun. The *nakaudo* sits in the place of honor; next comes the bride's father and male relatives. The bridegroom's relatives sit on the other side. Trays of food contain many fish soups of which the fish is always taken home. So little of the banquet food is supposed to be eaten that, both here and later at the groom's house, an ordinary meal of *miso* soup and rice with relish is served to the guests at the end of the party. Only *sake* is drunk on wedding occasions, and it is poured with great ceremony by serving girls. The bride joins the banquet later. She hardly touches her food and takes her gift box with her, in return for which her mother will bring home the food served to the bride at the groom's house.

After the banquet and a few exchanges of drinks the trousseau and gifts are moved onto a wagon, and the party is ready to start out. Usually a bus is hired on such occasions, for there is a special arrangement whereby the party is taken to and from the wedding for fifteen yen. The procession walks toward the bus while neighbors stare and discuss the bride in whispers.

At the groom's house similar preparations have gone on all day, and the guests are received at the gate by the groom's relatives. The house is spick and span. The same pattern is followed—tea, presentation of bride's gifts, banquet.

However, before this begins, while guests are seated in the *zashiki,* the bride and groom are taken into a separate room (or behind a screen in the same room) and the *san-san-ku-do* ceremony is performed under the direction of the go-between. This is the marriage ceremony of the "three-three-nine times" drink. Two children pour out the *sake* in three small pours from a special container into a tier of three cups one on top of the other. First the groom has a drink out of the smallest cup, then the bride, then the same is done with the second and the third cup. Drinks are also exchanged between the bride and the groom's father; and there are also exchanges with the *nakaudo* and his wife. A serving girl brings in some dried seaweed and cuttlefish of which a small amount is handed to each to be wrapped up in a tiny piece of paper and put away.

After the *san-san-ku-do* the *noshi* is brought into the banquet hall on a tray. The *noshi* is a small strip of dried fish in a red and white paper folded in a special pattern. This *noshi* is a more elaborate form of a similar paper also called *noshi* which is attached to all formal gifts including wedding gifts. It is presented to the groom's father, and the go-between announces that "the *noshi* has been received." No one seems to know just what this symbolizes, but apparently it indicates that the gift of the bride has been received. Like many other parts of the wedding ceremony, this is not indigenous to Kuma so that not only has the meaning disappeared but radical variations occur. For instance, according to some, *noshi* are exchanged between bride and groom, and sometimes the groom presents a *noshi* to the bride's family in which case the go-between announces that "the *noshi* has been presented." After this the bride's *tsunokakushi* is removed and the formal ceremony is over.

The bride joins the company to sit demurely through the banquet; the groom remains in the back room and will come out toward the end of the banquet. Until his arrival everything is very formal, and, although drinks are poured out, no one makes the rounds, everyone sitting in a formal position on his heels. At a better wedding there is congratulatory wedding chanting during the *san-san-ku-do* and once during the banquet.

At the end of the banquet when fish, presented by the bride, has been taken around by a serving girl along with a special *sake* cup, out of which each guest drinks, it is announced by the groom's father that the ceremony is over, and everyone is asked to relax and sit at ease. Men change their position, cross their legs, and begin to make the rounds exchanging drinks. The bride goes out to change into one of her trousseau *kimono,* and other women might also change at this point into other dressy, but less formal, clothes. Men will play *ken,* and music and dancing will commence. Soon after the singing and dancing begins, a group of *buraku* young men, with faces covered by towels, bring in the nearest stone Jizō on which they have pasted an obscene verse or two and a request for some *shōchū*. After depositing their burden amid shouts and jokes, they retire to the kitchen where some of the serving girls give them the desired *shōchū*. The Jizō is said to be good to keep the bride from running home. A few days after the wedding, the Jizō is replaced in his niche by some pathway and adorned with a new bib sewn by the bride.

During the singing and dancing stage of a wedding banquet, many rather broad jokes are made at the expense of the bride and groom. As the host supplies plenty of *sake* and *shōchū,* a great deal of liquor is drunk, and both men and women are soon dancing boisterously to the rhythm of two or three *samisen* and the handclaps of all who are not busy playing *ken* or exchanging drinks. The wedding is the extreme example of the pattern whereby a social gathering begins with stiff formality and ends with orgiastic abandon.

The party lasts until eleven or midnight. After the guests have been served supper and rice, they are ready to go home. Now the bride, as hostess, will serve tea made of the two measures brought to her by the groom and with the groom's family will come to the gate to see off her parents. Thus she assumes her role of daughter in the new household.

On the day following a wedding the girls who had been asked to assist come again to help clean up. The whole morning is spent putting the house in shape again. On this day there is a party given for the village officials, schoolteachers, and other people of consequence in the *mura*. The *buraku* as a whole (usually represented by the women) is invited the day after. These post-wedding parties are called *chanomi* and serve to introduce the bride to the community. Special formalized congratulatory wedding cakes are served at all three parties.

Three days (usually later but supposed to be the third day) after the wedding, bride and groom dress up in fine clothes for a visit to the *nakaudo*. They present him with a gift—a return gift for the one he gave at the wedding and one which must be better than his gift as it also serves as a return for his services as *nakaudo*.

From now on the *nakaudo* has close connections with the family. He will be invited to every child's naming ceremony and will probably attend as a mourner at funerals in the family. But, most important, he must continue to act as go-between for the two families related through the marriage. If there is trouble between bride and groom—if the bride goes home and stays too long—he must try to reconcile them. If this is impossible, he must arrange a separation as smoothly as possible.

Not all weddings are as elaborate as the foregoing description indicates. Some poorer families, and formerly nearly everyone in Suye, used *shōchū*, the local drink, in the *san-san-ku-do*, and much of the formality including the *noshi* and elaborate *banquet* food was lacking. As in dress, so in weddings: the ordinary farmer of today does many things only *samurai* were allowed to do in feudal times.

4

To understand our Japanese enemy during World War II, the cultural anthropologist Ruth Benedict believed that it was necessary to understand Japanese child-rearing practices and other customs, roles, and beliefs. Her The Chrysanthemum and the Sword was commissioned by the American government during the war and widely discussed by Japanese after the war. It has become the classic inspiration for many of the studies of national character in the years since 1945. In this excerpt she shows, through an examination of the Japanese concept of debt (on), how Japanese understood their duty to society. On bound Japanese in service both to their parents and to the Emperor and nation.

F R O M

The Chrysanthemum and the Sword

RUTH BENEDICT

REPAYING ONE-TEN-THOUSANDTH

O N is a debt and must be repaid, but in Japan all repayments are regarded as falling into another category entirely. The Japanese find our morals, which confuse these two categories in our ethics and in our neutral words like obligation and duty, as strange as we would find financial dealings in some tribe whose language did not separate "debtor" from "creditor" in money transactions. To them the primary and ever-present indebtedness called *on* is worlds apart from the active, bowstring-taut repayment which is named in a whole series of other concepts. A man's indebtedness (*on*) is not virtue; his repayment is. Virtue begins when he dedicates himself actively to the job of gratitude.

It will help Americans to understand this matter of virtue in Japan if we keep in mind the parallel with financial transactions and think of it as having behind it the sanctions against defaulting which property transactions have in America. Here we hold a man to his bond. We do not count extenuating circumstances when a man takes what is not his. We do not allow it to be a matter of impulse whether or not a man pays a debt to a bank. And the debtor is just as responsible for the accrued

Ruth Benedict, *The Chrysanthemum and the Sword.* Copyright © 1946 by Ruth Benedict. Reprinted with permission of Houghton Mifflin Company. Chapter 6, pp. 114–132. Footnotes omitted.

interest as he is for the original money he borrowed. Patriotism and love of our families we regard as quite different from all this. Love, with us, is a matter of the heart and is best when freely given. Patriotism, in the sense of putting our country's interests above everything else, is regarded as rather quixotic or certainly as not compatible with fallible human nature until the United States is attacked by the armed forces of an enemy. Lacking the basic Japanese postulate of great indebtedness automatically incurred by every man and woman born, we think that a man should pity and help his needy parents, should not beat his wife, and should provide for his children. But these things are not quantitatively reckoned like a debt of money and they are not rewarded as success in business is. In Japan they are regarded quite as financial solvency is in America and the sanctions behind them are as strong as they are in the United States behind being able to pay one's bills and the interest on one's mortgage. They are not matters that must be attended to only at crises such as a proclamation of war or the serious illness of a parent; they are one's constant shadow like a small New York farmer's worry about his mortgage or a Wall Street financier's as he watches the market climb when he has sold short.

The Japanese divide into distinct categories, each with its different rules, those repayments on *on* which are limitless both in amount and in duration and those which are quantitatively equivalent and come due on special occasions. The limitless repayments on indebtedness are called *gimu* and they say of it: "One never repays one ten-thousandth of (this) *on.*" One's gimu groups together two different types of obligations: repayment of one's *on* to parents, which is *ko,* and repayment of one's *on* to the Emperor, which is *chu.* Both these obligations of gimu are compulsory and are man's universal lot; indeed Japan's elementary schooling is called "gimu education" because no other word so adequately renders the meaning of "required." The accident of life may modify the details of one's gimu, but gimu is automatically incumbent upon all men and is above all fortuitous circumstances.

Both forms of gimu are unconditional. In thus making these virtues absolute Japan has departed from the Chinese concepts of duty to the State and of filial piety. The Chinese ethical system has been repeatedly adopted in Japan ever since the seventh century and chu and ko are Chinese words. But the Chinese did not make these virtues unconditional. China postulates an overriding virtue which is a condition of loyalty and piety. It is usually translated "benevolence" (*jen*) but it means almost everything Occidentals means by good interpersonal relations. A parent must have *jen.* If a ruler does not have it it is righteous for his people to rebel against him. It is a condition upon which one's gift of loyalty is predicated. The Emperor's tenure and that of his officials depended on

SCHEMATIC TABLE OF
JAPANESE OBLIGATIONS AND THEIR RECIPROCALS

I. *On*: obligations passively incurred. One "receives an *on*"; one "wears an *on*," i.e., *on* are obligations from the point of view of the passive recipient.

    ko on. On received from the Emperor.

    oya on. On received from parents.

    nushi no on. On received from one's lord.

    shi no on. On received from one's teacher.

    on received in all contacts in the course of one's life.

    NOTE: All these persons from whom one receives *on* become one's *on jin*, "*on* man."

II. Reciprocals of *on*. One "pays" these debts, one "returns these obligations" to the *on* man, i.e., these are obligations regarded from the point of view of active repayment.

    A. *Gimu*. The fullest repayment of these obligations is still no more than partial and there is no time limit.

        chu.   Duty to the Emperor, the law, Japan.

        ko.   Duty to parents and ancestors (by implication, to descendants).

        nimmu. Duty to one's work.

    B. *Giri*.   These debts are regarded as having to be repaid with mathematical equivalence to the favor received and there are time limits.

        1. *Giri*-to-the-world.

            Duties to liege lord.

            Duties to affinal family.

            Duties to non-related persons due to *on* received, e.g., on a gift of money, on a favor, on work contributed (as a "work party").

            Duties to persons not sufficiently closely related (aunts, uncles, nephews, nieces) due to *on* received not from them but from common ancestors.

        2. *Giri*-to-one's-name. This is a Japanese version of *die Ehre*.

            One's duty to "clear" one's reputation of insult or imputation of failure, i.e., the duty of feuding or vendetta. (N.B. This evening of scores is not reckoned as aggression.)

            One's duty to admit no (professional) failure or ignorance.

            One's duty to fulfill the Japanese proprieties, e.g., observing all respect behavior, not living above one's station in life, curbing all displays of emotion on inappropriate occasions, etc.

their doing jen. Chinese ethics applies this touchstone in all human relations.

This Chinese ethical postulate was never accepted in Japan. The great Japanese student, Kanichi Asakawa, speaking of this contrast in medieval times, says: "In Japan these ideas were obviously incompatible with her imperial sovereignty and were therefore never accepted in entirety even as theories." In fact jen became in Japan an outlaw virtue and was entirely demoted from the high estate it had in Chinese ethics. In Japan it is *jin* (it is written with the same character the Chinese use) and "doing jin" or its variant "doing jingi" is very far indeed from being a virtue required even in the highest quarters. It has been so thoroughly banished from their ethical system that it means something done outside the law. It may indeed be a praiseworthy act like putting one's name on a subscription list for public charity or granting mercy to a criminal. But it is emphatically a work of supererogation. It means that the act was not required of you.

"Doing jingi" is used in another sense of "outside the law," too; it is used of virtue among gangsters. The honor among thieves of the raiding and slashing swashbucklers of the Tokugawa period—they were one-sword men as contrasted with the two-sworded swashbuckling samurai—was "doing jingi"; when one of these outlaws asked shelter of another who was a stranger, that stranger, as an insurance against future vengeance from the petitioner's gang, would grant it and thereby "do jingi." In modern usage "doing jingi" has fallen even lower. It occurs frequently in discussions of punishable acts: "Common laborers," their newspapers say, "still do jingi and they must be punished. Police should see to it that jingi is stopped in the holes and corners where it flourishes in Japan." They mean of course the "honor among thieves" which flourishes in racketeering and gangsterdom. Especially the small labor contractor in modern Japan is said to "do jingi" when, like the Italian labor padrone at American ports at the turn of the century, he enters into outside-the-law relationships with unskilled laborers and gets rich off farming them out at a profit. The degradation of the Chinese concept of *jen* could hardly go farther. The Japanese, having entirely reinterpreted and demoted the crucial virtue of the Chinese system and put nothing else in its place that might make gimu conditional, filial piety became in Japan a duty one had to fulfill even if it meant condoning a parent's vice and injustice. It could be abrogated only if it came into conflict with one's obligation to the Emperor, but certainly not when one's parent was unworthy or when he was destroying one's happiness.

In one of their modern movies a mother comes upon some money her married son, a village schoolmaster, has collected from the villagers to redeem a young schoolgirl about to be sold by her parents to a house of prostitution because they are starving in a rural famine. The schoolmaster's mother steals the money from her son although she is not poor; she runs a respectable restaurant of her own. Her son knows that she has taken it but he has to shoulder the blame himself. His wife discovers the truth, leaves a suicide note taking all responsibility for the loss of the money, and drowns herself and their baby. Publicity follows but the mother's part in the tragedy is not even called in question. The son has fulfilled the law of filial piety and goes off alone to Hokkaido to build his character so that he can strengthen himself for like tests in coming years. He is a virtuous hero. My Japanese companion vigorously protested my obvious American verdict that the person responsible for the whole tragedy was the thieving mother. Filial piety, he said, was often in conflict with other virtues. If the hero had been wise enough, he might have found a way to reconcile them without loss of self-respect. But it would have been no possible occasion for self-respect if he blamed his mother even to himself.

Both novels and real life are full of the heavy duties of filial piety after a young man is married. Except in "modan" (modern) circles it is taken for granted in respectable families that the parents select their son's wife, usually through the good offices of go-betweens. The family, not the son, is chiefly concerned about the matter of a good selection, not only because of the money transactions involved but because the wife will be entered in the family genealogy and will perpetuate the family line through her sons. It is the custom for the go-betweens to arrange a seemingly casual meeting between the two young principals in the presence of their parents but they do not converse. Sometimes the parents choose to make for their son a marriage of convenience in which case the girl's father will profit financially and the boy's parents by alliance with a good family. Sometimes they choose to select the girl for her personally acceptable qualities. The good son's repayment of parental *on* does not allow him to question his parents' decision. After he is married his repayment continues. Especially if the son is the family heir he will live with his parents and it is proverbial that the mother-in-law does not like her daughter-in-law. She finds all manner of fault with her, and she may send her away and break up the marriage even when the young husband is happy with his wife and asks nothing better than to live with her. Japanese novels and personal histories are just as apt to stress the suffering of the husband as of the wife. The husband of course is doing *ko* in submitting to the break-up of his marriage.

One "modan" Japanese now in America took into her own rooms in Tokyo a pregnant young wife whose mother-in-law had forced her to leave her grieving young husband. She was sick and brokenhearted but she did not blame her husband. Gradually she became interested in the baby she was soon to bear. But when the child was born, the mother came accompanied by her silent and submissive son to claim the baby. It belonged of course to the husband's family and the mother-in-law took it away. She disposed of it immediately to a foster home.

All this is on occasion included in filial piety, and is proper repayment of indebtedness to parents. In the United States all such stories are taken as instances of outside interference with an individual's rightful happiness. Japan cannot consider this interference as "outside" because of her postulate of indebtedness. Such stories in Japan, like our stories of honest men who pay off their creditors by incredible personal hardships, are tales of the truly virtuous, of persons who have earned their right to respect themselves, who have proved themselves strong enough to accept proper personal frustrations. Such frustrations, however virtuous, may naturally leave a residue of resentment and it is well worth noting that the Asiatic proverb about the Hateful Things, which in Burma, for instance, lists "fire, water, thieves, governors and malicious men," in Japan itemizes "earthquake, thunder and the Old Man (head of the house; the father)."

Filial piety does not, as in China, encompass the line of ancestors for centuries back nor the vast proliferating living clan descended from them. Japan's veneration is of recent ancestors. A gravestone must be relettered annually to keep its identity and when living persons no longer remember an ancestor his grave is neglected. Nor are tablets for them kept in the family shrine. The Japanese do not value piety except to those remembered in the flesh and they conccentrated on the here and now. Many writers have commented on their lack of interest in disembodied speculation or in forming images of objects not present, and their version of filial piety serves as another instance of this when it is contrasted with China's. The greatest practical importance of their version, however, is in the way it limits the obligations of ko among living persons.

For filial piety, both in China and Japan, is far more than deference and obedience to one's own parents and forebears. All that care of the child which Westerners phrase as being contingent on maternal instinct and on paternal responsibility, they phrase as contingent on piety to one's ancestors. Japan is very explicit about it: one repays one's debts to one's forebears by passing on to one's children the care one oneself received. There is no word to express "obligation of the father to his children" and all such duties are covered by ko to the parents and their parents. Filial piety enjoins all the numerous responsibilities which rest upon the head of a family to provide for his children, educate his sons and younger brothers, see to the management of the estate, give shelter to relatives who need it and a thousand similar everyday duties. The drastic limitation of the institutionalized family in Japan sharply limits the number of persons toward whom any man has this gimu. If a son dies it is an obligation of filial piety to bear the burden of supporting his widow and her children. So also is the occasional providing of shelter to a widowed daughter and her family. But it is not a gimu to take in a widowed niece; if one does so, one is fulfilling a quite different obligation. It is gimu to rear and educate your own children. But if one educates a nephew, it is customary to adopt him legally as one's own son; it is not a gimu if he retains the status of nephew.

Filial piety does not require that assistance even to one's immediate needy relatives in the descending generations be given with deference and loving-kindness. Young widows in the family are called "cold-rice relatives," meaning that they eat rice when it is cold, are at the beck and call of every member of the inner family, and must accept with deep obedience any decisions about their affairs. They are poor relations, along with their children, and when in particular cases they fare better than this it is not because the head of the family owes them this better treatment as a gimu. Nor is it a gimu incumbent upon brothers to carry out their mutual obligations with warmth; men are often praised for having fully lived up to obligations to a younger brother when it is freely admitted that the two hate each other like poison.

Greatest antagonism is between mother-in-law and daughter-in-law. The daughter-in-law comes into the household as a stranger. It is her duty to learn how her mother-in-law likes to have things done and then to learn to do them. In many cases the mother-in-law quite explicitly takes the position that the young wife is not nearly good enough for her son and in other cases it can be inferred that she has considerable jealousy. But, as the Japanese saying goes, "The hated daughter-in-law keeps on bearing beloved grandsons" and ko is therefore always present. The young daughter-in-law is on the surface endlessly submissive but generation after generation these mild and charming creatures grow up into mothers-in-law as exacting and as critical as their own mothers-in-law were before them. They cannot express their aggressions as young wives but they do not therefore become genuinely mild human beings. In later life they turn, as it were, an accumulated weight of resentment against their own daughters-in-law. Japanese girls today openly talk about the great advantage of marrying a son who is not an heir so that they will not have to live with a dominating mother-in-law.

To "work for ko" is not necessarily to achieve loving-kindness in the family. In some cultures this is the crux of the moral law in the extended family. But not in Japan. As one Japanese writer says, "Just because he esteems the family highly, the Japanese has anything but a high estimation of the individual members or of the family tie between them." That is not always true, of course, but it gives the picture. The emphasis is upon obligations and repaying the debt and the elders take great responsibility upon themselves, but one of these responsibilities is to see to it that those below them makes the requisite sacrifices. If they resent these, it makes little difference. They must obey their elders' decisions or they have failed in gimu.

The marked resentments between members of the family which are so typical of filial piety in Japan are absent in the other great obligation which like filial piety is a gimu: fealty to the Emperor. Japanese statesmen planned well in secluding their Emperor as a Sacred Chief and in removing him from the hurlyburly of life; only so in Japan could he serve to unify all people in unambivalent service to the State. It was not enough to make him a father to his people, for the father in the household, despite all the obligations rendered him, was a figure of whom one might have "anything but a high estimation." The Emperor had to be a Sacred Father removed from all secular considerations. A man's fealty to him, chu, the supreme virtue, must become an ecstatic contemplation of a fantasied Good Father untainted by contacts with the world. Early Meiji statesmen wrote after they had visited the nations of the Occident that in all these countries history was made by the conflict between ruler and people and that this was unworthy of the Spirit of Japan. They returned and wrote into the Constitution that the Ruler was to "be sacred and inviolable" and not reckoned responsible for any acts of his Ministers. He was to serve as supreme symbol of Japanese unity, not as responsible head of a State. Since the Emperor had not served as an executive ruler for some seven centuries it was simple to perpetuate his back-stage rôle. Meiji statesmen needed only to attach to him, in the minds of all Japanese, that unconditional highest virtue, chu. In feudal Japan chu had been obligation to the Secular Chief, the Shogun, and its long history warned Meiji statesman what it was necessary to do in the new dispensation to accomplish their objective, the spiritual unification of Japan. In those centuries the Shogun had been Generalissimo and chief administrator and in spite of the chu that was due him plots against his supremacy and against his life were frequent. Fealty to him often came into conflict with obligations to one's own feudal overlord, and the higher loyalty frequently was less compelling than the lower. Fealty to one's own overlord was, after all, based on face to face ties and fealty to the Shogun might well seem cold in comparison. Retainers too fought in troubled times to unseat the Shogun and to establish their own feudal lord in his place. The prophets and leaders of the Meiji Restoration had for a century fought against the Tokugawa Shogunate with the slogan that chu was due to the Emperor secluded in the shadowy background, a figure whose lineaments every person could draw for himself according to his own desires. The Meiji Restoration was the victory for this party and it was precisely this shifting of chu from Shogun to symbolic Emperor which justified the use of the term "restoration" for the year 1868. The Emperor remained secluded. He invested Their Excellencies with authority but he did not himself run the government or the army or personally dictate policies. The same sort of advisors, though they were better chosen, went on running the government. The real upheaval was in the spiritual realm, for chu became every man's repayment to the Sacred Chief—high priest and symbol of the unity and perpetuity of Japan.

The ease with which chu was transferred to the Emperor was aided of course by the traditional folklore that the Imperial House was descended from the Sun Goddess. But this folkloristic claim to divinity was not so crucial as Westerners thought it was. Certainly Japanese intellectuals who entirely rejected these claims did not therefore question chu to the Emperor, and even the mass of the populace who accepted divine birth did not mean by that what Westerners would mean. *Kami,* the word rendered as "god," means literally "head," i.e., pinnacle of the hierarchy. The Japanese do not fix a great gulf between human and divine as Occidentals do, and any Japanese becomes kami after death. Chu in the feudal eras had been due to heads of the hierarchy who had no divine qualifications. Far more important in transferring chu to the Emperor was the unbroken dynasty of a single imperial house during the whole history of Japan. It is idle for Westerners to complain that this continuity was a hoax because the rules of succession did not conform to those of the royal families of England or of Germany. The rules were Japan's rules and according to her rules the succession had been unbroken "from ages eternal." Japan was no China with thirty-six different dynasties in recorded history. She was a country which, in all the changes she had embraced, had never torn her social fabric in shreds; the pattern had been permanent. It was this argument, and not divine ancestry, which the anti-Tokugawa forces exploited during the hundred years before the Restoration. They said that chu, which was due him who stood at the apex of the hierarchy, was due the Emperor alone. They built him up as high priest of the nation and that rôle does not necessarily mean divinity. It was more crucial than descent from a goddess.

Every effort has been made in modern Japan to personalize chu and to direct it specifically to the figure of the Emperor himself. The first Emperor after the Restoration was an individual of consequence and dignity and during his long reign he easily became a personal symbol to his subjects. His infrequent public appearances were staged with all the appurtenances of worship. No murmur rose from the assembled multitudes as they bowed before him. They did not raise their eyes to gaze upon him. Windows were shuttered everywhere above the first story for no man might look down from a height upon the Emperor. His contacts with his high counselors were similarly hierarchal. It was not said that he summoned his administrators; a few specially privileged Excellencies "had access" to him. Rescripts were not issued on controversial political issues; they were on ethics or thrift or they were designed as landmarks to indicate an issue closed and hence to reassure his people. When he was on his deathbed all Japan became a temple where devotees devoted themselves to intercession in his behalf.

The Emperor was in all these ways made into a symbol which was placed beyond all reach of domestic controversy. Just as loyalty to the Stars and Stripes is above and beyond all party politics so the Emperor was "inviolable." We surround our handling of the flag with a degree of ritual which we regard as completely inappropriate for any human being. The Japanese, however, capitalized to the hilt on the humanness of their supreme symbol. They could love and he could respond. They were moved to ecstasy that he "turned his thoughts to them." They dedicated their lives to "ease his heart." In a culture based as fully as Japan's has been on personal ties, the Emperor was a symbol of loyalty far surpassing a flag. Teachers in training were flunked if they phrased man's highest duty as love of country; it had to be phrased as repayment to the Emperor in person.

Chu provides a double system of subject-Emperor relationship. The subject faces upward directly to the Emperor without intermediaries; he personally "eases his heart" by his actions. The subject receiving the commands of the Emperor, however, hears these orders relayed through all the intermediaries that stand between them. "He speaks for the Emperor" is a phrase that invokes chu and is probably a more powerful sanction than any other modern State can invoke. Lory describes an incident of peacetime Army maneuvers when an officer took a regiment out with orders not to drink from their canteens without his permission. Japanese Army training placed great emphasis on ability to march fifty and sixty miles without intermission under difficult conditions. On this day twenty men fell by the way from thirst and exhaustion. Five died. When their canteens were examined they were found to be untouched. "The officer had given the command. He spoke for the Emperor."

In civil administration chu sanctions everything from death to taxes. The tax collector, the policeman, the local conscription officials are instrumentalities through which a subject renders chu. The Japanese point of view is that obeying the law is repayment upon their highest indebtedness, their ko-on. The contrast with folkways in the United States could hardly be more marked. To Americans any new laws, from street stoplights to income taxes, are resented all over the country as interferences with individual liberty in one's own affairs. Federal regulations are doubly suspect for they interfere also with the freedom of the individual state to make its own laws. It is felt that they are put over on the people by Washington bureaucrats and many citizens regard the loudest outcry against these laws as less than what is rightly due to their self-respect. The Japanese judge therefore that we are a lawless people. We judge that they are a submissive people with no ideas of democracy. It would be truer to say that the citizens' self-respect, in the two countries, is tied up with different attitudes; in our country it depends on his management of his own affairs and in Japan it depends on repaying what he owes to accredited benefactors. Both arrangements have their own difficulties: ours is that it is difficult to get regulations accepted even when they are to the advantage of the whole country, and theirs is that, in any language, it is difficult to be in debt to such a degree that one's whole life is shadowed by it. Every Japanese has probably at some point invented ways of living within the law and yet circumventing what is asked of him. They also admire certain forms of violence and direct action and private revenge which Americans do not. But these qualifications, and any others that can be urged, still do not bring in question the hold that chu has upon the Japanese.

When Japan capitulated on August 14, 1945, the world had an almost unbelievable demonstration of its working. Many Westerners with experience and knowledge of Japan had held that it would be impossible for her to surrender; it would be naïve, they insisted, to imagine that her armies scattered over Asia and the Pacific Islands would peacefully yield up their arms. Many of Japan's armed forces had suffered no local defeat and they were convinced of the righteousness of their cause. The home islands, too, were full of bitter-enders and an occupying army, its advance guard being necessarily small, would run the risk of massacre when it moved beyond range of naval guns. During the war the Japanese had stopped at nothing and they are a warlike people. Such American analysts reckoned without chu. The Emperor spoke and the war ceased. Before his voice went upon the radio bitter opponents had thrown a cordon around the palace and tried to prevent the proclamation. But, once read, it was accepted. No field commander in Manchuria or Java, no Tojo in Japan, put himself in opposition. Our troops landed at the airfields and were greeted with courtesy. Foreign correspondents, as one of them wrote, might land in the morning fingering their small arms but by noon they had put these aside and by evening they were shopping for trinkets. The Japanese were now "easing the Emperor's heart" by following the ways of peace; a week earlier it had been by dedicating themselves to repulse the barbarians even with bamboo spears.

There was no mystery about it except to those Westerners who could not grant how various are the emotions that sway men's conduct. Some had proclaimed that there was no alternative to practical extermination. Some had proclaimed that Japan could save itself only if the liberals seized power and overthrew the government. Either of these analyses made sense in terms of a Western nation fighting an all-out and popularly supported war. They were wrong, however, because they attributed to Japan courses of action which are essentially Occidental. Some Western prophets still thought after months of peaceful occupation that all was lost because no Western-type revolution had occurred or because "the Japanese did not know they were defeated." This is good Occidental social philosophy based on Occidental standards of what is right and proper. But Japan is not the Occident. She did not use that last strength of Occidental nations: revolution. Nor did she use sullen sabotage against the enemy's occupying army. She used her own strength: the ability to demand of herself as chu the enormous price of unconditional surrender before her fighting power was broken. In her own eyes this enormous payment nevertheless bought something she supremely valued: the right to say that it was the Emperor who had given the order even if that order was capitulation. Even in defeat the highest law was still chu.

5

*In this unusual and provocative study of the Japanese sense of
skin color, the Japanese sociologist Hiroshi Wagatsuma shows
how Japanese identity has been tied to an aesthetic standard.
Japanese, Wagatsuma suggests, have had to maintain a sense
of their own standards of beauty and their own aesthetic
values in order to assert their own national identity and resist
the cultural impact of both China and the West. As standards
for art and beauty change, in accord with "diversity of experiences," Wagatsuma seems to feel that the Japanese sense of
their own national identity will also change dependent upon
their national experiences.*

The Social Perception of
Skin Color in Japan

HIROSHI WAGATSUMA

Long before any sustained contact with either Caucasoid Europeans
or dark-skinned Africans or Indians, the Japanese valued "white"
skin as beautiful and deprecated "black" skin as ugly. Their spontaneous responses to the white skin of Caucasoid Europeans and the black
skin of Negroid people were an extension of values deeply embedded in
Japanese concepts of beauty. From past to present, the Japanese have
always associated skin color symbolically with other physical characteristics
that signify degrees of spiritual refinement or primitiveness. Skin color
has been related to a whole complex of attractive or objectionable social
traits. It might strike some as curious that the Japanese have traditionally
used the word *white* (*shiroi*) to describe lighter shades of their own skin
color. The social perception of the West has been that the Chinese and
Japanese belong to a so-called "yellow" race, while the Japanese themselves have rarely used the color yellow to describe their skin.

I

"White" skin has been considered an essential characteristic of feminine
beauty in Japan since recorded time. An old Japanese proverb states that

Hiroshi Wagatsuma, "The Social Perception of Skin Color in Japan,"
Daedalus, Spring 1967. Reprinted with permission of *Daedalus,* Journal
of the American Academy of Arts and Sciences, Boston, Mass. Footnotes omitted.

"white skin makes up for seven defects"; a woman's light skin causes one
to overlook the absence of other desired physical features.

During the Nara period (710–793), court ladies made ample use of
cosmetics and liberally applied white powder to the face. Cheeks were
rouged. Red beauty spots were painted on between the eyebrows and at
the outer corners of both the eyes and the lips. Eyelids and lips were
given a red tinge. Both men and women removed their natural eyebrows
and penciled in long, thick lines emulating a Chinese style. The custom
of blackening teeth spread among the aristocratic ladies. In the next
period (794–1185), when the court was moved to the new capital of
Heian (Kyoto), countless references were made in both illustration and
writing to round-faced, plump women with white, smooth skin. Necessary
to beauty was long, black, straight hair that draped over the back and
shoulders without being tied. One can illustrate this conception of white
skin as a mark of beauty from *The Tale of Genji* by Lady Murasaki, a
romance of the first decade of the eleventh century:

Her color of skin was very white and she was plump with an attractive face.
Her hair grew thick but was cut so as to hang on a level with her shoulders—
very beautiful.

Her color was very white and although she was emaciated and looked noble,
there still was a certain fulness in her cheek.

In her personal diary, the same author depicted portraits of several court
ladies:

Lady Dainagon is very small but as she is white and beautifully round, she has
a taller appearance. Her hair is three inches longer than her height.

Lady Senji is a small and slender person. The texture of her hair is fine, delicate and glossy and reaches a foot longer than her height.

Lady Naiji has beauty and purity, a fragrant white skin with which no one
else can compete.

Writing about the year 1002 in essays called *The Pillow Book,* the
court lady Sei Shōnagon described how she despised "hair not smooth and
straight" and envied "beautiful, very long hair." In *The Tale of Glory*,
presumably written in 1120 by Akazome Emon, a court lady, two beautiful women of the prosperous Fujiwara family are depicted: one with "her
hair seven or eight inches longer than her height," and the other with
"her hair about two feet longer than her height and her skin white and
beautiful." From the eighth to the twelfth century, the bearers of Japanese
cultural refinement were the court nobility who idled their lives away in

romantic love affairs, practicing the arts of music and poetry. The whiteness of untanned skin was the symbol of this privileged class which was spared any form of outdoor labor. From the eleventh century on, men of the aristocracy applied powder to their faces just as the court ladies did.

In 1184, the warriors took the reins of government away from the effete courtiers and abruptly ended the court's rather decadent era. To protect the *samurai* virtues of simplicity, frugality, and bravery, the warriors set up headquarters in the frontier town of Kamakura located far away from the capital. The warrior maintained Spartan standards, as is evidenced in the many portrait paintings showing rather florid or swarthy countenances. Women still continued, however, the practices of toiletry established previously in the court. In 1333 the warriors' government was moved from Kamakura back to Kyoto, where the Ashikaga Shogunate family emulated court life and re-established an atmosphere of luxury among the ruling class.

Standards of feminine beauty still emphasized corpulence of body, white skin, and black hair, which in this period was worn in a chignon. Preference was voiced for a woman with a round face, broad forehead, and eyes slightly down-turned at the corners. By this time, the old court custom of penciling eyebrows and blackening teeth had become incorporated into the puberty rites practiced for both boys and girls. Such rites were principally held by the warrior class but were later adopted by commoners. The writing of Yoshida Kenkō, a celebrated poet and court official who became a Buddhist monk in 1324, exemplifies the continuing preoccupation this period had with the white skin of women. Yoshida wrote the following in his *Essays of Idleness:*

The magician of Kume (as the legend runs) lost his magic power through looking at the white leg of a maiden washing clothes in a river. This may well have been because the white limbs and skin of a woman cleanly plump and fatty are no mere external charms but true beauty and allure.

Following a chaotic political period, the Tokugawa feudal government was established in 1603. It was to last until the modern period of Japan, more than two hundred and fifty years. Changes occurred in the ideals of feminine beauty during this period of continuing peace. Gradually, slim and fragile women with slender faces and up-turned eyes began to be preferred to the plump, pear-shaped ideal that remained dominant until the middle of the eighteenth century. White skin, however, remained an imperative characteristic of feminine beauty. Ibara Saikaku (1642–1693), a novelist who wrote celebrated books about common life during the early Tokugawa period, had the following to say about the type of female beauty to be found in Kyoto and Osaka:

A beautiful woman with a round face, skin with a faint pink color, eyes not too narrow, eyebrows thick, the bridge of her nose not too thin, her mouth small, teeth in excellent shape and shining white.

A woman of twenty-one, white of color, hair beautiful, attired in gentleness.

Thanks to the pure water of Kyoto, women remain attractive from early childhood but they further improve their beauty by steaming their faces, tightening their fingers with rings and wearing leather socks in sleep. They also comb their hair with the juice of the *sanekazura* root.

Another author, depicting the beauties of the middle Tokugawa period of the 1770's, wrote: "A pair of girls wearing red-lacquered thongs on their tender feet, white as snow, sashes around their waists, with forms as slender as willow trees." Tamenaga Shunsui (1789–1843), an author of the late Tokugawa period, never forgot to mention white skin when describing the beautiful women of Edo (Tokyo):

Her hands and arms are whiter than snow.

You are well-featured and your color is so white that you are popular among your audience.

This courtesan had a neck whiter than snow. Her face was shining as she always polished it with powder.

The use of good water and the practice of steaming the face were thought to make skin white and smooth. Rings and socks were worn in sleep to stunt excessive growth of limbs since small hands and feet were valued attributes of feminine charm. The juice of the *sanekazura* root was used to straighten the hair. These practices all confirm the continuous concern with white skin and straight hair. They also suggest, however, the possibility that many women were lacking in such standards of feminine beauty. The following quotation describes what was considered ugly:

Disagreeable features for a woman are a large face, the lack of any tufts of hair under the temple, a big, flat nose, thick lips, black skin, a too plump body, excessive tallness, heavy, strong limbs, brownish wavy hair and a loud, talkative voice.

These were the comments of Yanagi Rikyō, a high-ranking warrior of the Kōriyama fief, who was also a poet, artist, and noted connoisseur of womanhood in the late-eighteenth century. He contrasted these objectionable features with "the amiable features of a woman, a small and well-shaped face, white skin, gentle manner, an innocent, charming and attentive character." One might speculate that the supposed Polynesian or Melanesian strains, sometimes thought to have entered the Japanese racial mixture, would be responsible for flat noses, thick lips, or brownish, wavy hair. Such features are certainly not rare among Japanese, although they run directly counter to the Japanese image of beauty.

Because Mongoloid skin shows a very quick tendency to tan and to produce "black" skin, the Japanese can maintain lightness of skin only by total avoidance of sunlight. Not surprisingly, Tokugawa women made constant use of parasols or face hoods to hide their skin from sunlight and assiduously applied powder to face, neck, throat, and upper chest. In order to increase the whiteness and smoothness of their skin, women "polished" it in their baths with a cloth bag containing rice bran or the droppings of the Japanese nightingale. Application of other grains such as millet, barley, Deccan grass, and beans was also considered to have some "bleaching" effect on the skin. Juices taken from various flowers were also used for the same purpose, and many medicines were sold that promised "to turn the skin as white as the snow found on the peaks of high mountains."

When a woman's constant care of her skin achieved desired results, she would enjoy such praise as "Her face is so smoothly shiny that it seems ready to reflect," and "Her face can compete with a mirror," or "Her face is so shiny as to make a well polished black lacquered dresser feel ashamed."

From the beginning of the nineteenth century, the Kabuki actors set the standards of men's beauty. A rather feminine type of male with a slender figure, well-formed face, white skin, black hair, and red lips became a favorite object of feminine desire. Men possessing these elements of attractiveness would enjoy such a flattering remark as "You should be a Kabuki actor." By the middle of the nineteenth century, these characteristics began to be considered effeminate. A man with a more dusky skin and a piquantly handsome face became the preferred type.

The word *white* repeatedly used in the quotations taken from these various sources is the same Japanese word *shiroi* that is used to describe snow or white paper. There was no intermediate word between *shiroi* ("white") and *kuroi* ("black") used to describe skin color. When distinctoins were made, there would be recourse to such words as *asa guroi* ("light black").

II

Not long after the first globe-circling voyages of Magellan, Westerners appeared on the shores of Japan. Dutch, English, Portuguese, and Spanish traders came to ply their trade in Japanese ports. Both Spanish and Portuguese missionaries sought to establish Christianity in Japan. Before the Tokugawa government sealed off Japan from the West, the Japanese had ample opportunity to observe white men for the first time. In these early contacts, the Portuguese and Spaniards were called *nanban-jin* or *nanban* meaning "southern barbarians," words adopted from the Chinese who had names to designate all the "inferior savages" living to the north, south, east, and west of the Middle Kingdom. The Dutch were called *kōmō-jin* or *kōmō,* "red-haired people."

In several of the colored pictures of the day that included both Japanese and Europeans, the Japanese artists painted the faces of the Portuguese, Spanish, and Japanese men in a flesh color or light brown, but depicted the faces of Japanese women as white in hue. In a few other pictures, however, some Portuguese are given white faces like Japanese women, while other Portuguese are given darker facs. Seemingly, the Japanese artists were sensitive in some instances to some form of color differential among the foreigners. Many Portuguese and Spaniards were actually not so white-skinned as northern Europeans, and after the long sea voyage to Japan, they undoubtedly arrived with rather well-tanned skins. The Dutch in the pictures, on the other hand, seem to be given invariably either gray or white faces. When contrasted with the Japanese women near them, the Japanese feminine face is painted a whiter hue than that of the Dutch.

The differences between the Japanese and the Europeans in these old prints are clearly depicted in hair color and facial characteristics. The Portuguese, Spaniards, and Dutch are all taller than the Japanese and are given somewhat unrealistically large noses. Their double eye folds and their bushy eyebrows and mustaches seem slightly exaggerated. The Portuguese and Spanish hair is painted brown although a few are given black hair. The Dutch hair is usually depicted as either red or reddish-brown in color. Written and pictorial descriptions indicate that the Japanese were more impressed with the height, hair color, general hairiness, big noses and eyes of the foreigners than with their lighter skin color. Some pictures include portraits of the Negro servants of the Portuguese and Dutch. The faces of Negroes are painted in a leaden- or blackish-gray, and their hair is shown as extremely frizzled. The physiognomy of the Negroes is somewhat caricatured and in some instances closely resembles the devils and demons of Buddhist mythology.

Some Japanese scholars of Dutch science seem to have had a notion that the black skin and frizzled hair of Negro servants were the result of extreme exposure to heat and sunshine in the tropical countries in which they were born. In 1787, such a scholar wrote of what he had learned from his Dutch friends about their Negro servants:

These black ones on the Dutch boats are the natives of countries in the South. As their countries are close to the sun, they are sun-scorched and become black. By nature they are stupid.

The black ones are found with flat noses. They love a flat nose and they tie children's noses with leather bands to prevent their growth and to keep them flat.

Africa is directly under the equator and the heat there is extreme. Therefore, the natives are black colored. They are uncivilized and vicious in nature.

Another scholar wrote:

Black ones are impoverished Indians employed by the Dutch. As their country is in the South and the heat is extreme, their body is sun-scorched and their color becomes black. Their hair is burned by the sun and becomes frizzled but they are humans and not monkeys as some mistakenly think.

After the closing of the country by the Tokugawa government in 1639, the only contact of Japanese with Westerners, aside from the Dutch traders, would occur when shipwrecked Japanese sailors would occasionally be picked up by Western ships and taken for a period to a Western country. The reports about the English, Russians, and Spaniards made by these Japanese sailors upon their return commented much more on the hair and eyes of the Occidentals than upon the color of skin.

In 1853 Commodore Perry of the United States Navy came to Japan with his "black ships" and forced Japan to reopen her ports to foreign vessels. When Perry visited Japan for the second time in 1854, there were two American women on board. It was reported in a Japanese document:

On board is a woman named Shirley, 31 years old and her child Loretta, 5 years old. Their hair is red. They have high noses, white faces and the pupils of their eyes are brown. They are medium in size and very beautiful.

The portraits of Commodore Perry and five principals of his staff drawn by a Japanese artist show the Americans with noses of exaggerated size, large eyes, and brownish hair. Their faces are painted in a washed-out, whitish-ash color. In other pictures, however, both American and Japanese faces are painted with an identical whitish-gray, although the Americans are given brown hair and bushy beards. In some pictures showing the American settlements in Yokohama and Tokyo of the 1860's, the faces of both American and Japanese women are painted whiter than those of American and Japanese men. It may well be possible that the American men's faces were more sun-tanned and exposed to the elements during the voyage than the faces of the women who, observing canons of beauty much like those held by Japanese women, may have kept themselves out of the sun. Also, the artist may have simply resorted to convention by which women's faces were painted white.

In 1860 the Tokugawa government sent an envoy with an entourage of eighty-three warriors to the United States to ratify a treaty of peace and commerce between the United States and Japan originally signed in 1854. Some of the members of the entourage kept careful diaries and noted their impressions of the United States during their trip to Washington. Upon meeting the President of the United States, one *samurai* wrote: "President Buchanan, about 52 or 53 years of age, is a tall person. His color is white, his hair is white." The *samurai* leaders were surprised to attend formal receptions at which women were included and to find that American men acted toward their women as obliging servants. They were impressed with the daring exposure afforded by the décolletage of the formal evening gowns worn by women at these balls and receptions. In their diaries they noted their appreciation of American beauty, although they continued to express their preference for black hair:

The women's skin was white and they were charming in their gala dresses decorated with gold and silver but their hair was red and their eyes looked like dog eyes, which was quite disheartening.

Occasionally I saw women with black hair and black eyes. They must have been of some Asian race. Naturally they looked more attractive and beautiful.

Another man expressed his admiration for the President's niece, Harriet Lane, in true *samurai* fashion by composing a Chinese poem.

> An American belle, her name is Lane,
> Jewels adorn her arms, jade her ears.
> Her rosy face needs no powder or rouge.
> Her exposed shoulders shine as white as snow.

This American belle and her friends had asked another *samurai* at a party which women he liked better, Japanese or American. The *samurai* wrote in his diary:

I answered that the American women are better because their skin color is whiter than that of the Japanese women. Such a trifling comment of mine obviously pleased the girls. After all, women are women.

After seeing about a hundred American children aged five to nine gathered at a May festival ball, another warrior wrote of his admiration of their beauty:

The girls did not need to have the help of powder and rouge. Their skin with its natural beauty was whiter than snow and purer than jewels. I wondered if fairies in wonderland would not look something like these children.

On the way back from the United States, the boat carrying the Japanese envoy stopped at a harbor on the African coast, and the *samurai* had a chance to see the black-skinned Africans inhabiting the region. They noted with disapproval their impression of Negroid features:

The black ones look like devils depicted in pictures.

The faces are black as if painted with ink and their physiognomy reminds me
of that of a monkey.

III

In the early Meiji period, the Japanese began their self-conscious imitation of the technology of the West. Less consciously, they also began to
alter their perception of feminine beauty. In their writings, they referred
with admiration to the white skin of Westerners, but noted with disapproval the hair color and the hairiness of Westerners. Wavy hair was
not to the Japanese taste until the mid-1920's. Curly hair was considered to be an animal characteristic. Mrs. Sugimoto, the daughter of a
samurai, writes in her autobiography that, as a child with curly hair, she
had her hair dressed twice a week with a special treatment to straighten
it properly. When she complained, her mother would scold her, saying,
"Do you not know that curly hair is like that of animals? A *samurai's*
daughter should not be willing to resemble a beast."

The body hair of Caucasian men suggested a somewhat beastly nature
to Japanese women, and, probably for reasons of this kind, Japanese
women of the late-nineteenth century refused or were reluctant in many
instances to become mistresses to Western diplomats.

By the mid-1920's the Japanese had adopted Western customs and
fashions, including the singing of American popular songs and dancing
in dance halls. They watched motion pictures with delight and made
great favorites of Clara Bow, Gloria Swanson, and Greta Garbo. Motion
pictures seem to have had a very strong effect in finally changing habits
of coiffure and attitudes toward desirable beauty. During this period
many Japanese women had their hair cut and, in spite of the exhortations
of proud *samurai* tradition, had it waved and curled. They took to wearing long skirts with large hats to emulate styles worn by Greta Garbo.
The 1920's was a time of great imitation. Anything Western was considered "modern" and, therefore, superior. This trend lasted until the
mid-1930's when, under the pressure of the ultra-nationalist, militarist
regime, the ties with Western fads were systematically broken.

Already in 1924, Tanizaki Junichirō depicted a woman who represented
a kind of femininity that was appealing to "modern" intellectuals of the
time. She was Naomi in *The Love of an Idiot,* and her physical attractiveness had a heavy Western flavor. She was sought after by a man who
"wished if ever possible to go to Europe and marry an Occidental
woman." Since he could not do so, he decided to marry Naomi, who had
such Occidental features. He helped her refine her beauty and educated
her so that she would become "a real lady presentable even to the eyes
of the Occidentals." She became, instead, a promiscuous, lust-driven
woman who turned her mentor-husband into a slave chained to her by

his uncontrollable passion. An important aspect of Tanizaki's depiction of this Occidental-looking girl is the whiteness of her skin:

Against the red gown, her hands and feet stand out purely white like the core of a cabbage.

Her skin was white to an astounding degree. . . . All the exposed parts of her voluptuous body were as white as the meat of an apple.

There is a most interesting passage in this book, however, in which Tanizaki, with a note of disappointment, compares Naomi with a real European woman, a Russian aristocrat living in exile in Japan.

[The Russian woman's] skin color . . . was so extraordinarily white, an almost ghostly beauty of white skin under which the blood vessels of light violet color were faintly visible like the veining of marble. Compared with this skin, that of Naomi's lacked clearness and shine and was rather dull to the eye.

The subtle, not fully conscious, trend toward an idealization of Western physical features by the Japanese apparently became of increasing importance in the twenties. It remained a hidden subcurrent throughout the last war while Japan, as the "champion of the colored nations," fought against the "whites." In spite of propaganda emphasizing the racial ties between Japanese and other Asians, the "yellowness" of the Japanese was never quite made a point of pride. The rapidity with which Western standards of beauty became idealized after the war attests to the continuous drift that was occurring in spite of ten years of antagonism and military hostilities.

IV

Older Japanese who have lived overseas have been astounded upon visiting postwar Japan. The straight black hair of the past is all but gone. Even most geisha, the preservers of many feminine traditions, have permanents and wave their hair. Among ordinary women, one periodically sees extreme examples of hair that has been bleached with hydrogen peroxide or, more commonly, dyed a purplish or reddish hue. Plastic surgery, especially to alter eye folds and to build up the bridge of the nose, has become almost standardized practice among the younger movie actresses and, indeed, even among some of the male actors. There were examples of plastic surgery to be found before the war, but its wide popularity is something new.

Contemporary Japanese men interviewed in the United States and Japan all agreed in valuing the "whiteness" of skin as a component of beauty in the Japanese woman. Whiteness is very often associated in their minds with womanhood ("Whiteness is a symbol of women, distinguishing them from men"), with chastity and purity ("Whiteness suggests purity and moral virtue"), and motherhood ("One's mother-image is white"). Linked with concerns for the skin's whiteness are desires that it also be smooth with a close, firm texture, a shiny quality, and no wrinkles, furrows, spots, or flecks. Some informants mentioned the value of a soft, resilient, and subtly damp surface to the skin. This quality, called *mochi-hada* ("skin like pounded rice") in Japanese, has an implicit sexual connotation for some men.

Although many young men accept the primary preference for white skin, they also admit that sun-tanned skin in a young woman is of a "modern" healthy attractiveness. Some men contrasted such healthy charm to that of a "beautiful tuberculosis patient whose skin is pale and almost transparent," a type of helpless beauty that represented tragic charm during the 1930's. Associated with brownish, sun-tanned skin as a beauty type are large Western eyes, a relatively large mouth with bold lips, a well-developed body, and an outgoing, gay personality.

Such a creature with "Western" charm was held in direct contrast to the more traditional femininity of white skin, less conspicuous physique, gentle manner, and quiet character. One finds these contrasts and stereotypes juxtaposed in popular contemporary fiction. There is some ambivalence about light-colored skin in men. Light skin suggests excessive intellectualism, more effeteness, individuals who are impractical and concern themselves with philosophical questions of life, love, and eternity, and those who are unduly ruminative and lack the capacity to act.

Among the women interviewed, there was a general consensus that Japanese women like to be "white-skinned," but that there is a type of modern beauty in women with sun-tanned skin. The women believe that such women, however, when they marry and settle down, "stop being sporty and sun-tanned. Such a girl will take care of her skin and become white."

Several informants with working-class backgrounds said that, as children, they heard their mothers and other adult women talk about the "fragile, white-skinned women" of the wealthier class who did not have to work outside. They remembered a certain tone of both envy and contempt in their mother's voices. There is a tendency to associate "white" skin with urban and "black" skin with rural living.

In this connection, a Japanese social psychologist who had visited Okinawa several times told us that many Okinawans become self-conscious of their "black" skin when they meet Japanese from Japan. To Okinawan eyes, the Japanese appear to have "whiter" skin and, therefore, look much more refined and urban than do the Okinawans. There used to be a general association among the Japanese of "white" skin with wealth, "black" skin with lower economic status. The younger generations, however, increasingly tend to consider sun-tanned skin as the sign of the socially privileged people who can afford summer vacations at the seaside or mountain resorts.

With only a few exceptions, the women interviewed voiced the opinion that Japanese women like light-brown-skinned men, seeing them as more masculine than pale-skinned men. Many women distinguished between "a beautiful man" and "an attractive man." A beautiful man (*bi-danshi*) is white-skinned and delicately featured like a Kabuki actor. Although he is admired and appreciated almost aesthetically, he is, at the same time, considered somewhat "too feminine" for a woman to depend upon. There is sometimes a reference to the saying, "A beautiful man lacks money and might." On the other hand, an attractive man (*kō-danshi*) is dusky-skinned, energetic, masculine, and dependable. Women often associate light-brown skin in a man with a dauntless spirit, a capacity for aggressive self-assertion, and a quality of manly sincerity.

A few of the women interviewed parenthetically mentioned that a woman concerned with her own "black" skin might want to marry a white-skinned man, hoping thereby to give birth to light-skinned daughters. A few younger women in favor of white skin in a man said that a white-skinned man is "more hairy" (or perhaps hair stands out better against a light background), and hairiness has a certain sexual appeal. Other women, however, expressed their dislike of body hair on a man. Some women mentioned a liking for copper-brown skin tone. They associated this with manual outdoor labor, strong health, and masculinity, though not with intelligence. A reddish, shining face is thought to suggest lewdness in middle-aged fat men who have acquired wealth through shady activities. Such a figure stands in opposition to concepts of justice, sincerity, and spiritual cleanliness. The reddish face of a drinking man may look satisfied and peaceful to some women, though it is hardly considered attractive.

In these interviews with both men and women, the present attitudes toward Caucasian skin seem to fall into opposites of likes and dislikes depending, seemingly, upon the degree of an individual's receptivity toward or identification with Western culture. These two opposite attitudes may coexist within an individual, either appearing alternately or being expressed simultaneously. Somewhat more than half of both men and women interviewed in California and about two thirds of those interviewed in Japan considered Caucasian skin to be inferior to the Japanese from the standpoint of texture and regularity. This stereotype was among the negative attitudes expressed in the interviews.

Caucasians' skin tends to be rough in texture, full of wrinkles, spots, and speckles.

If you look at the neck of an old Caucasian woman with furrows and bristles, it reminds you of that of a pig.

When I try to visualize a Causacian woman, she is associated in my mind with skin of rough texture and unsmooth surface. Pores of her skin may be larger than ours. Young women may have smoother skin, but older women have bad skin.

A Eurasian child will.be very attractive if it takes a Japanese parent's skin and a Caucasian parent's facial structure, but the result of an opposite combination could be disastrous.

This notion concerning a Eurasian child seems to be fairly widely held among Japanese. The idea that Caucasian skin is "ugly" is also expressed in the following passage taken from the work of a contemporary Japanese novelist:

When a kissing couple was projected on a large screen in a close-up, then the ugliness unique to Caucasian female skin was magnified. The freckles covering the woman's cheek and throat became clearly visible. . . . On the fingers of a man caressing a woman, gold hairs were seen shining like an animal's bristles.

Some informants who favored Japanese "white" skin but not Caucasian suggested that Caucasian skin is *not white* but *transparent:*

This may be completely unscientific but I feel that when I look at the skin of a Japanese woman I see the whiteness of her skin. When I observe Caucasian skin, what I see is the whiteness of the fat underneath the skin, not the whiteness of the skin itself. Therefore, sometimes I see redness of blood under the transparent skin instead of white fat. Then it doesn't appear white but red.

I have seen Caucasians closely only a few times but my impression is that their skin is very thin, almost transparent, while our skin is thicker and more re-silient.

The Caucasian skin is something like the surface of a pork sausage, while the white skin of a Japanese resembles the outside of *kamaboko* [a white, spongy fish cake].

Some men and women commented on the general hairiness of Cauca-sians. American women do not shave their faces and leave facial hair un-touched. This causes the Japanese some discomfort since they are ac-customed to a hairless, smooth face. (Japanese women customarily have their entire faces shaved except for the eyebrows.) Some women felt that the whiteness of Caucasian men lowered their appearance of masculinity; others disliked the hairiness of Caucasian men which they thought sug-gested a certain animality.

Japanese who have had little personal contact with Westerners often associate Caucasians with "strange creatures," if not with animality. Caucasian actors and actresses they constantly see on movie screens and on television may be the subject of their admiration for "manliness," "handsome or beautiful features," or "glamorous look," but "they don't seem to belong to reality." "Real" Caucasians are felt to be basically discontinuous with the Japanese. As one informant said:

When I think of actual Caucasians walking along the street, I feel that they are basically different beings from us. Certainly, they are humans but I don't feel they are the same creatures as we are. There is, in my mind, a definite discontinuity between us and the Caucasians. Somehow, they belong to a different world.

Deep in my mind, it seems, the Caucasians are somehow connected with something animal-like. Especially when I think of a middle-aged Caucasian woman, the first thing which comes up to my mind is a large chunk of boneless ham. This kind of association may not be limited to me. As I recall now, once in an English class at school, our teacher explained the meaning of the word "hog" as a big pig. A boy in our class said loudly, "Oh, I know what it is! It's like a foreign (meaning, Caucasian) woman!" We all laughed and I felt we all agreed with the boy.

For most of the Japanese without much personal contact with Westerners, skin is only one of several characteristics making up the image of a Caucasian. Other components of this image are the shape and color of eyes, hair, height, size, weight of the body, and also hairiness. Japanese feelings toward a Caucasian seem determined by all these factors. Many people interviewed in Japan talked of their difficulty in discussing their feelings toward Caucasian skin as differentiated from other Caucasian physical characteristics. An image of a Caucasian with white skin, deep-set eyes, wavy hair of a color other than black, a tall, stout, hairy body, and large hands and feet seems to evoke in many Japanese an association with "vitality," "superior energy," "strong sexuality" or "animality," and the feeling that Caucasians are basically discontinuous with Asians.

   Positive attitudes toward Caucasian skin center on the idea that Caucasian skin is, in actuality, whiter than the so-called white skin of the Japanese and, therefore, more attractive. Two college students in California who had dated only Caucasian boys said Caucasian white skin meant to them purity, advanced civilization, and spiritual cleanliness. They felt that even white-skinned Japanese men were "not white enough" to attract them. Although there is no basis upon which to generalize, the following report by a student who had a sexual relationship with a white woman may deserve some note:

Perhaps I was a little drunk. Under an electric light I saw her skin. It was so white that it was somehow incongruent with her nature. Such a pure whiteness and this girl of some questionable reputation.

He associated the whiteness of a woman's skin with purity and chastity, and felt white skin incongruent with the woman's promiscuous tendency.

A Japanese hairdresser married to a Japanese American disagreed with the notion that Caucasian skin is "ugly." She said that Caucasian women tend to have larger facial furrows; these are more visible than smaller wrinkles, but otherwise "their skin is no better or worse than ours." She added, however:

After attending to several Caucasian customers in a row, when I turn to a Japanese lady, the change in color is very striking. She *is* yellow. It always comes to me as a kind of shock, this yellow color. Does it remind me of my own color?—I don't know. I think I know I am yellow. Do I still want to forget it?—maybe.

A sudden realization that Japanese skin color is darker when compared with the white skin of Caucasians has been the experience of several Japanese men and women in the United States:

When I stay among Caucasian friends for some time and another Japanese joins the group, I look at him, my fellow countryman, and he looks yellow or even "black" to me. This, in turn, makes me momentarily self-conscious. I mean, I feel myself different in the group.

My daughter is very "white" among the Japanese. Looking at her face, I often say to myself how white she is. As a mother, I feel happy. But when I see her among Caucasian children in a nursery school, alas, my daughter is *yellow* indeed.

It is interesting to note that Japanese who have spent time in the United States acquire the idea that Japanese are "yellow" rather than brown-skinned. Those we met in Japan, with only a few exceptions, hesitate or even refuse to describe their skin as "yellow." They know that the Japanese belong to the "yellow race" (*Ōshoku jinshu,* the technical term for the Mongoloid), but they cannot think of their skin as actually yellow, "unless," as some remarked, "a person comes down with jaundice."

Having few occasions to compare their skin color with that of other races, the Japanese apparently do not have any words available other than *black* and *white* to describe their skin. In modern Japan, *shakudō-iro* ("color of alloy of copper and gold") and *komugi-iro* ("color of wheat") are used to describe sun-tanned skin, but other words for brown and yellow are rarely employed. When I asked a thirty-year-old woman college graduate to describe the color of Japanese skin, she answered spontaneously, "Of course, it is *hada-iro* ['skin color']!" It is not known why the Japanese, after spending time among Caucasians, come to adopt the word *yellow* for their skin. This may be an attempt to adhere to common terminology, or it may be partially a continuation of a distinction between themselves and Southeast Asians, whom they consider to be darker-skinned.

The informant who had told us about the "yellow skin" of her daughter was asked if she felt unhappy about her daughter's "yellowness." Her answer was an emphatic no, although she admitted that the white skin of Caucasian women is beautiful. A college graduate, married to a university professor, she suggested her solution to race problems:

I think there should be three different standards of beauty to be applied separately to three groups of people of different colors. It is a confusion of these standards or the loss of one or two of them that leads to tragedy and frustration.

Many Japanese men, especially those in the United States, admit the beauty of white skin in Caucasian women, but also point out the sense of the inaccessibility of Caucasian women. Although the feeling of "basic discontinuity" between Japanese and Caucasians found among those without much contact with Westerners may become weakened as the Japanese spend time among the whites, it may sometimes persist in this feeling of basic remoteness and inaccessibility.

Looking at the white skin I feel somehow that it belongs to a different world. People understand each other a great deal but there is something which people of different races cannot quite share. It sounds foolish and irrational, I know, but somehow this is the feeling I have, looking at the white skin of a Caucasian woman.

White skin suggests a certain remoteness. When I went to Mexico, where most women are not white-skinned like the American, I felt more at home seeing them. I felt more comfortable.

Sometimes I feel that the white skin of the Caucasians tells me that after all I am an Oriental and cannot acquire everything Western, however Westernized I might be. It is like the last border I cannot go across and it is symbolized by the white skin. Is this my inferiority feeling toward the white people—I often wonder.

An extreme expression of such inferiority feelings about the Japanese skin color compared with that of the Caucasians is found in *Up to Aden,* a short story by an award-winning, French-educated, Catholic author Endō Shūsaku. Written in 1954 when he was thirty years old, this is Endō Shūsaku's first literary work. In it he emphasizes the basic discontinuity between European tradition and Japanese culture, focusing symbolically upon the hero's somewhat exaggerated feelings about physical differences between a white French woman and himself. The hero, a Japanese student on his way home from France, shares a fourth-class cabin on a cargo boat with a very ill African woman. The story is a beautiful montage of what the student sees and feels on the boat until it reaches Aden and of his reminiscences of his painful love for a French girl while he was still in France. The following are several quotations from the story:

"Race does not make any difference!" the [French] girl said impatiently. "The whites, the yellows or the blacks, they are all the same!" That was what she said. Race does not make any difference. Later she fell in love with me and I did not refuse her love Because there was this illusion that race does not make any difference. In the beginning, in love, we did not at all take into consideration that her body was white and my skin was yellow. When we kissed for the first time—it was in the evening on our way home from Mabyon where we had gone . . . dancing—I shouted almost unintentionally to the girl who was leaning against the wall with her eyes closed, "Are you sure? Are you sure you don't mind its being me?" But she simply answered, "Stop talking and hold me in your arms." If race did not make any difference, why on the earth did I have to utter such a miserable question, like a groan, at that time? If love had no frontiers and race did not matter, I should not have felt unself-confident even for a moment. In reality, however, I had to try instinctively not to envisage a certain truth hidden beneath my groan. I was afraid of it. Less than two months after that evening, the day finally came when I had to see the truth. It was in the last winter when the two of us made a trip together from Paris to Lyon. It was in the evening when for the first time we showed our skin to each other. . . . Breathlessly, we remained long in each other's arms. Golden hair had never looked to me more beautiful. Her naked body was of spotless, pure whiteness and her golden hair smoothly flowed down from her shoulders. She was facing toward a door. I was facing toward curtained windows. As the light was on, our naked bodies were visible in a mirror on an *armoire*. In the beginning I could not believe what I had seen in the mirror was really my body. My naked body had been very well proportioned for a Japanese. I was as tall as a European and I was full in chest and limbs. Speaking of the body form, I would not look inharmonious when holding a white woman in my arms. But what I saw reflected in the mirror was something else. Besides the gleaming whiteness of her shoulders and breasts in the lighted room, my body looked dull in a lifeless, dark yellow color. My chest and stomach did not look too bad, but around the neck and shoulders turbid yellow color increased its dullness. The two different colors of our bodies in embrace did not show even a bit of beauty or harmony. It was ugly. I suddenly thought of a worm of a yellow muddy color, clinging to a pure white flower. The color of my body suggested a human secretion, like bile. I wished I could cover my face and body with my hands. Cowardly, I turned off the light to lose my body in darkness. . . . "Hold me tight. We are in love and that is enough," she said to me once when we kissed at a street corner in dusk. But it was not enough that we were in love. By love only, she could not become a yellow woman and I could not become a white man. Love, logic and ideology could not erase differences in skin color. . . . White men had allowed me to enter their world as long as their pride was not hurt. They had allowed me to wear their clothes, drink their wine and love a white woman. They could not accept that a white woman loved me. They could not accept it because white people's skin is white and beautiful and because I am yellow and ugly. They could not stand a white woman falling in love with a man of such lifeless, muddy yellow color. Foolishly enough, I had not known or thought of it at all until this day [when the girl had announced her engagement to a Japanese man only to invite frightened blame and anger from her friends].

Lying down in the fourth class cabin, I watch the feverish dark brown body of a sick African in front of my eyes. I truly feel her skin color is ugly. Black color is ugly and yellow turbid color is even more miserable. I and this Negro woman both belong eternally to ugly races. I do not know why and how only the white people's skin became the standard of beauty. I do not know why and how the standard of human beauty in sculpture and paintings all stemmed from the white body of the Greeks and has been so maintained until today. But what I am sure of is that in regard to the body, those like myself and Negroes can never forget miserable inferiority felings in front of people possessing white skin, however vexing it might be to admit it.

Three years ago when I came to Europe in high spirits, and when I came through this Suez canal, I had not yet given much thought to the fact that I was yellow. In my passport it was written that I was a Japanese, but at that time in my mind Japanese were the same human beings as white people, both possessing reason and concepts. I had thought, like a Marxian, of class struggle and race conflict but I had never thought of color conflict. Class conflict may be removed but color conflict will remain eternally and eternally, I am yellow and she is white.

Though it seems somewhat painful for most Japanese to be frank about it (and many of them refuse to do so), there is among Japanese intellectuals a more or less unconscious, if not conscious, ambivalence toward the world of white people. Such an attitude is understandable if one takes even a brief glance at Japan's modern history. Japan, at first overwhelmed by an apprehension of the Western world's great power, caught up with the West in an amazingly short time. Then, feeling a sense of rejection over unequal treatment, Japan appointed itself a champion of non-white Asians. In this role, it boldly tried to win a place in the company of white imperialists. Failing disastrously after all, Japan found itself receiving a "democratic education" from its American teachers toward whom it felt the greatest rivalry mixed with admiration.

The diffuse ambivalence toward Western civilization may very well be focalized in the admiration, envy, sense of being overwhelmed or threatened, fear, or disgust that are evoked in the Japanese mind by the image of a hairy giant who, with his great vigor and strong sexuality, can easily satisfy an equally energetic and glamorous creature. Consequently, actual sexual experiences with a white woman may help some Japanese to overcome such feelings of inferiority toward Caucasians.

One of the persons interviewed remarked that his uncle once told him that during Japan's control over Manchuria many Japanese men enjoyed sleeping with white Russian prostitutes:

My uncle said, having a relationship with a white woman made these men feel different, more masculine or something. The feeling is different from that one has after having a relationship with an Asian woman.

Generally, however, Japanese men, as authors of travel books suggest, seem rather overwhelmed and discouraged by the large physique of a white woman. This is well portrayed by author Tamura Taijio, who is known for his bold description of human sexuality. In his reminiscences on twelve women, he describes a Russian prostitute he met in Shanghai in 1934 after graduating from a university:

Her stout body of large build also overwhelmed my feelings. . . . My arms were bigger than those of an average Japanese, but hers were much bigger than mine, almost beyond comparison. When I sat next to her, the volume and weight of her whole body made me feel inferiority and think that I was of a race physically smaller and weaker than hers. . . . "Shall we dance?" the woman talked to me perfunctorily. I put my arms around her and again I was frightened. The girth of her chest was all too broad. It did not belong to the category of chest I had known from the Japanese women. It certainly was something which wriggled in an uncanny way, something which made me wonder what she had been eating everyday. . . . "Come on!" she said. Between two heavy cylinders, like logs, covered up to thighs with black stockings, which were the only thing she wore, the central part of the woman swoll in a reddish color. It was a bizarre view. . . . It was no doubt beyond the imagination of the vegetarian Japanese how the meat-diet of these women made their sexual desire burn and blaze violently and irrepressibly.

In contrast to this complex of attitudes about Caucasoid racial traits, the Japanese attitudes toward the black skin and facial characteristics of Negro Americans encountered during the Occupation were generally negative, although a number of Japanese women married Negro men. The Japanese interviewed in California, being intellectuals and living in the United States, were all keenly aware of the recent racial issues. Most of them made such statements as:

I know people should not feel different about Negroes and I have no negative notions about them.

I have nothing against them. I don't think I have any prejudice against them.

These measured comments would be followed by a "but," and then would come various expressions, usually negative:

I feel resistance to coming closer to them.

It's almost a physical reaction and has nothing to do with my thinking.

It's almost like a biological repulsion.

It's the feeling of uneasiness and something uncanny.

These were the reactions of the Japanese to Negro features as a total *Gestalt* (eyes, hair, nose, and lips) but particularly to black skin.

I think it is simply a matter of custom or habit. We are not accustomed to black skin. I have a Negro friend, very black. I respect him as a scholar and we are close friends and yet I still feel I am not yet used to his black skin. It's something terribly alien to my entire life. It is much better now than it was two years ago when I first met him.

Coming to this country, I had not known that a Negro's palm was different in color from the back of his hand. I was playing cards with two Americans and one African student and I suddenly noticed the color of this African student's palm. I felt I saw something which I had never seen in my life. All that evening, playing cards, I could not help looking at his hands time after time. . . . I just could not get over it.

A year after my arrival, I was introduced to an American Negro for the first time. He was a very friendly person and immediately extended his hand toward me. At the very brief moment, I hesitated. No, I did not hesitate but my arm did. My arm resisted being extended forward. Like a light flashing through my mind, I said to myself, "there is no reason why I don't want to shake hands with this black man." I did shake hands with him and I do hope he did not sense my momentary hesitation. Since then I have never hesitated to shake hands with a Negro.

The idea that black skin is something novel to the Japanese and only for that reason difficult for them to get used to was also voiced by a Japanese woman married to a Negro American.

Frankly, I felt uneasy about it [black skin] in the beginning, but you see it every day, from morning to evening; there is nothing else you can do except to get used to it. I did get used to it. Especially since he was very nice and kind all the time. Once you get used to it, you no longer see it.

The same idea is stated in a novel by Ariyoshi Sawako, a contemporary Japanese author. Although written as a comment by the heroine, a Japanese woman married to a Negro, it most probably reflects the author's frank feminine reaction to Negroid features:

The Negro's facial features—black skin, round eyes, thick round nose, big thick lips—may very well look animal-like to the eyes of those accustomed only to a yellow or a white face. Living long enough among the Negroes, however, one comes to realize how human their faces are. . . . The color of the Negro skin gives one an overwhelming impression but once one gets over it, one notices how gentle their facial features are.

Incidentally, this novel, with the English subtitle *Not Because of Color*, is of special interest for us. Ariyoshi spent a few years in the United States as a Rockefeller Fellow. She then returned to Japan and wrote this novel, in which she describes the life of a Japanese woman married to a Negro in New York's Harlem. She also depicts a few other uneducated Japanese women married to Negro, Puerto Rican, and Italian Americans, as contrasted with a highly intellectual Japanese woman married to a Jewish college professor and working at the U.N. As suggested by the subtitle, Ariyoshi seemingly wanted to emphasize that—in spite of the prejudiced opinion of many white Americans and Japanese—laziness, apathy, lack of conjugal stability, and many other inferior characteristics attributed to Negro Americans are not racially inherent qualities, but the products of their degraded social status. The author accurately describes common Japanese reactions to Negro-Japanese marriages and their offspring. The heroine's mother, learning that her daughter wants to marry a Negro soldier, says:

Our family has been honored by its warrior ancestry. Though we were not well-to-do, none of us has ever shamed the name of our family. And you, a member of our respectable family, wish to marry a man of such blackness! How shall we apologize to our ancestors? If you wish to marry an "American," that might be a different matter. But marrying that black man!

Embraced by such a black one, don't you feel disgusted? I am afraid of him. Why don't you feel strange?

When the heroine takes her daughter to downtown Tokyo, people around them loudly voice their reactions to her child with Negro blood:

Look, the child of a *kuronbo* ["black one"].

Indeed, it's black, even when it is young.

She looks like a rubber doll.

She must have taken only after her father. So black. Poor thing.

Animal Husbandry, written by Ōe Kenzaburō when he was still a French literature student at the University of Tokyo in 1957, is the story of a Negro flyer on a B-29 bomber in World War II. The flier bails out of the plane when it is shot down and lands on a mountain. Caught by Japanese villagers, he is kept in a stable like an animal. Eventually some of the villagers butcher him because they are afraid.

The story describes not only the village children's fear of an enemy soldier and their associations of a Negro with an animal, but also their discovery of his "humanity" and their timid affection for him. As is already clear from the title, the Negro soldier, "with bristle-covered heavy fingers . . . thick rubber-like lips . . . springy black shining skin . . . frizzled short hair . . . and . . . suffocating body odor," was often associated with an animal. For example, "The wet skin of the naked Negro soldier shone like that of a black horse."

A third story to be mentioned here is the work of Matsumoto Seichō, a widely read author of numerous mystery and documentary stories. In this short story, two hundred and fifty Negro soldiers enroute to Korea break out of Jōno Camp in Northern Kyushu one night and attack civilian houses around the camp. Many women are raped. Two other companies of American troops are called out to subdue the disturbances; most of the soldiers are brought back to the barracks within several hours and sent to the Korean front a few days later. A Japanese man whose wife had been assaulted by a group of Negroes divorces his wife and begins working at the Army Grave Registration Service, as a carrier of corpses. One day, he finally finds what he has been looking for: the corpses of two Negro soldiers he remembered by their obscene tattoos. They were among those who raped his wife. Out of his anger, hatred, and desire for revenge, the man stabs the corpses with an autopsy knife. The Negroes in this story are frequently associated with animals and also with the primitive natives of the African jungle:

The sound of drums at a village festival was heard from far. It reminded them [Negro soldiers] of the rapture of their ancestors, who beat cylindrical and conical drums at ceremonies and in hunting, and whose same blood was running through them. . . . The melody in the distance was following the rhythmic pulsing of the human body. Unavoidably it stimulated their dancing instinct and they began moving their shoulders up and down and waving their hands in fascination. They started breathing hard, with their heads tilted and their nostrils enlarged. . . . Thick sounds and rhythm of drums woke the hunters' blood in them.

Their bodies were all dark like shadows but their eyes shone like patches of white paper. . . . His white eyes shone like the inside of a sea shell but the rest of his face was black, his nose, cheeks, jaw and all. . . . His thick lips were pink and dull in color. . . . Hair was kinky as if scorched. . . . Their bodies exhaled a strong foul smell of beasts. . . . When he took off his shirt, his upper body looked like that of a rhinocerous, with rich heaps of black flesh. The skin looked almost ready to squeak when moved, like tanned leather of black color. . . . When naked, his body was swollen, abdomen hanging low. It was cylindrical like a monkey's body.

Other Japanese interviewed considered that the Japanese attitude toward black skin is more than just a simple reaction to something novel. According to this view, black skin is associated in the Japanese mind with many undesirable traits; other Negroid features are also the opposite of what Japanese have long valued as desirable physical characteristics:

Blackness is often combined with death, vice, despair and other kinds of negative things. "A black-bellied man" is wicked. "Black mood" is depression.

When something becomes dirty and smeared, it gets black. White skin in our minds symbolizes purity and cleanliness. Then, by an association, black skin is the opposite of purity and cleanliness. . . . Black skin after all suggests something unclean. It is not the natural state of things.

Speaking of a Japanese face, we do not appreciate such features as a pug nose, snub nose, squatting nose, goggle eyes, thick lips, kinky hair. They are despised and often made a laughingstock. They often suggest foolishness or crudity and backwardness among Japanese. What is preferred is all the opposite of these. But just think. Aren't they what the Negroes usually have?

The following report by a graduate student who had sexual relations with a Negro woman shows that guilt feeling over sexuality can become focused on the blackness of skin, conceived as dirty:

I was not in love with her, nor was she with me. It was a play. To say the truth, I was curious about a Negro, after hearing so much about them. When it was over, however, I had to take a shower. The idea shocked me because it was ridiculous but I was caught by an urge. It was almost a sudden compulsion, to wash my body off, and I did.

Unlike the Japanese interviewed in California, those who were questioned in Japan expressed their feelings toward Negro Americans and Africans without reservation. They were undifferentiatedly seen by them as "black men with inhumanly black skin, goggle eyes, thick lips, kinky hair, strong body odor, and animal-like sexuality and energy." The feelings toward such an image were invariably negative. Many said that they felt indignation toward the white American discrimination against Negroes. Some were very fond of Negro musicians. Negro baseball players were well liked. And yet, as one said, their "basic feelings are repulsion and disgust toward Negro features"; these feelings were frequently justified as a "physiological reaction, which one's reasoning cannot control."

Such strongly negative attitudes toward Negro physical characteristics certainly pose problems for the mixed-blood children of Negro American fathers and Japanese mothers, although nobody has yet made a systematic study of the lives of these children in postwar Japan. Three lower-class Japanese with less than six years of primary education independently voiced an astonishing notion when interviewed; they believed that if a Japanese woman gave birth to the black baby of a Negro man, her next baby, and probably the third one also, of a Japanese father would show some black tinge on the body. In other words, in the mind of these men, impregnation of a Japanese woman by a Negro man was associated with "blackening" of her womb as though by ink, so that the second and even the third baby conceived in it would become "stained."

The type of Negro the Japanese think attractive or handsome, or the least objectionable, is a light-skinned individual with Caucasian features. For this reason, they all find Hindu Indians with their Caucasoid facial structure generally more acceptable, even though the Hindus' black skin still groups them with African and American Negroes. The Japanese are not ready to appreciate a very Negroid Negro as attractive; the newly emergent trend among the Negro Americans has not yet made any impression in Japan.

The Negro in the Japanese language is either *koku-jin* ("black person") or *kuronbo* ("black ones"); the former is a neutral word, but the latter has a definitely belittling, if not derogatory, tone. According to a philologist, the origin of *kuronbo* is Colombo, a city of Ceylon. In the seventeenth century, Colombo was pronounced by the Japanese as "*kuronbo*" or abbreviated as "kuro," probably because of the association with the word *black* (*kuro*) since the servants on the Dutch boats, identified as "people from Colombo," were actually black-skinned. The word *bo*, originally meaning a Buddhist priest's lodge and then the priest himself, came also to mean a boy or "sonny." A suffix to certain words with the meaning of "little one," such as *akan-bo* ("a little red one": "a baby") and *sakuran-bo* ("cherry"), *bo* also creates belittling or even contemptuous connotations in other words, such as *wasuren-bo* ("a forgetful one"), *namaken-bo* ("lazy one"), or *okorin-bo* ("quick-tempered one"). By the same token, *kuron-bo* ("a black one") carries the connotation of childishness.

Most Japanese born before 1935 first discovered Negroes by singing "Old Black Joe" and other Stephen Foster melodies in music classes at school or by reading the Japanese translation of *Uncle Tom's Cabin*. Although they might have related the lot of Negro Americans to a vague notion of injustice, such a life remained for most Japanese children a remote world. Another sort of encounter with black people, with more direct reference to their color, was evidenced in a cartoon serialized for many years in a popular magazine for children, *Adventurous Dankichi*, and in a popular song, "The Chief's Daughter," dating from the 1920's. Dankichi was a Japanese boy who put to sea one day to go fishing and, while asleep, drifted to an island somewhere in the South Pacific. On the island, Dankichi outwitted the black natives by his cleverness and ingenuity and became their king. He wore a crown on his head and rode on a white elephant near rivers inhabited by crocodiles.

This fantasy cartoon blended ideas about South Pacific islanders and primitive tribes in Africa. Originally cannibalistic and war-like, these people could become loyal though somewhat simple-minded subjects when tamed and educated. It is worth noting that this was the kind of image of "black people" to which most Japanese children of the prewar period were exposed. "The Chief's Daughter" created an image of carefree South Sea islanders with black skin who danced away their lives under the swaying palm trees.

> My lover is the Chief's daughter.
> Though her color is black
> She is a beauty in the South Seas. . . .
> Let us dance, dance under the palm trees
> Those who don't dance, no girls will care to marry. . . .

In 1958 and 1959, there was a sudden fad for a small plastic doll called *Dakko-chan* ("a caressable one"). It was a jet black and very much caricaturized Negro child of about one foot in height when inflated; its hands extended in such a way that it could cling to a person's arm or a pole. It was so widely sold that almost every house had one, and the manufacturers could not keep up with the demand. A great many teen-agers as well as younger children carried it around with them on the streets. It was, indeed, a cute little doll, but it did not help the Japanese form an image of a more dignified adult Negro.

v

Since a very early time in history, the Japanese have valued the skin color they consider "white." The Japanese "white" skin is, above all, *unsun-tanned* skin, while Mongoloid skin is, in actuality, very sensitive to the tanning action of the sun. Japanese, particularly the women, tried hard to remain "white," jealously guarding their skin from exposure to the sun. An old Japanese expression observes, "In the provinces where one can see Mt. Fuji, one can hardly see beautiful woman." The districts traditionally known for their white, smooth-skinned native beauties are, consequently, Izumo, Niigata, and Akita. These are all located on the Japan Sea coast where in long, snowy winter weather one rarely enjoys sunlight. Conversely, where one can see Mt. Fuji, one also enjoys a warm Pacific climate year-round and a certain continuous sunshine which can tan unguarded skin.

Mainly due to modern Japan's contact with the Western world, the Japanese became aware of the "white" skin of the Caucasians, "whiter" than the "whitest" skin of the Japanese. This could cause disappointment when they compared themselves with the Caucasians, whom they sought to emulate by guided modernization programs of industrialization, as well as in spontaneous leisure-time fads and aesthetic pursuits. During the earlier contact, the charm of the Caucasian white skin was counterbalanced by reactions to light-colored hair and eyes, and body hair—distasteful traits in terms of Japanese aesthetic standards. Under the post-

World War II impact of American culture, a preference for Western facial structure and hair style brought the Japanese sense of physical aesthetics ever closer to that of Caucasians. The historical inferiority-superiority complex of this extremely Westernized Eastern nation seems today to reflect mixed attitudes toward Caucasian skin. There is the notion that Caucasian skin is "ugly" in texture and quality, thus maintaining a Japanese skin supremacy, while at the same time admitting the better appearance of the refined Caucasian facial structure.

Up to the present, the color of Negroid skin and other physical features find little favor in Japanese aesthetics. One may argue that it is simply because the Japanese are not accustomed to black skin; but one can also contend that "blackness" has been symbolically associated in the Japanese mind, as elsewhere, with things evil or negative and that the image of a Negro hitherto created in Japan has been that of a primitive, childish, simple-minded native. Relatively little note has been taken to date of the emergence of a new Africa under its modern leaders.

It remains a curious fact of Japanese identity that there is relatively little kinship expressed with any Asian countries other than China, toward which present-day Japan feels less and less cultural debt. Japanese eyes, despite cases of plastic surgery, may keep their Oriental look, but through these eyes Japanese see themselves as part of the modern Western world conceptualized in Western terms. Some Japanese wish to change their physical identity from that of a Japanese to something else, but are countered by a vague sense of resignation that such a change is not possible.

Still in search of their national identity, the Japanese are experiencing some difficulties in maintaining and protecting the standards of Japanese beauty and handsomeness from the onslaughts of standardized images produced by the Western cinema. Preoccupied with changing standards, the Japanese may be slow to note a new convergent perception of beauty entering the West, which includes traditional Japanese aesthetic standards in art, architecture, and even in Mongoloid physical beauty. Physical attractiveness is gradually losing its unitary cultural or racial basis in most societies. Art or beauty cannot be maintained in a fixed, single standard. Each changes with the diversity of experiences.

PART TWO
The Sense of the Past

6

What role did traditional values and beliefs play in Japan's rapid modernization? In his classic study of Tokugawa Religion, Robert N. Bellah attempts to find the Japanese equivalent of Max Weber's "Protestant Ethic." In the following selection Bellah sums up his conclusions about the role that loyalty played in the Meiji government's extraordinary efforts to adopt Western institutions and carry out far-reaching reforms at all levels of society.

FROM

Tokugawa Religion

ROBERT N. BELLAH

I WOULD like to take up two or three questions which are relevant to our argument but whose full exploration lies outside the scope of this book before making my final comments on the relation of religion to the rise of modern Japan.

By limiting the analysis arbitrarily to the Tokugawa Period two major aspects of the problem of the relation between religion and the rise of industrial society in Japan have had to be left out. The first of these is a historical study of the formation of what we have called the central value system, which we believe to have existed in its essentials at least by the beginning of the Tokugawa Period. The second is an analysis of the modern period, especially Meiji, with respect to the way in which the values and motivations we have been discussing actually did contribute to the rise of an industrial society. Both of these studies would have to be undertaken in at least as much detail as this one if our conclusions were to be fully convincing. Since that is not at present possible, here we can only suggest some of the ways these gaps might be filled.

The central value system, as we have used the term, is meant to designate the most generalized orientations toward human action, especially in defining role expectations, which are found in a society. Relatively little is known about the processes leading to the formation of such central value systems, though Weber's comparative work points to the important role of religion in their development. Since we have not dealt with the formation of the central value system but have taken it as given

Robert N. Bellah, *Tokugawa Religion*, pp. 178–197. Reprinted with permission of Macmillan Publishing Co., Inc. Copyright 1957 by The Free Press, a corporation. Footnotes omitted.

for the period we were primarily concerned with, no contribution to the problem of the relation of religion to the formation of the central value system has been made here. We have, however, dealt with two other types of relation between religion and the central value system. Every central value system seems to imply or require certain concomitant religious beliefs and actions. That is, there must be some metaphysical grounding, some view of the world, which makes that value system meaningful in the largest context, and thus motivates people to adhere to it; and there must be forms of religious action which will allow people to meet the threats of death, guilt and meaninglessness, of basic alienation, in such a way that the integration of their personalities is maintained and their commitment to the central value stabilized. In Chapter III we attempted to set forth the basic forms of religious belief and action which seem to be concomitant with the Japanese value system. Though some historical remarks were made, we essentially ignored the historical dimension and discussed the general religious orientations that were in existence at the beginning of the Edo Period. Finally, the last type of relation between religion and the central value system with which we are concerned is that between the central value system and what we may call "pietist" movements. Such movements arise usually as intense forms of the basic religious tradition and attempt to inculcate a more strict adherence to the central value system, especially in times of moral laxness Chapters IV, V and VI have given an ample selection of such movements from the Tokugawa Period. We have attempted to show that such movements, starting from a primarily religious interest nevertheless made important contributions to political and economic rationalization. But there is a sense in which all the intensification which the religious movements brought about was merely the development of tendencies inherent in the central value system. Looking at it from this point of view it is the central value system which is the most important variable and which is most in need of explanation. Though this has not been the subject of this study, during the course of the work a number of observations on this subject have come to mind which it might be well to include at this point.

From the earliest period of Japanese history we have evidence for a very high regard for loyalty to one's lord. Many incidents in the *Kojiki* and *Nihongi* indicate as much. For example, the *Nihongi* recounts that a follower of Jimmu Tennō in his voyage across the inland sea sacrificed himself by jumping into the water in order to quell a storm and save his lord. This was a society in which there was endemic warfare and the relation of lord and follower, especially in a military context, came to have a pre-eminent importance. From a somewhat later period (7th century), we may quote from a long poem written after the death of Prince Takechi, which, after recounting his military prowess, says,

> Because of our lord who has gone
> To rule the Heavens above
> In what endless longing we live,
> Scarce heeding the days and months that pass!
>
> Like the water of the hidden pool
> On the bank of the Haniyasu Lake
> They know not whither to go—
> Sore perplexed are they, the servants of the prince!

The emphasis on loyalty to one's lord in a society of this general type is not restricted to Japan, nor is the intense personal loyalty implied in the poem we have just quoted. We need but to look to the Anglo-Saxon poem, *The Wanderer,* for a close parallel:

> All joy has departed. Truly does he know this who must long forgo the advice of his dear lord. When sorrow and sleep both together often bind the wretched lonely man, it seems to him in his mind that he embraces and kisses his liege lord, and lays hands and head on his knee, as sometimes in days of yore he enjoyed the bounty from the throne. Then awakens the friendless man; he sees before him the dark waves, the sea-birds dipping, spreading their wings, frost and snow falling, mingled with hail. Then are the wounds of his heart the heavier, the sore wounds after his dear one; his sorrow is renewed.

This society of the Anglo-Saxon had the same high regard for loyalty that the ancient Japanese had. It was a disgrace to live if one's lord had died in battle. A warrior was to give his life for his lord, if need be, in return for all that he had received from the lord. Whitelock tells us that "when the claims of the lord clashed with those of the kindred . . . the duty to the lord should come first." She points out that such attitudes were by no means new among the Germanic peoples and quotes Tacitus:

> Furthermore, it is a lifelong infamy and reproach to survive the chief and withdraw from the battle. To defend him, to protect him, even to ascribe to his glory their own exploits, is the essence of their sworn allegiance. The chiefs fight for victory, the followers for their chief.

Nor did they cease to exist under Christianity and she quotes Cnut's laws, probably from the pen of Archbishop Wulfstan:

> For all that ever we do, through just loyalty to our lord, we do to our own great advantage, for truly God will be gracious to him who is duly faithful to his lord.

In both Japan and the West these semitribal conceptions of the lord and follower relation persist in the Middle Ages and form one source of the "feudal" values of the respective cultures. In each case this period sees a transition away from purely personal loyalty to loyalty to a status. From this point on the two cases are not parallel. The intense value of warrior loyalty continue to play some role in the West in various transformations and with varying significance in the different national groupings, but in late feudal and early modern times other values become much more important. In Japan on the contrary these values continued to hold primacy and to be elaborated for classes and situations far removed from the tribal battle field.

In the West universalism in many contexts transformed or replaced the ethic of warrior loyalty. For example, the old particularistic loyalty was replaced by the new impersonal ideology of nationalism which emphasized a more universalistic loyalty. In Japan, on the contrary, particularism remained unchallenged. Japanese nationalism remained peculiarly particularistic due to its focus on the imperial family, reigning for ages eternal, the main family of which all Japanese families are branch families. In the West in spite of various uneasy alliances the universalism inherent in Christianity ultimately acted as a solvent on most relations of particularistic loyalty outside the nuclear family. In Japan national Shintō was hardly more than an expression of particular loyalty and Confucianism acted as strong reinforcement of it rather than a solvent. Buddhism had its greatest effect on the ethic of warrior loyalty in the ideas of selflessness and asceticism which strengthened rather than dissolved it. The ideal of the Japanese warrior was by no means the carousing hedonistic robber baron of the late Middle Ages in Europe. The separation of the warrior ideal from hedonism or desire for plunder which have characterized the warrior ethic in so many times and places is of the greatest importance in making possible the adaptation of that ethic to classes other than the warriors. The Buddhist monk in his selfless devotion to his religious duties has been taken as an ideal for the warriors, as for instance when Minamoto Yoritomo writes to Sasaki Sadashige in December of 1191:

> *Samurai* warriors should take responsibility for safeguarding the Ruler and the country in the same devoted way as Buddhist priests obey to Buddha's precepts. Seeing that the country is now under the civil and military rule of the Kamagura *shōgun,* all the *shōgun's* retainers, irrespective of the relative extent of fiefs granted to them, should serve their supreme lord with the uniform spirit of devotion and at any moment be prepared to lay down their lives in repayment of the favours received. They should not regard their lives as their own.

Confucianism also had a profound effect on the Japanese warrior ethic. It should be remembered that the character frequently used to write the word *samurai* was the Chinese *shih. Shih* as used in the Confucian classics is translated by Waley as "knight." The society of pre-Ch'in China has often been called "feudal" and whether or not this term is appropriate, there were certain similarities between it and Japanese society which were not shared by the later imperial China. For example, the *shih* of the classics could more easily be related to the Japanese *samurai* than could the scholar-gentry official of the later period. What is important is that, though certain elements of a warrior status remained part of the ideal of the *shih*, Confucius and Mencius had already gone far toward universalizing this ideal. Learning, virtue, and responsibility for the governing of the people were all important components of it. This ideal also had an element of asceticism or at least frugality and distaste for profit. Loyalty ranked very high in the values of the *shih*, which served to make a convenient link with the *samurai* ethic, but the important thing about the influence of this Confucian thinking on the Japanese ethic was that it tended to broaden it beyond purely military concerns to include intellectual, economic and governmental interests. The partial development of a military warrior stratum into a class of bureaucratic officials, as occurred in the Tokugawa Period, is made more understandable if these transitional aspects of the Confucian ethic are taken into account. Another consequence of the transformation of the warrior ideal into the ideal of a "good man" is that it contributes to the possibility of the generalization of that ethic to classes other than the warriors. The great difference from China is that whereas there the military aspect tended to atrophy and particularistic loyalty to one's lord, though important, was not primary, in Japan the military aspect remained important even if it had to be only symbolic and the idea of loyalty to one's lord continued to override all other ethical concepts. Another important influence of Confucian thinking in Japan was its emphisis on filial piety which helped to rationalize the Japanese idea of the family in terms of "political" values without at the same time being able to make familistic values as central as in China.

To summarize these speculations on the development of the Japanese value system, we may say that its roots go far back into the tribal past but that it took its definite form during the troubled centuries of the Middle Ages. Basically the ethic of a warrior class, under the influence of Confucianism and Buddhism it became sufficiently generalized so that it could become the ethic of an entire people. The continuity of the imperial line and of the national religion served to symbolize an almost "primitive" particularism. The high evaluation on military achievements and the fulfillment of one's lords commands became generalized beyond the warrior class into a high valuation of performance in all spheres. These, at any rate, are the hypotheses I would make after a cursory survey of the problem. If they turn out to be correct it is apparent that religion and religiously based ethics played a great part in this development.

We may now turn just as briefly and just as hesitantly to a consideration of the relation between the ethic which has been analyzed in this
study and the development of the Meiji and modern periods. We might
begin with a consideration of the 1868 Restoration itself. It was, as we
have noted in Chapter II, carried through largely by the lower *samurai*.
In Chapter IV we discussed the ideology of *sonnō* and *kokutai* which gave
legitimation to the movement for the overthrow of the *bakufu* and the
restoration of the imperial monarch, and noted that this ideology was not
in conflict with the *samurai* ethic, *Bushidō*, but entirely consonant with
it. The specific historical cause leading to the Restoration was the problem of how to deal with the encroachments of the Westerners. The battle
cry of the Restoration was *sonnō-jōi*, revere the emperor and expel the
barbarians, which implied that the *bakufu* had been lax in allowing
foreigners to encroach upon Japan, and that all loyal Japanese would join
in getting rid of the *bakufu* as the first step in getting rid of the foreigners.
The point I am trying to make is that the Restoration was carried through
by the *samurai* for at least explicitly political reasons. Of course economic
causes had some part: in Chapter II a number of the economic weaknesses of the Tokugawa system were pointed out. But the *bakufu* did
not fall because of a financial crisis, it was not unable to function
economically. The ideology of the Restoration was not motivated by
economic considerations and had no economic demands. Moreover, although the merchant classes had been affected by the proimperial propaganda and may well have wished the end of the *bakufu,* they did not take
an active part in its overthrow. True, they supplied money to the loyalist
cause, but so did they to the *bakufu,* and it is to be doubted if this implied
much concerning their political thinking one way or the other. They
were accustomed to accommodating political superiors when they demanded money, whoever those superiors might be.

There is little doubt that the increasing disparity between performance
and reward had a great deal to do with the movement for the Restoration,
but this disparity built up pressures primarily in the lower *samurai* class,
not in the "bourgeoisie." The 1868 Restoration, as has been pointed out
before, cannot be understood as a "bourgeois revolution," as the attempt on
the part of an economically restricted middle class to overthrow "feudalism" and win economic freedom. It would be difficult to find a trace of
such a desire on the part of the *chōnin*. E. Herbert Norman, who
combed the Tokugawa Period in an effort to find anyone who expounded
a democratic-liberal political ideology, was almost forced to give up the
attempt when he discovered Andō Shōeki, who did make a rather sweeping attack on the feudal system and its ideological base. But this man was
not a merchant, he was an isolated thinker, without influence, whose
works were not even published. Of course there were many complaints
from the merchants about particular policies of the *bakufu* and covert

lampooning of the government was common. But there was no crystalliza-
tion of this into any ideological form, much less organizational. The merchants were basically loyal to the old government or the new. They were
hard-working, frugal, and in most cases honest, but, as we have seen in
the discussion of Shingaku and elsewhere, they were oriented to receiving
directions from the rulers, to whom they relegated policy-determining
functions. The fact that the merchants were not the spearhead for change
and were not oriented to taking initiative in new and challenging circumstances is of the first importance in understanding the process of the
modernization of Japan. If the merchants were not so, certainly neither
were the farmers or artisans. Only one class was in a position to lead the
nation in breaking new ground: the *samurai* class. From the nature of its
situation, its locus of strength was the polity, not the economy. Thus both
the Restoration and the subsequent modernization of Japan must be seen
first in political terms and only secondarily in economic terms. I am
insistent on this point because the tendency to regard economic developments as "basic" and political developments as "superstructure" is by no
means confined to Marxist circles but permeates most current thinking on
such matters.

Modernization, however, though it includes the notions of modernization of government, as well as education, medicine, etc., is so heavily dependent on economic factors that it is almost synonymous with industrialization. It is poor logic to draw from this the conclusion that the motivation
for modernization must be primarily economic. Actually it seems clear that
a great deal of the motivation for modernization in Japan was political
rather than economic, concerned with the increase of power, for which the
increase of wealth was but a means. The fact that it was the new Meiji
government which took the lead in the introduction of new industries and
carefully fostered the beginnings of the *zaibatsu* with subsidies and other
support fits in with this point of view. Heavy industry was uneconomic in
the technical sense from the beginning and continued to be so even to the
present. It was always dependent on government support and the great
concerns which controlled Japan's heavy industry were always to be understood as a sort of political capitalism tied in with government in a dozen
ways, and in the long run, more told than telling. It is interesting to note
that the basic principles of this political attitude toward the economy were
well worked out already in the Tokugawa Period, as was shown in Chapter V.

So far we have attempted to show that it was only the *samurai* class
which could have led a movement for basic social changes in Tokugawa
Japan, that its motivation for doing so was primarily political—the desire
to restore the emperor and increase the national power—and that utilizing
their newly created modern state apparatus they encouraged the development of the economy with, again, the primary aim of increasing national

power. How, then, was the economy developed, what groups took leadership and what groups responded to the government's desires in these directions?

It is not surprising that in the leadership of the new industries above all were to be found the *samurai*. The old legal distinctions between classes had been abolished and there was no prohibition on *samurai* entering industry, rather it was encouraged, and the government was especially helpful to *samurai* who wished technical training. The *samurai* had those qualities of initiative and leadership which the merchants of Tokugawa days had relatively little opportunity to develop. Furthermore, it was left natural in a society where status considerations were still strong that those of formerly high status should fill the important positions, and many of the most important of the new positions were in the economy. But all of this, it seems to me, would not have availed to make industrialists and businessmen out of former *samurai* if the *samurai* ethic had been that romantic militarism of the late European nobility. That it was not so I hope is abundantly clear from the analysis of *Bushidō* in chapter four. Bernard Makihara, in a most interesting honors thesis, has shown that the "*samurai* spirit" was still a strong force activating the Meiji industrialists and finds the ethic of *Bushidō* a powerful factor in "capitalist" development. For example, he quotes the house rules of the *samurai* Iwasaki, founder of Mitsubishi, which is a most interesting adaptation of the *samurai* ethics to the situation of the modern industrialist:

Article 1. Do not be preoccupied with small matters but aim at the management of large enterprises.

Article 2. Once you start an enterprise be sure to succeed in it.

Article 3. Do not engage in speculative enterprises.

Article 4. Operate all enterprises with the national interest in mind.

Article 5. Never forget the pure spirit of public service and *makoto*.

Article 6. Be hard-working and frugal, and thoughtful to others.

Article 7. Utilize proper personnel.

Article 8. Treat your employees well.

Article 9. Be bold in starting an enterprise but meticulous in its prosecution.

If the *samurai* class supplied a large number of capable and vigorous entrepreneurs, what about that other important human component which seems to be a precondition for industrialization, a disciplined labor force? I hope that it is apparent from what has been said in this study already that an obedient, hard-working and frugal labor force was to be found in abundance among both the farmers and the city classes. Actually the division between entrepreneurs and labor force, outside of the larger enterprises, is somewhat misleading when applied to Japan. The vast majority of businesses were of very small size, with five workers or less, and were basically family enterprises. It was these small businesses with the help of electrical equipment later on, which produced the bulk of Japan's light goods, always the main export and the basis of the economy. In these small businesses the "entrepreneur" was merely the family head, certainly in most cases a farmer or townsman rather than a *samurai,* and the "labor force" was the family members and perhaps a few additional workers largely assimilated to the family pattern. The rigid discipline, long hours and incredibly low overhead of these establishments were certainly one of the primary sources of Japan's economic rise, and these are impossible to understand without an idea of the peasant and *chōnin* ethic and the peculiar way the family fits into them. It is interesting to note that competition was not any more conspicuous in the realm of small industry than in the field of large industry. The small enterprises were usually under the direction of large trading firms, or were organized in trade associations under government direction. Improvements of standards or shifting of type of production was usually a result of compliance with orders from above, often directly from the government, rather than the sensitive response to a competitive market situation. Of course the large firm or government was sensitive to such market situations, especially relative to the export trade, but this has quite a different meaning than if each small business were thus sensitive. The economy continued to be penetrated by political values.

To summarize the cursory glimpse of the post-Tokugawa situation, we may say that the central value system which was found to be present in the Tokugawa Period remained determining in the modern period, in perhaps even more intense and rationalized form. The adaptations of that central value system which had been worked out as the status ethic of the various classes proved very favorable for handling the new economic responsibilities which fell to each class. In spite of the growth of a modern economy the polity remained the dominant sphere of national life and the economy was permeated with political values.

At many points in this study implicit or explicit comparisons with China have been made. This has usually been prompted by the fact that so much of the cultural and religious tradition is common to both, whereas the process of modernization took such a different course in China and Japan. We have usually attempted, wherever this subject has come up, to use the basic value systems of the two societies as a primary reference point in explaining the differences. We have said that China was characterized by the primacy of integrative values whereas Japan was characterized by primacy of political or goal-attainment values. While it is clearly beyond the scope of this study to give an adequate comparison of the two value systems, a somewhat more extended statement of what is meant by integrative values in China might assist the reader in understanding the logic behind those comparisons that have already been made.

A society characterized by the primacy of integrative values is more concerned with system maintenance than with, for example, goal attainment or adaptation; more with solidarity than with power or wealth. The pattern variables which are coordinate with the integrative subsystem are particularism and quality. This implies with respect to human relations that one is more concerned with particularistic ties, of which kinship is the type case but which may include common local origin, etc., than with universalistic attributes. It also implies that one is more concerned with qualities than performance, in Chinese terms, with "virtue" rather than deeds. Kinship relations perhaps more than any others symbolize the values of particularism and quality, and a great deal of Chinese society can be seen as the symbolic extension and generalization of kinship ties. Even the imperial government was strongly "familistic" in its structure, though at the same time a powerful locus of political values. In concrete terms the Chinese saw the problem of system maintenance in terms of a determinate set of human relations that only needed to be kept in a state of mutual adjustment for a harmonious and balanced social system to result. An adjusted equilibrium was indeed the ideal of Chinese society.

Just as we have seen that system maintenance was an important if secondary value in Japan, so goal attainment with its consequent emphasis on performance was an important if secondary value in China. The main locus of these "political" values was naturally enough in the imperial government. The comparison of the place of political and integrative values, of the polity and the integrative system in China and Japan, can perhaps be revealing of both the similarities and the differences of the two countries. The relative importance of loyalty and filial piety may be taken as an important index of this contrast. As we have already seen, in Japan loyalty clearly superseded filial piety. In China:

> . . . if one chose to join the official rank, one had "to transform filial piety into loyalty to the sovereign"; but . . . when these two virtues seriously conflicted it was the duty of the son as son that should receive first consideration. This is further evidence that the family system was the foundation of traditional Chinese society and filial piety the basis of its moral principles.

Not only did the value of filial piety take precedence over loyalty, but loyalty itself had a very restricted focus. We have seen in Japan that loyalty permeated the whole society and became an ideal of all classes. In China, on the other hand, it did not even apply strongy to the whole gentry class but only to those in office:

> One does not have a chance to choose one's father. That is something determined by fate. But one can choose one's sovereign, just as a girl, before her marriage, can have a choice as to who should be her husband. It was a common saying that "the wise bird chooses the right tree to build his nest; the wise minister chooses the right sovereign to offer his service." It is true that traditionally all the people of the Chinese Empire were theoretically subjects of

the emperor. But it is also true that traditionally the common people had not the same obligation of allegiance toward the emperor as those who entered the official ranks of the government. It was to the officials that the relationship between sovereign and subject was specially relevant. So even in the time of unification when there was only one sovereign, one could still choose whether to join the official ranks or not, just as the girl might choose to remain single, even though there were only one man whom she could marry. In Chinese history, if a scholar chose to remain outside the official ranks, he was a man, as a traditional saying puts it, "whom the Son of Heaven could not take as his minister, nor the princes take as their friend." He was a great free man, without any obligation to the emperor except the paying of taxes.

Such an attitude toward one's political superior would be quite without support in the Japanese value system. In fact, while political power penetrated to the lowest units of society in Japan, it was much more circumscribed in China:

The daily life of the masses was regulated by social authority, while political authority was usually confined to the activity of the *yamen*. The court, except in the case of a few tyrants, did not interfere in the going concern of society. In general a good monarch collected a definite amount of taxes and left the people alone.

Not only was the generalization and extension of political power thwarted by the narrow range within which that power operated, but even in its own home ground, the imperial bureaucracy, that power was constantly being constrained by familistic and integrative considerations. Whereas the interest of the emperor may have been in the building up of national power and in taking strong, goal-oriented steps in that direction, he was constantly hampered by a bureaucracy which was not oriented to political goal-attainment values, but to the maintenance of an existing system of interests. The history of every "reform" effort in modern Chinese history (before the recent change of regime) is a tale of just such a situation, and this holds whether before or after the 1911 revolution. A perhaps overdrawn but vivid account of this situation is given by Fei:

. . . Chinese officials did not share in the political power of the emperor but served their monarch by neutralizing and softening down his power rather than by supporting it. With his nephews in court, the uncle was protected even in secret rebellious activities. According to Chinese tradition, officials did not work seriously for the government, nor did they like to continue as officials for a long period. Their purpose in entering the government was to gain both immunity and wealth in this order. The Chinese officials when in office protected their relatives, but, when this duty to the family had been performed, they retired. Retirement and even a hermit's life were the ideal. In retirement there was no longer any authority to be served with watchful care, while the relatives who had gained protection from their kinsman official owed him a debt of gratitude.

Now he need only enjoy his social prestige and grow fat and happy. As we say in China, "To come back to one's native soil, beautifully robed and loaded with honors, is the best thing in life."

Of course not all officials acted in this way. There are many examples of officials who were loyal in the extreme and earnestly attempted to build up the national power. They never, however, were able to dominate the government and put through a thoroughgoing modernization program as the young *samurai* were in Japan. They were always more or less checkmated by those committed to the maintenance of the old system. Even within the framework of integrative values there is room for considerable rationalization. Weber has pointed this out in his study of the Confucian ethic. To take a concrete example, it has been written of Tseng Kuo-fan, one of the more outstandingly honest and loyal of the late Ch'ing officials:

> He sought daily to improve himself by constant examination of his own mistakes and short-comings. . . . The same habits of rigid self-examination are shown in the letters which he wrote to his parents, to his brothers, and to his sons; and in the admonitions he gave to the young to live lives of frugality, diligence, and integrity.

Here is indeed a rational, this-worldly ethic, the ethic of the Confucian literati. But the aim of this ethic is neither to amass wealth, nor to increase national power. Rather it is designed to maintain the adjusted equilibrium of Chinese society. Therefore it lacks the dynamism which could overcome the traditionalism of the masses or transfer the primary allegiance from the family to some larger collectivity. The rationalism inherent in the Confucian ethic seems to need to be linked with a value system in which political values have primacy if it is to have an influence in the direction of modernization. This was the case in Japan and perhaps in presentday China.

Perhaps the most interesting result of this way of comparing the value systems of China and Japan is that it maintains that they both have a strong emphasis on political and integrative values, on loyalty and filial piety, but that there is a difference with respect to primacy of stress. This comparison then is used to explain in part the dramatic differences in social development. Thus the difference in social consequences is seen not in terms of the presence or absence of certain key values, but entirely in terms of the way in which values are organized.

We are now in a position to return to some of the considerations of Chapter I and summarize the results of the present investigation for the general problems set forth there.

Our first general conclusion is that a strong polity and dominant political values in Japan were distinctly favorable to the rise of industrial society. This is not what one would necessarily have expected if one extrapolated only from the European material. The orthodox view of European economic history has generally considered the "interference" of the state in the economy as inimical to economic development, though specific policies were often viewed as favorable. A general consideration of the relation of the polity and political values to economic development in the West might significantly alter the traditional view. Nevertheless, it seems likely that the role of the polity was considerably less important in European economic development than in Japanese. The Japanese case takes on special significance when compared with other non-Wesern societies. All of these societies faced certain problems in common which were different from those of the West. Whereas in the West industrialism was built on centuries of slow accumulation of capital and techniques, the non-Western societies faced industrialism as an existent fact. They did not have to go through the slow process of accumulation which the West had, nor could they if they had wanted to. The capital required for modern industrialization was too great to be supplied by the existing economic mechanisms in these societies. What has happened is that in almost every case, whatever industrialization has occurred has been government-controlled or government-sponsored, because only the government has been able to marshal the requisite capital. Under these circumstances it is obvious that the strength of the polity and political values are crucial variables. Of all the major non-Western societies Japan stands out as unique in its possession of a strong polity and central political values, and it is this above all, in my opinion, which accounts for the differential acceptance of industrialization.

A consideration of the cases of Russia and China may lend further credence to this view. These societies, since they have become Communist, have certainly had strong polities and strong political values. The Soviet Union is, in fact, almost the type case of a society emphasizing goal attainment. Though Russia is a marginal case, if we include it under the category of non-Western, it is the only non-Western nation besides Japan which has been able to become a major industrial power through its own efforts. China, more clearly a non-Western society, since its shift from the traditional integrative values to the Communist political values has shown a marked spurt in industrialization and can be expected to join Japan and Russia as the third great non-Western society to industrialize. Kemalist Turkey offers a non-Communist example of the importance of a strong polity in the process of modernization. On the other hand, if we consider a society such as Indonesia, we find that although what industrialization there is is under government direction or sponsorship; a weak polity and a low emphasis on political values are important factors in the extreme hesitancy, inefficiency and weakness of the movement toward industrialization. Whatever the specific form they take, and the Japanese and Communist examples are of course very different, political values and a strong polity would seem to be a great advantage and perhaps even a prerequisite for industrialization in the "backward" areas of today's world. Unfortunately any strongly goal-oriented society is perilously close to totalitarianism, if we take that term to define the situation in which political considerations tend to override all other considerations, as all of our three examples indicate.

Our second general conclusion is that religion played an important role in the process of political and economic rationalization in Japan through maintaining and intensifying commitment to the central values, supplying motivation and legitimation for certain necessary political innovations and reinforcing an ethic of inner-worldly asceticism which stressed diligence and economy. That it may also have played an important part in the formation of the central values which were favorable to industrialization is at least a strong possibility.

Religion reinforced commitment to the central value system by making that value system meaningful in an ultimate sense. The family and the nation were not merely secular collectivities but were also religious entities. Parents and political superiors had something of the sacred about them, were merely the lower echelons of the divine. Fulfillment of one's obligations to these superordinates had an ultimate meaning. It ensured the continuation of future blessings and of that ultimate protection which alone could save the individual from the hardships and dangers of this transitory world.

Alternatively another set of religious conceptions was offered which also reinforced the central value system. This view accepted the structure of Japanese society and its values as in accordance with the nature of reality. Fully and wholeheartedly carrying out one's part in that society and living up to its values meant an identification with that ultimate reality. This losing the self and becoming identified with ultimate nature, a line of religious thought deriving from Mencius, also promised release from the basic frustrations of existence in a state of enlightenment. Actually the two views usually went together, they were the two lenses through which Japanese religion viewed the world; though they can be analytically separated, in practice the difference between them was usually not noticed.

Though the primary religious reinforcement of the central value system occurred in the family and national cults, a series of religious movements arose in the Tokugawa Period which developed independent institutional forms and reached large numbers of people. Some of these have been considered a length in this study. They must be seen as symptomatic of the increasing intensity of the commitment to the central values in Tokugawa times and as in turn contributing to that intensification. Doctrinally they were usually fairly simple versions of the religious conceptions we have just reviewed. They were often syncretic in origin and more concerned with piety and ethical conduct than with the fine points of doctrine. Religion in both its general and sectarian aspects, then, contributed to the integration of sociey in terms of a set of values which we have seen as singularly conducive to the industrialization of Japan under the special conditions in which that industrialization took place.

Furthermore, religion played a major role in political rationalization by emphasizing certain overriding religio-political commitments which could supersede all lesser obligations, thus supplying motivation and legitimation for the Restoration of the emperor, in spite of the fact that this Restoration involved breaking with many loyalties and customs of the past. This trend was clothed in nativistic and fundamentalist garb as is so often the case when religious movements are seeking to legitimize social change. Just as the Protestant Reformation proclaimed, "Back to the Bible" and Reform Islam "Back to the Koran," so the Shintō Revival movement proclaimed "Back to the *Kojiki*." Though State Shintō in modern times was in certain respects a hothouse plant, there can be no doubt that reverence for the emperor has been a major ideological force in Japan and has served to legitimize changes which would otherwise have roused the strongest sentiments of opposition. The origins of these attitudes are not restricted to a few scholars of the Kokugaku but were widely and deeply distributed in Tokugawa times. The biography of Ishida Baigan, who was certainly no Kokugakusha, provides but one example. That powerful religious motivation is often an imporant factor in major political change is also indicated by the close association of Protestantism and democracy in the West and by the charismatic ideology of Communism, for most purposes to be considered as a religion, without which Communist political success would be unthinkable.

Finally, we must consider the relation of religion to that ethic of inner-worldly asceticism which is so powerful in Japan. The obligation to hard, selfless labor and to the restraint of one's own desires for consumption is closely linked to the obligations to sacred and semisacred superiors which are so stressed in Japanese religion, as also to that state of selfless identification with ultimate nature. As we have had repeated occasion to see, Japanese religion never tires of stressing the importance of diligence and frugality and of attributing religious significance to them, both in terms of carrying out one's obligations to the sacred and in terms of purifying the self of evil impulses and desires. That such an ethic is profoundly favorable to economic rationalization was the major point of Weber's study of Protestantism and we must say that it seems similarly favorable in Japan. The importance of such an ethic is clearly relevant to the general social and cultural circumstances. An inner-worldly ascetic ethic has been described for Manus and for Yurok, but clearly neither of these primitive societies was in a position to industrialize. Furthermore, it is probably not uncommon among certain types of merchant class. Geertz has described the inner-worldly asceticism of the Muslim merchants of Java, which is certainly related to their economic success, but hardly sufficient to guarantee a successful industrialization in Indonesia. On the other hand, such an ethic certainly seems favorable if not essential to industrialization, at least in its early stages. It is found not only in Protestantism and Japan, but in Communism. In each case the importance of religious rationalization and reinforcement is very considerable.

After all that has been said about the "functions" of Japanese religion we are finally forced to consider the meaning of those functions in terms of religion itself. If we give Japanese religion "credit" for contributing to the miraculous rise of modern Japan, we must also give it "blame" for contributing to the disaster which culminated in 1945. Such a conclusion has implications for the relation of religion and society in general. Every religion seeks to proclaim a truth which transcends the world, but is enmeshed in the very world it desires to transcend. Every religion seeks to remake the world in its own image, but is always to some extent remade in the image of the world. This is the tragedy of religion. It seeks to transcend the human but it is human, all too human. And yet tragedy is not the last word about religion, and 1945 is not the end of Japanese religion. As long as religion maintains its commitment to the source of ultimate value, which is to say as long as it remains religion, the confrontation of religion and society continues. Holding to that commitment religion turns every human defeat into victory.

7

In the following selection Thomas Smith also assesses the role that traditional values played in Japan's adaptation of new techniques. By the use of traditional values, Smith concludes, the Meiji leaders were able to find the sanctions that allowed them to industrialize. In his view, Meiji leaders had no choice; only by using old values could Meiji leaders find "sanction for their monopoly of power."

Old Values and New Techniques in the Modernization of Japan

THOMAS C. SMITH

ODERN technology was introduced into Japan under the sanction of traditional Japanese values. I do not suggest that there was logical necessity in this: that from the values we could infer modernization; nor do I suggest that nothing new was added. But despite amplification and reinterpretation, it was, none the less, traditional ideas that Japanese leaders used to justify change. Japanese mythology, long neglected by political theory, became the core of an ideology that made national power a necessity. At a time when Japan found herself impotent yet plunged into the middle of a world power struggle, mythology was called upon to endow the nation with one kind of greatness: the emperor was descended by unbroken lineage from divine ancestors, and he was father of a nation conceived as an extended family: what other nation could make *that* claim? A nation unique and precious as this was, could not fall behind others in power—economic and political as well as military—even if inherited institutions had to be scrapped wholesale to keep abreast. Otherwise the claim to greatness must eventually collapse. Belief in the claim, which was bolstered in everyday life by making a cult of the patriarchal family with its values of obedience and hierarchy, gave the nation the will and discipline to transform an almost purely agrarian society into a predominantly industrial one within a generation. No Asian nation has yet duplicated this feat.

Do we credit the old values with too much? I think not: telescoping

Thomas C. Smith, "Old Values and New Techniques in the Modernization of Japan," *Far Eastern Quarterly*, Vol. 14 (May 1955), pp. 355–363. Reprinted with permission of the publisher. Footnotes omitted.

centuries of social time into decades requires powerful sanctions that cannot be improvised. The alternative to building on the past was waiting for gunboats and ideas to destroy it and then there might be nothing to build with; in any case, for decades and perhaps generations, the envisioned forced march to modernization must be an agonizing crawl.

But if old loyalties provided the sanctions for change, they were not in turn strengthened by it. Having sanctioned technological and institutional change without themselves being able to change—how can a claim to divine origins be modified?—they gradually lost power to command belief. Let me cite a few examples of how their works robbed them of faith. Rationalist thought, which an educational system dedicated to the advancement of science and technology could not but promote, increasingly called into question the Japanese political myth. Modern industry gave rise to new and harsher class antagonisms that made the familial ideal of society harder to cherish. The authority of the family and the power of its symbols declined as the family lost economic functions to the market and as the difference in outlook between generations widened with accelerating change. Nevertheless, the primary old values—throne and family—did not collapse, for they were continuously reinforced by stronger and more efficient measures of indoctrination and thought control by the state.

The groups in control of the state had no choice but to sustain the old values as best they could. Without them there was no sanction for their monopoly of power or for the fearful and wrenching effort of industrialization. If that effort should collapse, so must Japan's always precarious international position, bringing loss of foreign markets, unemployment, perhaps even social revolution; for Japan's industrial economy was built in critical part on the exploitation of other peoples' resources, and the scope of exploitation had continuously to be extended to maintain the momentum of economic growth and allay deep-lying class conflicts. And because foreign aggrandizement brought resistance and moral condemnation from others, Japanese leaders insisted the more vehemently on judging themselves by their own unique standards. There was no way out: the weaker old values became, the more they were needed. To push ahead at any cost demanded either supreme nerve or blind faith, and in the end (as is so often the case) the two were one. The price the nation paid for *these* qualities of leadership was frightful: to be led without enthusiasm into challenging half the world to arms by men whose belief in the old values was most nearly absolute and whose brush with the outside world and modern thought most superficial—men whose rural origins and army careers had kept them "pure."

But long before this the nation was paying a price in malaise. Japanese life was racked by the mounting tension of living by old values in a world to which they no longer belonged. Tension did not take the form of an ideological struggle between parties that stood by the old values and parties that would overthrow them. This might have relieved the tension; in any case, for some the tension would have been *between* them and others and not inside. But except for Marxist intellectuals, no important segment of the Japanese population openly disavowed the official ideology; no one could without becoming an enemy of the state and, worse, breaking with his cultural past. But fewer and fewer people wore the straight-jacket of orthodoxy comfortably: despite nearly universal protestations of loyalty and belief, there was secret or unconscious alienation.

It is easier to guess than to prove the existence of inner conflict because Japanese dissembled it. Still, there were unwitting flashes of candor and even some quite intentional. Take this passage from the novel *Sore kara,* by Natsume Sōseki, in which a young man reflects on his father:

His father had received the moral upbringing usual for *samurai* before the Restoration. This training was unsuited to the realities of contemporary life, but his father, who was true to its precepts neither in conduct nor feeling clung to it in theory and for appearances sake. He had gone into business and had been driven by egotism and avarice which over the years had corrupted him. He was quite unaware of this. Although he was not the man he had been, he was always professing that it was his same old self that acted and had brought his affairs so satisfactorily to their present state. But Daisuke felt that no man could satisfy the hourly demands of modern life and remain true to a feudal ethic. Whoever tired, whoever strove to maintain two disparate selfs, must suffer the torment of war between them.

Or consider the case of Ishikawa Takuboku, one of Japan's most popular modern poets. Takuboku wrote a novel in which the hero (who is himself) thinks existing society utterly corrupt and worthy only of destruction. While writing this novel, Takuboku wrote to a friend that he badly needed money from its publication to discharge a long-neglected duty to his elder brother. What this duty was we do not know, but the term he used was *giri*—one of the central concepts of ethics as taught in Japanese schools; and Takuboku was at this time a teacher, and his hero was the principal of a village elementary school. I am convinced that conflicts like that of Takuboku, who seems both a rebel against society's conventions and a slave to them, went so deep and wide that few aspects of modern Japanese culture would not reveal them to analysis. Let me cite a few random and gross examples of what I mean.

Everyone knows that a recurring theme in Japanese drama is the inner struggle of the individual torn between duty and desire—between the imperatives of conventional morality and contrary impulses from experience. I am not about to suggest that this is a novel or uniquely Japanese theme; but when it becomes perhaps the dominant theme of a popular theatre we suspect that a great many people are tormented by the problems it treats, and we can see why this was so in Japan. *Kabuki* was the product of a wealthy merchant class which, deprived of political power and social honor by the warrior class, embroidered living with the enjoyment of the sharpest sensual pleasures—riotous color, melodrama, wine, women, and song. Pursuit of these pleasures was as contrary to the stern ethic of the dominant warrior class as the colorful ukiyoe prints of bourgeoise culture were different from the severe black and white paintings of Zen masters. And since the warrior ethic dominated Tokugawa society, pursuit of these pleasures involved the bourgeoisie in essentially the same conflict that assumed larger proportions and caught more people later on, as the warrior class modernized the country and sought at the same time to make its own moral code the ethic of the nation. I say it was essentially the same conflict, for, despite the drastic social changes modernization brought, *Kabuki* did not change its themes or its repertoire nor did it lose its popularity.

My second example is from the field of politics. Except on the far left, which did not count in the parliamentary struggle, no political party openly challenged the theory that all political authority derived from the emperor. For the "liberal" parties that embraced this theory as well as the conservative, it had serious disadvantages: it placed Japanese cabinets, whose ministers were responsible only to the emperor, ultimately beyond their control. To overcome this inconvenience, one party or another, almost continuously from 1880 to about 1935, advanced the view, strongly resisted by the military, the bureaucracy and the conservative political parties, that cabinet ministers should be responsible to parliament: the emperor would still appoint them but now from the majority party in the lower house. Those who held this view disclaimed any intention of encroaching on the power of the emperor, and they proved it to their own satisfaction by giving the doctrine of the emperor as father of the people an ingenious if unconvincing twist. Since the emperor was a wise and benevolent father who desired nothing but the welfare of his loving and filial subjects, there could be no conflict between throne and people. And to make the government responsible to parliament was to bring the two closer together and to make the single will of both, now sometimes frustrated by selfish (and presumably unfilial) ministers, more effective. This argument was advanced by parties that represented hard-headed modern businessmen who, while well aware of the stabilizing value of the throne, were from time to time embarrassed, frustrated, and bullied by the governments that manipulated its occult powers. The argument was in essence a radical attack on authoritarian government hidden in a statement of the purest and fussiest orthodoxy. There was no dishonesty in this; just divided minds and hearts.

We might give still other examples: the drive to rationalize operations in business firms organized on the family principle; indoctrination in the values of the hierarchical family in an essentially equalitarian educational system; emperor worship and class struggle in the labor movement. But we must go on to consider two problems our argument raises. First, why did Japanese leaders combine beliefs upon which they placed the highest value with a technology destructive of them? Of course, they did not fully appreciate the contradiction; but holding the beliefs they did, why did they value the new technology at all? It is no answer to say that they saw in it a means of enhancing Japan's power and prestige; the question *still* remains, for there were fanatically patriotic men who sought these same ends by rejecting the new technology. Second, how was the combination of old values and new techniques, once effected, sustained? By action of the state, of course; but what sustained the purpose of the state as its social base was transformed? My answers to these questions must be very general, tentative, and incomplete.

As to the first question, consider the interests joined by the Meiji Restoration, the political revolution of 1867 that started Japan on her career of modernization. At that time Japan's feudal rulers were overthrown in the name of the emperor by dissatisfied low-ranking warriors backed by a developing capitalist class. The grievances of these warriors were in part grudges nursed by a centuries-old feudal vendetta between eastern and western barons and in part economic dissatisfactions bred of rising prices and falling incomes as the land economy, on which warrior wealth and position were based, gave way before commercial capitalism. There was *nothing* in either of these grievances that helps explain the revolutionary use low-ranking warriors made of power once they had it: why, for example, they swept away the feudal political structure by which warriors monopolized power to establish a modern bureaucratic state in its place. The answer I think is that the warrior's capitalist allies were not interested in substituting one group of feudal rulers for another. They were for the most part rural industrialists and merchants who found feudal government, with its closed class system, its manifold restrictions on enterprise, and its bias in favor of tamed city guild-merchants, hateful. These men not only backed the Restoration movement with money; they gave it direction, turning what might otherwise have been a struggle to reorganize the feudal system into a movement to destroy it.

But why, then, did the slogans and ideology of the revolution look to the past? Why not some native variant of "liberty, equality, and fraternity" instead of "revere the Emperor"? For one thing, the capitalist element, although able to influence the Restoration movement, was not strong enough to dominate it. Under Tokugawa feudal rule even very wealthy commoners did not have the self-confidence, freedom of movement, and prestige to organize and lead an opposition movement; they could do no better than follow warriors who did. And because the warriors, who were the elite carriers of the traditional virtues, led the revolution, it was justified in the only way it could be for them, not as a break with the past but as a spiritual return to it. But there was another reason for this: the warrior's allies had one foot in the future, but the other was firmly planted in the past. As merchants and industrialists, they looked forward to sweeping change. But they were also landlords who exploited land through a system of patriarchal tenant relationships based on protection and patronage, loyalty and obedience, the structures of which not only gave them dominant social and political power in the village but supported their mercantile and industrial operations as well. While they wished to be free of the trammels and inequalities of feudalism, they did not wish to weaken the traditional structure and spirit of the village. What they wished was a more efficient and enlightened authoritarianism—one that would give them economic scope and opportunity for social advancement and at the same time stand as a bulwark against radical agrarian change.

This is what they got; but it became increasingly hard to preserve, for the enlightened efficiency of the new regime eventually weakened its authoritarian base. This brings me to the second question: what sustained authoritarian government?

Although modern technology must, it seems, ultimately transform the whole of a traditional society and all its values, it does not transform all sectors at the same rate. Typically, change in rural areas is slower than in cities, and in Japan it has been exceptionally slow. The reason for this, I think, is at least in part the character of Japanese agriculture.

One way industrial development may radically change agriculture is by depriving it of essential labor and so forcing the mechanization of farming. This has not occurred in Japan because rural population growth has offset —and in some areas more than offset—emigration to the city. No doubt this growth is due in part to the elimination or softening of Malthusian checks. But equally important in my opinion is that the typical holding in Japan is so small and badly fragmented that mechanization is blocked, and the peasant family faced with a labor shortage has no means of meeting it but natural increase. This is not always possible; biology sometimes lets the family down. But it is in most cases because the family adapts to the demands of biology—by adopting sons-in-law, permitting second wives, holding the young child-bearing generations in the family indefinitely. There is more than a hint of this adaptability and its consequences in the remarkably close correlation, confirmed by many demographic studies, between the size of the family and the size of its holding—that is, the amount of labor it needs.

Population growth, in part forced by the smallness of the holding, sustained the small holding in the face of a growing demand from industry for labor. Indeed, the average working holding has become somewhat smaller during the past century of industrial development and, as a result, although the family has been broken up as a unit of production elsewhere, it has *not* in agriculture. The typical family uses no more than a few days of hired labor a year, and all its adult members work at the same occupation under closely similar conditions, as share-holders in a single enterprise. And because the enterprise operates on the narrowest margin—costs are high and income low with hand labor—solidarity, obedience, and authority are for the peasant family conditions of survival.

Since machines cannot supplant nor wage labor compete with family labor in agriculture, the development of capitalist farming is blocked even though, as farming becomes increasingly commercial, land ownership tends to concentrate (although typically on a small scale). The man who by lending and foreclosing lays field to field, acquiring more land than he can work with family labor, almost invariably lets the surplus to families of tenants. The result is increasingly sharp distinctions of wealth and income in the village, but the solidarity of the village is never shattered, as that of the medieval English village was, by division of the population increasingly into capitalist farmers and agricultural laborers. With rare exceptions, the village remains predominantly a community of small farmers—some landlords, some tenants, and others owner-cultivators but all faced with essentially the same problems of small-scale farming. Not that conflicts of interest do not occur: but for the most part they take the form of personal quarrels, and although larger, class antagonisms undoubtedly exist, they are usually submerged by an overriding sense of community solidarity. I wish to comment further on this point after noting two other factors that contribute to the spirit of solidarity.

The first concerns landlord-tenant relations, a complex subject that I must unconscionably simplify. Before the occupation land reform the Japanese landlord rented a holding to a tenant who managed it; the landlord's return depended on the skill and resourcefulness of the tenant as a farmer; for he could not collect rent unless the tenant, who almost never had savings, made enough from current operations to pay it. He could normally evict the tenant for nonpayment of rent; but unless the tenant and not nature or the market were at fault, he rarely exercised this right, for there was no reason to think another tenant could do better, and it was not easy to deprive a whole family known to him and everyone else in the village of the means of life. So in bad years he reduced the rent instead and, the return from agriculture being highly variable from year to year, he made this concession repeatedly. Therefore, even when rent was theoretically a fixed payment in money or kind, it varied in practice from year to year with yields, so that the landlord was to some extent a partner of the tenant whose interests he could not infringe beyond a certain point without hurting his own. Moreover, such events in the tenant's family as sickness and death affected the tenant's ability to pay rent in full almost as directly as the weather, and the landlord had to make similar allowance for them. Since this forced him to take an interest in and assess events at the very center of the tenant's family life, landlord-tenant relations were social as well as economic. The relationship was not always friendly, but it was rarely overly hostile, for it was subject to conventions of polite and considerate conduct enforced by community opinion.

The second factor I wish to mention is the cultivation of rice. Rice is cultivated in Japan everywhere soil, climate, and terrain permit, which is to say on at least part of most holdings and all of some. And because rice must be made to stand in water during much of the growing season to get maximum yields, there is need in almost every village for a vast and complex system of ditches, dams, dikes, ponds, tunnels, and water gates that can be constructed and maintained only by community effort. No man who grows rice, therefore, owns or controls all of the essential means of production himself nor may make all of the more critical decisions of farming independently. A man may wish, for example, to turn an unirrigated field into paddy, but he will not be allowed to do so if this would impair the water supply of others; and he will refrain from insisting on his wish because he has been taught he must, and village opinion will be ranged solidly against him if he does not. The habit of bowing to group opinion where water is concerned carries over, we may suppose, to other matters—if for no other reason than that any serious breach of harmony in the village strikes at the communal foundations of agriculture.

To return now to the significance for us of community solidarity: the sense of it makes the village a powerful agency for suppressing individualism and dissent, for blocking innovation and maintaining custom's hard cake into which most lives and personalities in rural Japan are molded.

I have one further point to make and it also concerns the concentration of Japanese agriculture on the cultivation of rice. This concentration is characteristic of individual holdings as well as agriculture as a whole, and consequently there is far less specialization in farming than one might think in a country with the large urban market of Japan. Most peasant families, therefore, supply all or nearly all of their own food, and since the labor force is large in relation to its output, what is consumed takes a very large part of what is produced. Of the total agricultural income of the average peasant family in 1935, about one-third was in kind—that is, was not marketed. This means that the peasant's involvement in the market, the limits on which seem absolute, is far from complete and that commercial values do not penetrate a very large area of his economic relations, which remain embedded in custom-bound social groupings.

It is perhaps possible now to see what permitted the state to sustain the old values. Among the urban population modernization generated new attitudes destructive of them—class consciousness, individualism, skepticism; but the peasantry remained a vast hinterland of conservatism. And, owing to the intensive use of labor in agriculture, the demographic ratio between city and country did not alter with industrialization as radically as in many countries: in 1930 agricultural labor in Japan was 50.3 per cent of the total labor force as compared to 18.8 per cent in the U.S. in 1940, 16.3

per cent in Germany in 1933, and 6.2 per cent in England in 1938. I am suggesting, of course, that the peasantry provided a social base by virtue of which the state was able to impose the worship of old gods upon the entire nation.

But why, we may ask, did the agrarian sector remain decisive politically when it had ceased to be so economically? This question brings us back to Japan's struggle against the West. Launching upon industrialization late and poorly endowed with resources, Japan was bound to build heavily on foreign markets and resources already preëmpted; so she was bound to intrude and intruding to face fierce resistance which she must either defy or retreat before. And since she could not retreat—not without grave social risks and the risk of remaining powerless—she defied. Defiance brought success, but success intensified resistence, calling for a strengthening of old loyalties to overcome inner uncertainties and discipline the nation to a new effort. Pressure from the outside did not grow continuously; there were periods of relaxation; and nothing testifies so convincingly to the importance of foreign relations for the persistence of old values than the fact that in these periods the old values were seriously challenged by other values from the West. But the international honeymoon never lasted long and the '20's were invariably followed by the '30's. These wild oscillations between uncritical acclaim of the West and xenophobia were not mere fickleness: they were rooted in the real claims of two cultures that could not be reconciled because one was the foundation of a state always imperiled by states built on the other.

8

Modern urbanization first appeared in the old castle towns of Tokugawa Japan. In this essay John Hall shows why much of Japan's modern development took place in the old feudal centers. He also explains why the urbanization and bureaucratization of the samurai was so important for Japan's modernization.

The Castle Town and Japan's Modern Urbanization

JOHN WHITNEY HALL

JAPAN's role in Far Eastern history has been unique in many respects. Traditionally an integral part of the Chinese zone of civilization, Japan has nonetheless demonstrated a marked ability to remain independent of continental influence. In recent years Japan's remarkable record of adjustment to the conditions imposed upon her by the spread of Western civilization to the Orient has raised the provocative question of why Japan, of all Far Eastern societies, should be the first to climb into the ranks of the modern industrial powers. Is it possible, as one scholar has suggested, that Japan "has been the country which has diverged the most consistently and markedly from Far Eastern norms, and these points of difference have been by and large, points of basic resemblance to the West"?

To seek an answer to this fascinating problem in culture comparison is beyond the scope of this short article. Yet with this question in mind it may be profitable to pursue an approach to Japanese history through one of its key institutions. Perhaps by confining our attention to a single facet of historical development it will be possible to gain some useful insights into the process of cultural evolution in Japan, particularly into the historical factors which were so influential in the years of transition which followed the "opening" of the country to the West in 1854. For such purposes the city presents itself as a convenient object of study.

The city has been a distinct and important segment of society in both East and West. Characteristically it has constituted, in the words of Mumford, a "point of maximum concentration for the power and culture of a

John Whitney Hall, "The Castle Town and Japan's Modern Urbanization," *Far Eastern Quarterly,* Vol. 15 (November 1955), pp. 37–56. Reprinted with permission of the publisher. Footnotes omitted.

community." Most often the city has served as a source of progressive leadership, the center from which forces of innovation and change have spread into the community as a whole. The city as a cultural institution is both universally prevalent and historically significant. In the case of Japan it affords an especially rewarding object of study not only for the measure it provides of Japan's internal social and economic development but for the light it sheds on Japan's relative position between the cultural extremes of East and West.

Japanese cities prior to the impact of industrialized civilization upon them were essentially "oriental" in their composition and their social and economic functions. As in China such cities were larger by far than their European counterparts. But they seldom attained their size on the basis of trade alone. As in the case of most Eastern cities, a prime reason for their existence was that of civil administration and military defense. Yet while the morphology of Japanese cities and their role in national life reflected their oriental environment, it is also apparent that in their evolution they followed a pattern much more similar to that of the West than of China. In contrast to China where, since Han times, the function and structure of cities remained comparatively unchanged dynasty after dynasty, Japan presents a picture of continuing urban modification and expansion. Thus in Japan the major cities which succeeded in making the transition to modern times were, with few exceptions, completely undeveloped at the beginning of the sixteenth century. Furthermore, most of these did not reach maturity until the early eighteenth century and even then did not settle into a static, unchanging mode of existence. The city in Japan may be viewed as a constantly growing and evolving organism which, while it may never have constituted the dramatic challenge to the traditional land-based political and economic order as in Europe, was capable of rapid modification under the impetus of Western influence.

Before pursuing these observations further, however, it would be well to point out some of the limitations which must attend a study of this kind. Even within a society as comparatively homogeneous as that of Japan, cities have seldom been identical either in type or structure. Cities and towns have arisen from many diverse causes. Their historical evolution has followed several distinct paths according to the complex interweaving of changes in political, economic or religious conditions within the country. Geographic regionalism, especially in the contrasting features of the highly advanced central core of Japan and the generally retarded fringe areas, has provided a constant factor of diversity. Thus any attempt to trace the course of urban development as a single uniform process must run the risk of oversimplification. On the other hand, during many periods of Japanese history, one or another type of town has tended to predominate, and hence has stood out as the representative urban institution of its era. This is especially true of the period which immediately preceded the appearance of the modern industrialized city in Japan. During roughly three centuries, from the 1570's to the 1870's, the castle town, or *jōkamachi,* assumed an importance out of all proportion to other types of urban communities. The story of the rise of the castle town and its eventual modification under the forces of internal decay and Western influence may be taken as the central theme of Japan's modern urbanization.

The story of the castle town has its origins in the early Middle Ages in Japan, in the era of transition from the classical age of aristocratic rule to the feudalism of the rising military class. In medieval Japan, the Sinified monolithic government adopted from China during the seventh century and the old style administrative towns which housed the court bureaucracy fell into decay. After the twelfth century both Nara and Kyoto lost their significances as centers of political authority and fell apart into a number of loosely clustered towns: Nara as a locus of temples; Kyoto as a place of residence for court families. The provincial capitals, the *kokufu,* for the most part, reverted to the villages from which they had sprung. Lacking the massive walls of the Roman outposts in Europe, even the remains of their public buildings quickly disappeared from sight. This decline of the central government left few large concentrations of political or ecclesiastical power, since early feudal society in Japan was decentralized and its constituents were individually weak.

Beginning with the twelfth century, Japan entered a new phase of urban development along lines which followed the rise of new religious or military centers and the new economic requirements of a decentralized feudal society. Growth was slow. Kamakura appeared momentarily as a flourishing administrative seat but faded with the fall of the Hōjō. Not until the late fourteenth century did new towns of any consequence make their appearance. Fed by an expanding manorial economy, Nara and Kyoto began to recover some stature as commercial centers. Muromachi flourished as the location of the Ashikaga shogunate. Beyond these, local feudal headquarters such as Kagoshima, Yamaguchi, and Bingo Funai, religious centers such as Ishiyama, Sakamoto, and Ujiyamada, and commercial towns such as Hakata, Muro, Hyōgo, and Sakai attested to the expansion of the power of feudal and religious institutions and to the growth of domestic and foreign trade.

Scholars who have attempted to identify this phase of urban growth in Japan with comparable stages in the rise of European cities are uniformly agreed that the fourteenth-century Japanese towns remained far more dependent for their support on the agencies of political or ecclesiastical authority than did the newly emergent towns of Europe. Whether this was the result of some basic "characteristic" of Japanese society or merely a product of the tardy development of commercial economy is hard to determine. But for whatever reason it is apparent that the medieval town and the commercial and service community in Japan looked for security not in the building of walls, but in the patronage and protection of the aristocracy or the politically powerful temples, shrines, and military houses. More clearly a result of economic backwardness was the relative lack of differentiation of the town from the surrounding agrarian community. In fourteenth-century Japan traders and artisans continued to maintain strong ties with the land, functioning both as landlords and as members of trade or craft guilds. Self-government was slow to develop and in most areas was inspired by a more vigorous movement towards village self-rule.

During the fifteenth century, however, with the breakup of the Ashikaga hegemony and the consequent wars of succession and feudal rivalry, a growing spirit of freedom became evident in both countryside and town. The troubled times of Japan's civil wars provided the lower classes with both the occasion for independence and the opportunities for self-advancement. While the feudal wars brought destruction and turmoil, they served also to encourage social mobility and widespread economic growth. The causes of such growth are not easily enumerated, but the accompanying signs were clearly visible in technological improvements affecting agriculture and mining, the increase in foreign and domestic trade, the spread in the use of currency and in the agencies devoted to the handling of credit and exchange, and in the gradual absorption of the fragmented manorial economies into the larger blocks of feudal or ecclesiastical holdings.

By the sixteenth century such factors of economic growth and feudal competition had accounted for the emergence of the town into new prominence. New bonds of dependence were forged between castle and trading town as the shogun or the great *shugo* lords attempted to buttress their economic positions against the lesser feudal barons of the countryside. Notable was the attempt of the Ashikaga shogunate to maintain its superiority over its vassals through its use of the merchants of Sakai. In the ensuing years Sakai, Hirano, Hakata, and a few other port cities of central Japan won a degree of freedom from feudal control. Sakai in particular, the "Venice of Japan" to the Jesuits of the late sixteenth century, took on the form made familiar by free cities of Europe: a port governed by its chief burghers, protected by walls and moats, and by its own militia.

The appearance of such cities as Sakai has occasioned considerable speculation among Japanese and Western historians regarding the direction which Japan's social and economic institutions were taking in the mid-1500's. Early writers such as Takekoshi were extravagant in their views, claiming to see in the rise of trading cities the beginning of the end of feudalism in Japan. But more considered studies have demonstrated the weakness of these independent urban communities. Sakai was, after all, the achievement of a relatively unique region of Japan which, especially in its economy, had advanced far beyond the rest of the country. It is obvious that Japan as a whole lacked the basic requirements which could support a more widespread growth of free cities as Europe had done. Furthermore, the conditions which had favored such a growth in central Japan were to diminish in subsequent years. In sixteenth-century Japan religious organizations, which in Europe helped counterbalance feudal authority, were on the decline. Foreign trade, that source of vital energy for a free commercial class, was at best a precarious activity for the Japanese, placed so far from Chinese and Southeast Asian ports. Even in its most prosperous years much of the foreign trade carried on by Japanese adventurers was made possible only through the use of capital supplied by feudal or religious institutions. The ease with which the feudal authorities were able to control and then to monopolize foreign trade before the middle of the next century was a clear indication of the failure of such trade to become the support of urban freedom in Japan.

The "freedom" of such cities as Sakai was indeed illusory, based, as it was, less upon any prolonged struggle against feudal authority or on any overwhelming economic resources than upon the accidents of feudal rivalry and the weakness of the Ashikaga shogunate. Once the crumbling shogunate was replaced by new military coalitions, once Nobunaga and Hideyoshi turned towards the "free" cities, they fell, and Sakai among them. Perhaps the surest commentary on the "free cities" of the sixteenth century Japan was their subsequent history. Not one was to continue its dominant role through the succeeding Tokugawa period into the modern age.

In Japan of the sixteenth century the truly significant institutional development was not the free city nor the rising merchant community, but rather the maturation of a new type of feudal ruler, the daimyo. The rise of the modern daimyo produced one of the major turning points in the history of Japanese political and social institutions. During the late years of the civil war period the daimyo had been increasing constantly in size and effective strength. Then after the mid-sixteenth century, as the daimyo joined ranks in far-reaching military alliances, and eventually in an overall national unity, all opposition to feudal authority fell before them. The cities as well as the Buddhist church submitted. Japan was, in the words of her own historians, thoroughly "refeudalized."

But the word "refeudalization" is hardly adequate to describe the radical changes which swept Japan during the late sixteenth century. These years were distinguished not by some conservative retrogression within Japanese society but by a dynamic burst of activity which had few parallels in the history of Japanese institutions. The new feudal lords and the domains, or *han*, which they held represented the harnessing of social and material energies on a new unprecedented scale. Forged out of the great civil wars of the fifteenth century, the daimyo domains were the product of a process of military and political consolidation which brought increasingly large areas under the unified control of individual feudal rulers. They were supported by new advances in agricultural technology and by extensions in the area under cultivation which released into the hands of the feudal lords new potentials of wealth and military power. They won their way by the perfection of new developments in the art of warfare: the mastery of the use of muskets and cannon, the improvement of the means of fortification and the shift to the use of large mass armies. Finally, they were both the result and cause of far-reaching changes which affected the social organization of the peasantry and of the feudal ruling class. Characteristic of the daimyo was their ability to devise new means of social control which enabled them to draw increasingly on the manpower resources of the countryside and on the loyal services of their military vassals.

It has been suggested that the larger of the daimyo domains resembled petty principalities. Needless to say, however, not all Japan was consolidated into domains of sufficient size to warrant such a description. Many parts of the country remained politically fragmented, either because of adverse geographical conditions or because they occupied buffer zones lying between large rival concentrations of feudal power. By 1560 over two hundred daimyo had made their appearance, and the major plains of Japan had been reduced to stable blocks of control by the more powerful of these feudal lords. Although much fighting remained to be done, the contours of daimyo control had been established and the basis was laid for the movement towards "national unification."

The story of Japan's political unification in the last years of the sixteenth century is well known. Beginning with the formation of regional alliances among daimyo, it progressed under the leadership of the "three unifiers," Oda Nobunaga, Toyotomi Hideyoshi, and Tokugawa Ieyasu. By 1603 a national hegemony had been effected by the ascendancy of a new shogunal power able to reduce the competing daimyo to vassalage. The resultant political structure, referred to as the *baku-han* system by Japanese historians, was a curious blend of centralization and local feudal autonomy. In it direct shogunal authority extended from the powerful Kantō base of the Tokugawa house to include much of central Japan and most of the buffer zones, while the daimyo proper, though acknowledging their obligations of vassalage and subservience to the basic laws of the land, retained a generous amount of independence in local affairs.

The completion of this daimyo-based centralized feudalism had a profound effect upon the subsequent character of Japanese society, particularly upon its urban development. For the next three centuries all the cities of Japan were brought firmly under feudal control. Former religious centers or commercial and post station towns shared the common experience of incorporation into shogunal or daimyo territories. Those which survived as important cities saw the erection of huge castles in their confines or found themselves placed under the direct authority of feudal magistrates.

Thus Kyoto, Sakai, and Nagasaki became nonmilitary cities within the shogun's territories. But the most numerous urban units of the time were the castle towns which made up the military and administrative headquarters of the shogun and daimyo. Among these the vast majority were completely new cities occupying locations which, up to the time of their selection, supported little more than farming or fishing villages. The erection of the castle towns of the late feudal period out of the undeveloped countryside required a tremendous outlay of resources on the part of the daimyo. The achievement was made all the more remarkable by the dramatic suddenness with which these operations were carried out. Most of the first-ranking castles and castle towns such as Himeji, Osaka, Kanazawa, Wakayama, Tokushima, Kōchi, Takamatsu, Hiroshima, Edo, Wakamatsu, Okayama, Kōfu, Fushimi, Takasaki, Sendai, Fukuoka, Fukui, Kumamoto, Tottori, Matsuyama, Hikone, Fukushima, Yonezawa, Shizuoka, and Nagoya were founded during the brief span of years between 1580 and 1610. It would be hard to find a parallel period of urban construction in world history.

The castle town naturally derived its location and structural arrangement from the requirements laid down by the daimyo and the central shogunal authority, for the same forces which had given rise to the new combinations of feudal power gave shape to the castle towns. Thus as wider and wider domains were consolidated, the daimyo moved their headquarters from the narrow confines of mountain defenses to larger moat-and-tower fortresses placed at the strategic and economic centers of their holdings. In most instances the daimyo selected locations from which their castles could dominate the wide plains which formed the economic bases of their power and from which they could control the lines of communication stretching into the countryside. Here the daimyo was able to assemble and support his growing corps of officers and foot soldiers. In almost every instance the final establishment of the daimyo's castle town headquarters was preceded by the erection of less spacious establishments which were abandoned as the daimyo increased in power and stature. Oda Nobunaga's progress from Gifu to Azuchi and his subsequent attempt to acquire Osaka as his headquarters is merely the best known of such moves.

The new *jōkamachi* symbolized first of all the new concentrations of military power achieved by the daimyo. In the domains, defenses formerly scattered in depth were now pulled back to single central citadels where the massed resources of the daimyo could be held in readiness and where protective walls could be thrown up at sufficient distance from the vital nerve centers of military operations to protect them from musket and cannon. The shogunal edict of 1615 which ordered the destruction of all but one castle in each province was merely the culmination of a lengthy process of consolidation in which the functions of many smaller installations were combined into a limited number of oversize establishments.

In the province of Bizen, to take a typical example of an area which eventually came under the control of a single daimyo, there were at times during the fifteenth century between twenty and thirty castles. Yet by the time of the 1615 order only four remained. Of these, the lesser three were destroyed, leaving Okayama, which commanded the entire Bizen plain, as the headquarters of the daimyo of Bizen. The citadels which resulted from this process were huge by any standards of their day. It is probably no exaggeration to say that the greatest of the Japanese fortresses, Edo and Osaka, had no peers in terms of size and impregnability. For Japan, no clearer indication was needed of the ascendancy of feudal military might than these castles which at regular intervals towered over the Japanese countryside.

Intimately associated with the construction of the new consolidated fortresses of the late sixteenth century were a number of major changes in the structure of feudal society. In the first place the elimination of the numerous smaller castles had resulted in the decline and eventual elimination of numerous petty baronies scattered throughout the shogunal and daimyo territories. Within the new domains the daimyo became increasingly absolute as they consciously diminished the independence of their vassals. For this reason, and as a result of new military and tactical requirements, it became the policy of the daimyo to draw their vassals and retainers, both high and low, more and more into residence within the confines of the central citadel. The pattern made familiar by the enforced residence of daimyo in the environs of the shogun's castle at Edo had already become established practice at the daimyo level. The citadel thus of necessity became a town.

This physical displacement of the feudal class from countryside to castled towns held even more fundamental social implications. As the petty lords and feudal gentry left the land and congregated at the center of daimyo authority, a new line of distinction was drawn between the cultivators, those remaining on the land, and the feudal aristocracy, those members of the daimyo's retinue gathered at his castle headquarters. The process was not sudden, but continuous over several decades. It was most dramatically brought out by Hideyoshi's nationwide land resurvey begun in 1582, and the "sword hunt" of 1588. Thereafter the privilege of wearing two swords had become the badge of social distinction which gave to its possessor life and death power over the subject classes. By the end of the sixteenth century the castle and its attached feudal military elite had become a distinct unit and the chief reason for the existence of large concentrations of people in the years to follow. The *jōkamachi,* at first fundamentally garrison towns, had become the home of an entire class, the *bushi* or samurai.

The castle towns thus individually and collectively became the physical embodiment of the Tokugawa feudal elite. Edo, the shogun's capital, sym-

bolized the hierarchal unity of the daimyo under the Tokugawa house, as
the several daimyo built residences in the shadow of the castle and proceeded on a regular basis to pay yearly homage to the supreme feudal
authority. The daimyo's castle towns were but miniatures of this pattern.
The morphology of the castle town was in essence a cross-section of the
pattern of Japanese feudal society. The castle town was built by and for
the daimyo and his vassals. The castles, which occupied the center of these
cities, were built to protect the aristocracy. No outer wall enclosed the
whole community as in Europe, although outer moats were not infrequent.
Around the central keep lay the residences of the daimyo's vassals, generally in two zones. The higher officials were placed in a group closely
strung around the keep within the security of the main rampart and inner
moat. A second belt, farther removed, lay unprotected except perhaps by
the outer single moat and sometimes an earthen barricade. Here were the
quarters of the lesser vassals. Between the two groups of vassals resided
the daimyo's privileged merchants and artisans, while at the edge of the
outer belt lay a ring of temples and shrines whose substantial buildings
provided a sort of outer cordon of defense points controlling the major
roads and points of access to the city. In such a community the lines of
feudal hierarchy were clearly drawn and strictly maintained.

One of the most distinctive features of the castle town was the large
number of samurai resident in it. On the average they accounted for approximately fifty per cent of the town's entire population. But the figure
was frequently greater; for instance, in Sendai it was near seventy per cent
and in Kagoshima it was over eighty per cent. What this meant in total
numbers of samurai and family members will be evident from a few
examples. In Okayama, a city of slightly over 38,000 inhabitants in 1707,
10,000 were of the samurai class, another 8,000 were hangers-on of one
kind or another. The census of 1872 for the city of Sendai listed 29,000
inhabitants of a total of 50,000 in the samurai class. In Tottori, a city of
approximately 35,000 in 1810, 25,000 were of this category.

The *jōkamachi* were built first and foremost as garrison towns and military headquarters of their domains. But they rapidly became points of
concentration for many other functions important to the feudal rulers of
the day. Thus as civil war gave way to a new political unity, the daimyo's
headquarters became increasingly concerned with matters of local administration. It has been pointed out that one of the outstanding features of
Tokugawa feudal administration was its "public character," in which a
regular bureaucracy managed the affairs of taxation, judicature and maintenance of law and order. This public bureaucracy was eventually achieved
by the conversion of an essentially military hierarchy of officers and men,
which constituted the daimyo's corps of vassals and retainers, into an administrative officialdom. The great castles of Japan came to house the

central and local administrative headquarters of the nation. From them political authority radiated outward into the countryside.

The castle towns also quickly assumed importance as points of economic accumulation and consumption. The degree of economic concentration achieved in the *jōkamachi* is perhaps best understood in terms of the tremendous outlay of manpower and material required to construct the fortress and its accompanying residences and temples. The castle town symbolized from the first the ability of the daimyo to draw from his domain vast productive resources and to recruit the services of numerous commercial and industrial agents. Once having accomplished the initial task of castle construction, moreover, the need for economic concentration did not disappear. The daimyo and their vassals, having taken up permanent residence in the new towns, became dependent upon their commercial agents who could supply the sinews of warfare and the necessities of daily living, agents able to bridge the gap between town and countryside. The feudal aristocracy of the Tokugawa era, living in cities at a level of subsistence and consumption far above that of the meager self-sufficiency of the village, was made increasingly dependent upon the services of a merchant class.

Thus the same movement which brought the samurai to the castle headquarters of the daimyo also brought merchants out of the older port or religious cities and scattered trading towns. The result was a radical rearrangement of commercial activity in Japan. Daimyo, eager to attract to their castles the services of merchants and artisans, offered liberal conditions to those who would join them. The old guild system of medieval Japan was broken down as merchants took advantage of "free" markets provided in the castle towns. Thus as the daimyo rose to power the older centers of trade declined and new communities, surrounding the new castles, began to flourish.

This process, whereby the merchant community of the sixteenth century became increasingly attached to centers of feudal authority, has generally been described as coercive. It would be hard to deny the coercive aspects of the measures taken by the great centralizers such as Nobunaga and Hideyoshi as they clamped restrictions upon the merchants of Sakai or Hakata. But for most of Japan coercion was not the key factor. In the less economically advanced areas the daimyo provided local merchants and artisans with new and attractive opportunities. Under the stimulus of the insatiable demands for military supplies and food stores made by the warring feudal lords there came into being a new and more aggressive service class, many of whose members were actually drawn from the warrior class. By allying itself with the rising feudal aristocracy, this new class of merchaints was able to break the restraints of the medieval guild system and meet the daimyo's needs for an expanding economy. In the early years of their ascendancy the daimyo counted their commercial agents

among their most valuable resources. It was even customary for a daimyo
to take his merchant adherents with him when he moved the location of
his headquarters. Thus as the castle towns took shape, they became the economic centers of their domains. In them were concentrated the service
groups which in turn acted as exploitive agents for the daimyo and *bushi*.
In the *jōkamachi* the other half of the population consisted of merchants,
artisans, and service personnel. These were the *chōnin* of Tokugawa times.

In both the shogunal territories and daimyo domains, castle town merchants had the advantage of patronage and protection. Within the domain,
the daimyo drew a sharp line between castle town merchants and the
residents of the countryside. Commerce was strictly limited to the central
city and, under special circumstances, to the few towns which had functioned as urban centers before the emergence of the daimyo. The villages
were confined to agricultural and handicraft production. Within the
domain the castle town merchants performed two prime tasks: the wholesale accumulation of produce from the hinterland, and the linkage of the
domain economy to the national market. The first function gave rise to
monopoly associations under daimyo patronage. The second brought into
existence the class of rice mercants and domain financiers who maintained
the produce warehouses at Osaka or other exchange centers. The desire
of every daimyo to make his domain self-sufficient and prosperous was a
constant stimulus to the castle town merchants.

As with the *bushi*, disposition within the castle town revealed graphic-
ally the relative status of the *chōnin* within the community. In such towns
the early commercial settlers, those first to enter the daimyo's service,
constituted a privileged group. Among them the daimyo's chartered merchants, the *goyō shōnin*, enjoyed a degree of tax exemption and social
advantages which belied the low status eventually assigned to the merchants as a class. For the sake of convenience and protection these groups
were located in the belt between the two main zones of samurai residences.
Late arrivals were obliged to take up positions on the outskirts, along the
main roads leading to and from the town. It is sometimes maintained by
Japanese historians that the Tokugawa period merchants lived under a
system of local self-government. But the self-government they enjoyed
consisted of little more than the privilege of managing certain private areas
of their activity under their own headmen. In fact it is hardly possible to
distinguish any fundamental difference between the procedures utilized
by the Tokugawa rulers in their administration of the village and of the
town.

From their castles most daimyo divided their realms into two distinct
parts, the villages (*mura*) and the city blocks (*machi*). The same sort of
control mechanism was used to govern both parts. Within the city, each
block was supplied with guards and gates which converted it into a
separate administrative unit. Each block like its counterpart, a village, was

responsible for its own good conduct under its own representatives, whose titles of office often corresponded to those used in the villages. Individual citizens were made subordinate to the laws of the daimyo and shogun under the system of joint responsibility, the *goningumi*. The merchant community as a whole was managed by its own headman or headmen who performed their duties under the scrutiny of the shogunal or domain magistrates. In Tokugawa Japan all cities were administered ultimately by the city magistrate (*machi bugyō*) placed there by either shogun or daimyo.

It was inevitable, perhaps, that as the feudal authorities perfected their administrative machinery, the *chōnin* were brought under an increasingly heavy burden of legal responsibilities and social restrictions. Relegated increasingly to a low status as the Tokugawa adopted the concepts of Confucian social theory, the *chōnin* found almost every aspect of urban life and commercial activity placed under the scrutiny and regulation of the administrative class. Thus the merchant community passed from an early period of relative freedom to one of increasing regimentation. The protected location in the shelter of the castle turned into a prison. And even foreign trade, which might have offered an escape from feudal oppression, became a shogunal monopoly. Yet it must be remembered that there was always a limit to such oppression. In the final analysis, daimyo and shogunal policy towards the merchants was tempered by the degree to which the feudal class had become dependent upon their services. After the mid-seventeenth-century merchants were permitted to organize themselves into new guilds and protective associations. In this way, the Tokugawa merchants, though deprived of foreign markets, continued to prosper as the middlemen between castle town and countryside.

A final aspect of the centralization achieved by the daimyo in their castle towns was attained at the expense of local religious institutions. The story of Nobunaga's dramatic conquest of the Buddhist church in Japan is well known. Less familiar is the history of the clash of ecclesiastical and feudal interests at the level of the local domain. Yet for the daimyo, the conquest over hostile religious bodies in his locality was also a prerequisite for secure possession of the domain. In each locality, as formerly independent religious centers were brought under daimyo control, we find the local headquarters of Buddhist and Shinto sects being moved to the castle town. There the priests came under the direct patronage and surveillance of the daimyo and his magistrate of religious bodies. Even the location of religious buildings was frequently a matter of decision based on the strategic needs of the daimyo. In its growth the castle town became the focal point of the domain's religious institutions.

But of even greater importance in focusing religious sentiment upon the castle town was the adoption of the tenets of Confucianism, under which the shogun and daimyo became the divinely ordained rulers of the people. By weakening the hold of Buddhism over the minds of their subjects and by emphasizing the spiritual foundations of loyalty to the feudal authorities, the new rulers of Japan were able to achieve a new degree of popular support and solidarity within their domains. The feudal lords of the Tokugawa period, supported by their Confucian advisors and all the pageantry of aristocratic life, were able to exalt themselves in the eyes of their subjects. The cities in which they maintained their castled residences became in essence local capitals for the populace of the domain.

These, in profile, were the castle towns which sprang up with such vitality during the late sixteenth century to become the major cities of the Tokugawa period. Created by the newly ascendant feudal leaders in the course of their militant march to local and national unification, the *jōkamachi* were a unique institutional product of the new political and social organization consummated under the *baku-han* system. In terms of their total numbers, the *jōkamachi* were not necessarily more numerous than other types of towns and cities of the Tokugawa period. The commercial communities which continued to serve the major monasteries or which grew up around the ports and post-stations of the internal transportation network were far more prevalent. But most such communities were small and still largely rural in their orientation. In the final analysis all such towns were held under administrative and economic controls which emanated from the nearby castle town.

The supremacy of the *jōkamachi* in Tokugawa times is best demonstrated by a review of the size and number of those which attained a population of over 10,000. Admittedly, population data for the Tokugawa period are of uncertain accuracy. For one thing census figures, though assiduously kept, seldom listed the samurai population. Thus an exact population list is hardly attainable. Besides the incomplete statistics which do exist, however, students of Tokugawa population figures have suggested a rough rule of thumb to aid in gaining a general picture of the size of *jōkamachi*. Under this formula the inhabitants of castle towns would generally number somewhat more than ten per cent of the total population of the domain, which in turn was roughly equivalent to the assessed size in *koku* of the domain. Thus it would take a *han* of 100,000 *koku* assessment, of which there were just under fifty, to support a town of 10,000 inhabitants. A conservative estimate would place between thirty and forty castle towns, each the center of an extensive agricultural region, in the 10,000-or-more class. And this should be compared with the ten or so cities of noncastle origin which had population of the same size.

The above population figures do not, of course, apply to the early years of the Tokugawa period when the castles were still in construction and the city inhabitants not fully assembled. But under the peaceful conditions which followed the cessation of civil warfare, Japan's economy expanded rapidly, and with it her feudal cities. By 1700 most cities had reached their maximum growth. The pattern of Tokugawa urban development had fully matured. Edo was approaching the one-million mark. Osaka and Kyoto stood at around 300,000. Kanazawa and Nagoya had populations of nearly 100,000. Perhaps ten per cent of Japan's population lived in cities of over 10,000 inhabitants. The city had become a major factor in Japanese life, in the government and economy, and in the formation of popular cultural and intellectual attitudes. In this respect the continued dominance of the castle town among the cities of Tokugawa Japan was to become increasingly significant. In the years after 1700 the pattern of urbanization created by the feudal aristocracy was to place a deepening imprint upon the evolution of Japanese urban society.

First of all we must acknowledge the continuing effects of the strong centralized feudal authority symbolized by the castles. The *jōkamachi* were, as we have noted, primarily garrison towns, the loci of shogunal and daimyo military power. They were secondarily administrative centers, seats of feudal political authority. The high percentage of aristocracy—of military and official personnel—resident in the castle towns was a constant indication of the degree to which government served the interests of the elite and impringed upon the lives of its subjects. Yet, while in many ways the ascendancy of feudal authority must be looked upon as a stifling and restrictive influence, this is not the whole story. The city-centered local administrations established by the daimyo represented important advances in the technique of local administration. Life in Tokugawa Japan became infinitely more regularized and subject to written law than under earlier feudal regimes, and this in turn was a step in the direction of more modern public administration.

This standardization of governmental procedures and policies had yet another important effect upon Japanese society. The establishment of domain capitals became a powerful force in bringing about a uniform cultural and economic development throughout Japan. It was characteristic of the *jōkamachi* that their size depended not upon their proximity to the more developed core region of Japan but upon the size of the domain. Kagoshima, Kanazawa, and Akita, cities on the fringe, were in the same relation to the size of their domains as Nagoya or Hiroshima. No doubt a certain provincialism was inevitable in a feudal society such as that of Tokugawa Japan. But we find that throughout the nation the castle cities took on a remarkable uniform guise as the necessities of alternate attendance of the daimyo and their retinues at Edo circulated the ideas and practices of the center to the periphery, and as the enforced trade through Osaka and Edo knit the merchants of the realm more closely together.

But the elements of systemization and uniformity were not the only significant products of the urbanization which occurred under feudal stimulus. The factor of urban growth itself was to have far-reaching influence upon the various levels of Japanese society. Eventually it was to call into question the very ability of the feudal authorities to maintain their existence. The city, its life and its institutions, was in reality basically antagonistic to the type of land-centered military regime envisaged by the Tokugawa authorities. The urban environment, from its inception, was destined to have a contradictory effect upon the feudal class. With respect to the daimyo this became evident as they succumbed to the amenities of a life of ease in their castle towns and in the great metropolis of Edo. Certainly it was hard to recognize in the daimyo who gave up their domains to the Meiji government in 1869 the descendants of the hardy warlords of the late sixteenth century. As for the *bushi,* the establishment of castle towns served to complete their final separation from the land. In the cities the gentry warriors of the earlier days became increasingly removed from the actualities of the countryside both in their way of life and in their legal relationship to the land. By the eighteenth century, except for a few locations, the *bushi* had been stripped of any direct jurisdiction over their fiefs by the expanding power of the daimyo. Though as a class they nostalgically clung to the concept that they were a landed aristocracy, they had been converted, in reality, to little more than salaried officials of the daimyo. As their bureaucratic functions multiplied, their security became increasingly identified, not with the land, but with governmental service. Separated from the duties of actual land management, they became a thoroughly urbanized group living increasingly in sedentary style.

The assembling of the daimyo's vassals in the castle towns reflected yet another condition which was to have a depressive effect upon the morale of the *bushi* class. As peace and prosperity permeated the Japanese islands, as the settled life of the cities took the place of the more rugged life of the country, the military services of the *bushi* became increasingly superfluous. Large numbers of urbanized *bushi* were obliged to maintain themselves in mock military readiness. The shogunal and domain bureaucracies were overstaffed manyfold as peacetime occupations were provided for a class whose numbers had been determined by the necessities of civil warfare on a grand scale. The result for many was a life of hypocrisy and indolence. For the country as a whole it brought into being the curse of *"yakuninerie,"* as one observer so colorfully described Japan's particular brand of over-bureaucratization.

The economic hardships faced by the populous feudal class of Japan as it was obliged to maintain itself on fixed land incomes in the face of the mounting costs of urban life have been amply dealt with in Western literature. We need observe here only that these difficulties and the counter-efforts made by the authorities, whether in the nature of establishing new domain-sponsored commercial monopolies or of providing household handicraft opportunities for the distressed samurai, had the net effect of driving the *bushi* towards a more commercialized existence and of undermining the traditional way of life of the feudal aristocracy.

The story of the spread of money economy and the remarkable growth in commercial and craft activities which occurred during the Tokugawa period is also well known and requires no elaboration here. Few aspects of Tokugawa society were to remain unaffected by the rise in wealth and numbers of the *chōnin* communities in the feudal cities. Yet the fact that throughout these years the strength of feudal authority remained high forced upon the Japanese merchant a political passivity not generally seen in the West. Certainly it is undeniable that the urban commercial segment in Japan failed to become, at least by European standards, a significant antifeudal force. If anything, the leading merchants became, as time went on, more strongly allied with the feudal order, more dependent upon feudal privilege, and hence less inclined to oppose the dominant political order.

But if the Tokugawa merchant did not awaken to his possibilities of revolutionary leadership, the indirect effects of his enterprising commercial activities were great. In each locality the castle city with its core of merchants constituted a powerful stimulus to the economic development of the countryside, encouraging the spread of commercial agriculture and handicraft production. As commercial production interfered with land economy or was substituted for it, as trade became an alternative to agriculture, the feudal economic order was weakened. By the end of the Tokugawa period signs of fundamental change were beginning to appear in the structure of the Japanese urban economy. Within the administrative cities the machinery of feudal control began to weaken. Within the domains new towns of primarily economic importance began to compete with the privileged merchants of the castle towns.

Nor can we overlook the importance of the many cultural and intellectual innovations which accompanied the establishment of the *chōnin* communities of the Tokugawa period. The bourgeois culture, particularly of the three great cities of Edo, Osaka and Kyoto, became increasingly self-contained and sophisticated. In the art and literature of the *chōnin* and in the development of practical sciences and "Western learning," it was possible to descern the first stages of intellectual revolt against the feudal order and the Confucian system of thought. Such developments, moreover, were to carry an impact beyond the confines of the *chōnin* class. The *jōka-machi*, by bringing the *bushi* and *chōnin* into close proximity, eventually provided the basis for a fusion of interest between merchant and samurai. It was in this zone of fusion that the origins of the modern Japanese bourgeoise were to be found.

Perhaps the fundamental reason why the feudal cities of Japan did not play a more clear-cut role of political leadership is to be found in their structure. Combining, as they did, military, administrative, economic, and religious functions, they did not represent a single unified social group or aspiration. Yet by the end of the Tokugawa period such a unity of aspiration was being forged under the pressure of political crisis and economic distress. The city had become a point of maximum concentration for those many tensions which were eventually to break the bonds of feudalism in Japan. By the mid-nineteenth century, the feudal city had reached an obvious impasse, a limit in its ability to develop under the conditions imposed upon it by the Tokugawa regime. Bound by the rigid political, social, and economic doctrines of the daimyo system, limited by the technology of transportation, manufacture, and finance, the Japanese castle city was in unhealthy decline. The daimyo were in debt, the samurai ill-fed, the city poor in rebellious spirit. The ties between city and countryside were dangerously strained. Decay was everywhere visible. Yet it was in the depths of such decay that Japan's new leadership was stirring. In the zone of fusion of interest and outlook between the merchant and samurai resentment against the Tokugawa regime was mounting.

The revolution of the Meiji era brought in its wake political and economic changes of greatest consequence. The conditions which supported urban populations changed almost overnight. With the abolition of the shogunal and daimyo systems and the establishment of universal conscription, the large concentrations of *bushi* in remote areas ceased to be a necessity. With the abolition of the *han* and the opening of the entire nation to free economic development, with the creation of new ports of foreign trade, Japan's economic centers shifted rapidly. In this era of sudden change the Tokugawa city and the institutions it had fostered played a noteworthy role.

Fundamental to the remarkable flexibility demonstrated by Japanese society in the transition period was the fact that in the castle towns the feudal ruling class had been largely removed from the land. Thus it was assured that there could be no politically powerful landed class remaining after the abolition of the daimyo. The *bushi* did not constitute an entrenched land-based gentry as in China, able to back up their interests in the face of modern change. Without an economic base, the resentment they felt toward the reforms which deprived them of their feudal privileges was soon dissipated. Instead, they were forced to ride with the times, to join the new government or to seek security in the new economic opportunities which were offered them. They became the backbone of Japan's modern civil, military, and police bureaucracy, of her industrial management and labor force, and of her modern urban intelligentsia. In other words, they were a leaven for change rather than an obstacle.

Released from the inertia of social conservatism which a landed gentry might have provided, Japan after the Restoration moved swiftly in the direction of modern reform. In this process the castle city of Tokugawa times represented both an element of continuity with the past and a point of departure for far-reaching changes. In the first instance the *jōkamachi*, seats of feudal power, remained in modern Japan the local centers of national authority. Edo, the capital of the Tokugawa shogun, renamed Tokyo, was to remain the capital of new Japan. Today thirty-four of the forty-six prefectural capitals were *jōkamachi* in Tokugawa times, and in most instances the modern prefectures have taken the names of their capital cities rather than the old domain or provincial names. Throughout Japan prefectural capitals still constitute the major cultural and educational centers of their locales. Here are concentrated the schools, hospitals, newspapers and radio stations. Before the War many of them also acted as divisional military headquarters. Thus the castles which dominated the cities of Tokugawa Japan continued to stand as symbols of strong centralized bureaucratic power in the modern Japanese state.

But the great cities of Tokugawa Japan were also to lead in the process of adjustment to the new economic requirements of the modern state. From the economic point of view not all of the major *jōkamachi* were able to shape their own destinies. After the Restoration certain areas, notably along the line running through the center of Japan from Tokyo to Fukuoka, developed almost to the exclusion of the rest of the country. As Japan's modern transportation system took shape, areas rose or fell in economic importance as they were serviced or bypassed by railroads or shipping lines. Thus those castle towns on the Japan Sea or in the extreme north tended to make a slower adjustment to modern conditions. When given the chance, however, the *jōkamachi* demonstrated that they were in possession of the requirements necessary for modern commercial and industrial expansion. Situated at the major communication nodes, located on large rivers or close to the sea, in possession of land capable of cheap reclamation for industrial use, and linked to a large hinterland already closely tied to the city, the chief castle towns of the Tokugawa period made the transition to modern times to stand among the major urban centers of the new era. Today, more than one hundred years after the opening of Japan to the West, half of the sixty cities of over 100,000 population are former *jōkamachi*.

9

In this and the essay following, an American and a Japanese historian attempt to analyze the meaning of Japanese nationalism for her rapid modernization. Kenneth Pyle uses a number of recent typologies of nationalism to place "Japanese nationalism" in a world context, whereas Matsumoto Sannosuke notes the importance that Japan's peculiar intellectual-historical background played in the growth of Japan's modern nationalism. When reading both of them we can again see the continuing dialogue between Japanese particularism and Western universalism.

Some Recent Approaches to Japanese Nationalism

KENNETH B. PYLE

THE study of nationalism, the most powerful political emotion in the modern world, has often become enmeshed in polemic and ideological combat. In Japan during the past century, evaluations of the historical role of nationalism have tended to oscillate between extremes. Some of its first serious students in the late nineteenth century, writers like Kuga Katsunan and Miyake Setsurei, opposing the prevalent Westernism, were convinced that nationalism was a necessary ingredient of Japanese survival; and they would have agreed with Tocqueville's aphorism that "the interests of the human race are better served by giving every man a particular fatherland than by trying to inflame his passions for the whole of humanity." Since 1945, however, in a mood of national self-alienation, many Japanese writers have shared Veblen's turgid conclusion, "Born in iniquity and conceived in sin, the spirit of nationalism has never ceased to lead human institutions to the service of dissension and distress. In its material effects it is altogether the most sinister as well as the most imbecile of all the institutional incumbrances that have come down out of the old order." Once seen as necessary and beneficial, nationalism came in the post-war period to be villified or simply ignored amidst the scholars' preoccupation with their anti-establishment liberal heroes. With some no-

Kenneth B. Pyle, "Some Recent Approaches to Japanese Nationalism," *Journal of Asian Studies*, Vol. 31 (November 1971), pp. 5–16. Reprinted with permission of the publisher. Footnotes omitted.

table exceptions, nationalism has been slow to receive in Japan the thoughtful, dispassionate study it needs.

Outside of Japan, where a more detached attitude toward Japanese nationalism is possible, perhaps the greatest obstacle has been the difficulty of conceptualizing it and, hence, of finding a satisfactory approach to its study. There is possibly no more troublesome term in social science to define; and this has led some scholars to conclude that nationalism is perhaps not a fruitful problem for study. Thus, although over fifteen years have passed since Brown wrote what he frankly called "an introductory historical analysis" of Japanese nationalism that he hoped would lead others to serious work on the subject, few studies have been undertaken. This is unfortunate because the development of nationalism is surely one of the major organizing themes of modern Japanese history. At our present stage of knowledge, some of the most pressing questions we are asking about modern Japan await answers as to the sources, the nature, and the effect of nationalism. Despite this general lack of specific studies, there is perceptible a new interest in this subject, often evinced in the course of research on quite different topics that only "happened" to involve nationalism (as nearly all topics on modern Japan do). It may prove useful by way of introduction to the essays presented in this symposium, to consider this new interest, to characterize some of the best recent approaches, and to see where we are in our understanding of the subject.

If we may be somewhat arbitrary, it is possible to distinguish in the recent literature six distinct approaches to the development of nationalism:

1. Perhaps most familiar is the approach of the pure intellectual historian who is concerned with nationalism primarily as a set of ideas stressing the sovereignty, the mission, and the welfare of the nation-state. This "idea approach" is in the tradition of the classic studies of nationalism by Hayes, Kohn, and others. Insofar as it is concerned with the dynamics of nationalist growth, it tends to focus on the transmission of ideas, tracing their diffusion and development from one individual or group to another.

In this view, which is entrenched in modern historiography, modern nationalism is seen as emerging from pre-1868 thought. Thus Wilson, for example, writes in the beginning of his study of Kita Ikki that "modern national consciousness in Japan developed out of the ideas of later Tokugawa-period thinkers representing, in particular, the Mito, Dutch studies (*rangaku*), and "practical learning" (*jitsugaku*) schools of thought . . ." Similarly, Minear stresses the Tokugawa intellectual heritage, particularly Kokugaku and Mitogaku, in explaining the origins of Hozumi Yatsuka's nationalism. This approach is characteristic of pure intellectual history, where ideas have a life of their own and new ideas emerge out of the womb of antecedent ideas.

Some writers have objected that the idea approach is too limited to embrace the phenomenon of modern nationalism, for while nationalism is, as Kohn defined it, "a state of mind," it is also the result of a process of social change—a process, as I would define it, by which large numbers of people of all social classes are psychologically integrated into active membership in and positive identification with the nation-state. Minear himself seemed to sense this limitation when he wrote in the conclusion to his study of Hozumi: "The problem facing the intellectual historian is that he can go only so far: he can say what the ideology was, but he cannot say why it received general acceptance."

It was precisely this failure of intellectual history to deal with the activating social forces of nationalism that lay behind a second approach. Deutsch objected to the classic studies of nationalism in Europe because "nationalism came to be widely accepted as a mere 'state of mind' with few tangible roots." Johnson in his study of peasant nationalism in China was even more critical of the traditional approach: "An exclusive concern with nationalism as nationalists themselves define it is of almost no use for purposes of general analysis; and it ignores the question of timing" in the onset of nationalist movements.

2. We may call this second way of studying nationalism, which is apparent in some Japanese historians' work but so far never pursued in a systematic way, the functional or social communications approach since it is inspired, above all, by Deutsch's *Nationalism and Social Communication*. This approach is less concerned with the ideological content of nationalism than with the dynamics and process of its growth. It seeks precision both in identifying the pressures that cause populations to form nation-states and in isolating the conditions under which groups of human beings are transformed into national citizens.

Deutsch argued that the essence of nationalism lay in "the ability to communicate more effectively, and over a wider range of subjects, with members of one large group than with outsiders." This ability which he likened to "mutual rapport, but on a larger scale," is similar to what Lerner called "high empathetic capacity" and to what others have called "psychic mobility." At first glance, this approach seems more applicable to Europe where Deutsch, finding that "all the usual descriptions of a people in terms of a community of languages, of character, or memories, or past histories are open to exception," needed some other factor to explain the formation of a nation from diverse backgrounds. In the case of Japan, where a strong sense of a common cultural heritage existed from early times and therefore provided an enduring and cohesive basis of nationality, such "special" explanations might seem unnecessary. But, on closer look, the functional approach is useful in explaining the timing of nationalist movements. After all, the factor of cultural homogeneity does not help us explain, as Johnson points out (with a note of hyperbole) "why, for example, the Japanese were more nationalistic in 1930 than in 1830, since at both times they spoke the same language, held roughly the same religious views, and painted the same kind of pictures."

In studying the emergence of national communities out of European feudal society, Deutsch stresses the growth of towns, development of a commercial economy, and the consequent enlargement of basic communications grids. Although many writers have alluded briefly to factors significant in mobilizing a national awareness in Japan, we still know too little about the process. Dore speaks of the content of Tokugawa education and its diffusion as having a "nationalizing effect." Literacy greatly enhanced the citizenry's capacity for empathy; samurai, whatever their fief affiliation, came to share a common intellectual culture; and "the growth of Confucian scholarship and the teaching profession provided new national channels of communication which ignored fief boundaries."

In the modern period, the effectiveness of both the universal compulsory education system and the national conscript army in promoting a group consciousness that transcended regional and class limitations has been noticed by many writers. These two institutional reforms were in part designed to lift loyalties to the national level and eventually both became vehicles for purposeful nationalist indoctrination. But they also contributed to the growth of national consciousness in unplanned ways. The army, for example, by drawing peasant youth out of their villages to distant garrisons, served to mobilize the less politically aware and to contribute to an identity of interest.

Some attention, too, has been given to the way in which modern communications, by overcoming local isolation, mobilized national consciousness. With the development of railroads (nearly 5,000 miles of track had been laid by 1905) came a new physical mobility. Already by 1890 Shimbashi station accommodated up to 10,000 passengers a day; and Lafcadio Hearn observed in 1895 that mobility was a distinguishing feature of Japanese society: "Nothing is more characteristic of (Japanese) life than its extreme fluidity. . . . In their own country the Japanese are the greatest travelers of any civilized people." Yanagida Kunio pointed out a dramatic increase during the Meiji period in marriages that united men and women who had grown up great distances apart. More important, Japanese who did not travel were increasingly able to participate vicariously in distant events. This new psychic mobility was made possible by establishment of telegraphic service, a modern postal system, and mediums of mass communication—especially newspapers published after 1890 for a national audience.

Another factor often stressed in the functional approach is the impact of the international environment. Political awareness was heightened by Japan's emergence as a nation-state in competition with other nation-states. The unequal treaties imposed in the 1850's, the Triple Intervention in 1895, and the disarmament treaties of the 1920's and 1930's are examples frequently cited of the international state system's impingement on the domestic political environment which mobilized national loyalties. The function of war in awakening and stimulating national consciousness has likewise been recognized. Perhaps most impressive in this regard was the Sino-Japanese War of 1894–95, which drowned the doubts and dissensions of the preceding decades in a flood of national exhilaration. No less important was the influence of the cultural aspects of the international environment. The influx of Westerners and their civilization served as an object of comparison for the Japanese and tended to draw attention to the distinctive nature of their own culture and created extreme sensitivity to the problem of defining Japanese character. (Kuga Katsunan, one of the first Japanese to study the nature of nationalism in the West, contrasted the origins of European and Japanese nationalism by emphasizing the influence of Napoleonic aggression in the former case and the influx of Western culture in the latter. It was, he said, *buryoku* in one case and *bunryoku* in the other.)

3. A third view, which I shall call the "structural approach," identifies in traditional social groups certain structural features together with their supporting ethics that were conducive, or even tantamount to, the development of nationalism. Both Benedict, who stressed the ethics of *on* and *giri* and the Japanese "confidence in hierarchy," and Bellah, who has stressed the Japanese pattern of "particularistic groupism," believe that the traditional structure of group life provided the basis for modern nationalism.

This approach, however, is most clearly worked out in the historical dimension by Craig. He is inclined to downgrade the usual emphasis on Kokugaku thought and the coming of the West in the onset of nationalism in the late Tokugawa period. Instead he stresses "internal changes in the nature of feudal relations" and contends that "much of the emperor-centered Meiji nationalism as well as Bakumatsu sonnō thought was essentially a form of transmuted Tokugawa loyalty." Tracing the late Tokugawa development of an impersonal loyalty, directed more toward the domain than the person of its lord, he describes this loyalty as "almost, if not quite, . . . 'han nationalism.' I say not quite because, on the one hand, this tight in-group feeling was limited to the samurai class and perhaps to the upper stratum of peasant officials and, on the other hand, because it was much more structured than the diffuse feeling usually suggested by the word 'nationalism.' " Where other students have seen a weakening of traditional loyalty and the appearance of a new national one, Craig sees rather an intensification of traditional loyalty, although because it was directed more toward a status than a person "it was potentially, at least, what may be termed free floating loyalty. It was certainly this character that permitted the symbolic shift from the daimyo to the emperor and the shift in content from han nationalism to nationalism proper."

It is the essence of the structural approach that it claims the similarity of nationalism and other forms of group loyalty and sees national loyalties as an outgrowth of other loyalties. Because in some situations, as in the case of the Satsuma Rebellion, both sectionalism and nationalism were at work and circumstances caused them to work in opposition, historians are prone to emphasize the antithetical nature of different loyalties, to regard sectional loyalties as conflicting with national ones. But nationalism, as David Potter argued, "may be the terminal result of a full development of strong sectional forces, while sectionalism may be an emergent nationalism which has not yet matured." What is stressed here is that strong loyalties, whatever their object, are conducive or even indispensable to the development of nationalism. "If loyalty is a generalized way of responding," Harold Guetzkow writes, "the stronger the loyalty pattern in a given individual—no matter what its object—the easier it will be to build loyalties." From this point of view, nationalism may be seen not as breaking down, destroying, and supplanting family, local, and regional loyalties but rather incorporating, subsuming, and even pyramiding them. Thus Smith speaks of the Meiji leaders using the traditional language of loyalty and obligation "to make all little loyalties lead up to one great loyalty to the Emperor."

The structural approach thereby challenges one of the most widely accepted propositions about nationalism, which is that the growth of national loyalty depends upon destruction of local and regional ties. Modern nationalism, goes a typical explanation, "cannot be understood except in terms of the weakening and destruction of earlier bonds, and of the attachment to the political state of new emotional loyalties and identifications. It cannot be understood, that is, apart from those rents and clefts in the traditional structure of human loyalties, caused by economic and social dislocation, which left widening masses of human beings in a kind of psychological vacuum."

The structuralists, however, vary in their understanding of how long traditional loyalty patterns remained the basis of nationalism. Craig, for example, in his essay on Fukuzawa, maintains that after the turn of the century "a more modern nationalism" took hold. Presumably, he refers to a more diffuse feeling, more widely shared by different sectors of society than the old loyalty which had been highly structured and limited primarily to the old samurai class. Diffusion of nationalism after 1900 was achieved through education, the armed services, and "an ever more centralized political system." "But even this new patriotism," he concludes, "was substantially shaped by the old loyalty."

Many structuralists would argue that nationalism as a cohesive political force continued to depend heavily on the traditional structure of group ties—particularly in the countryside. In part this was possible because industrialization did not break up the peasant village and values of obedience and solidarity remained vital in agrarian society.

If national loyalties could be constructed from lesser loyalties, presumably the structure could also be dismantled. Thus structuralists argued that after World War II, when national political institutions and symbols were discredited, "Japanese nationalism was released from the central force that had until then controlled it and was automatically dispersed into its original sources, namely the family, the villages, and small local groups." Maruyama calls this a process of "demobilization" but stresses that "the spiritual structure of past nationalism did not become extinct, nor did it undergo a qualitative change, rather it would be correct to say that the change was quantitative: nationalist feelings were atomized, disappearing from the political and becoming embedded in the lower strata of national life." Presumably then it could be argued that barring social change of the kind that weakened hierarchies of personal and primary group loyalties, this structure could once again with relative ease be "mobilized" to serve nationalist ends. Morris, indeed, argues that ultra-nationalist elements were able to survive in post-war Japan because of "the highly personal basis of their loyalties."

4. A fourth approach to the study of nationalism—perhaps it is the most common one—is based on "interest theory." That is, nationalist doctrine is treated as an ideological weapon used by the government and by the dominant social groups in the interest of their own pursuit of power. Squaring neatly with the prevailing Marxist orientation of historians in Japan, this view presents a rather simple and straightforward understanding of the sources of nationalist growth and, unfortunately, has served perhaps to diminish further inquiry into the nature of modern nationalism. The growth of nationalism is seen primarily as the result of indoctrination and clever manipulation of traditional symbols to serve the interests of the elites. Where the structural approach has been particularly useful in describing aspects of nationalism in the early Meiji period, interest theory has special application to the twentieth century when government made use of education, the media, and the armed forces to inculcate the nationalist orthodoxy. In addition to indoctrinating conscripts and doctoring school texts, the government built a network of local organizations, under the control of the Home Ministry, which helped Tokyo mobilize nationalist sentiment in the countryside. For example, the Ministry made a concerted effort after the Russo-Japanese War to join village youth groups into a national organization under its control.

Although the interest theory approach puts prime emphasis on the role of government, dominant social groups may also be seen as promoting na-

tionalism in the service of their own interests. Besides the political, bureaucratic, and military elites, landlords and businessmen have also been
seen as instrumental in upholding the collectivist ethic upon which nationalist movements were founded. Dore and Ouchi, while dismissing Barring-
ton Moore's simple equation of landlords with ultranationalist leadership,
hypothesize that they were nonetheless important in the more conservative
nationalist movements of the 1920's. Marshall shows that members of the
Japanese business elite contributed substantially to the formulation and
maintenance of the nationalist ideology because they found its themes of
self-abnegation, group solidarity, and paternalistic authority useful in sanc-
tioning their newly acquired power and prestige. The business ideology, in
order to ease the traditional stigma on commerce and to justify the businessman's position in society, laid stress on his patriotic devotion and his
self-denial in the fulfillment of duty to the nation.

It may legitimately be objected that the interest theory approach is sometimes simplistic. One often gets the impression from it of Japanese nationalist ideology as something cooked up in the backroom by Itō and the oligarchs and fed to an obedient, deceived citizenry. The effectiveness of
government indoctrination is easily exaggerated and the remarkable receptivity to this official effort by people outside of the government is often
overlooked. The pressure to conform to the nationalist orthodoxy, Jansen
points out, came not so much from the government as from "forces within
Japanese society. Colleagues, neighbors, publicists, relatives—these were
the people who hounded the Kumes, the reformers, and the liberals."

Still, if a more complex causation is assumed, self-interest may be shown
to play an important role in promoting the growth of national loyalty.
Nationalism among certain groups may be prompted, in part, by their
perception of their own interests as coinciding with the nation's. Morton
Grodzins writes in his *The Loyal and Disloyal* that "populations are loyal
to the nation as a byproduct of satisfactions achieved within nonnational
groups, because the nation is believed to symbolize and sustain these
groups. From this point of view, one is loyal not to nation but to family,
business, religion, friends. One fights for the joy of his pinochle club
when he is said to fight for his country."

It may have been particularly true in Japan that nationalist sentiment
often masked concern for self-interest for, as Maruyama points out, private
interest tended to lack sanctions; and self-gain had to be rationalized with
reference to the nation. One is reminded of Soseki's ironic portrayal of a
businessman in *Sore kara* who was forever justifying his profit in terms of
service to the nation and of his son's wry remark that "if one can make as
much money as Father has by serving the nation, I wouldn't mind serving
it myself." In arguing against the conventional interpretation of Meiji
entrepreneurs as "community-centered" and as motivated by selfless samurai spirit, Yamamura has convincingly demonstrated that many of them

were relentless and even unscrupulous in their pursuit of profit. Nevertheless, from our perspective here, it is probably a mistake to regard nationalism and concern for self-interest as antithetical or even easily distinguishable. The Charles E. Wilson mentality ("What is good for GM is good for the country") is perhaps even more pervasive in Japan than in the United States.

5. There is a fifth way of studying nationalism which generally focuses on irrational impulses and which we may call the "strain theory" approach. It sees nationalism as provoked by malintegration of society and by psychological "strain." The rapidity of change and the unevenness of the pace between sectors is seen as subjecting society and the individual to severe stress. In particular, the introduction of modern technology and the consequent transition from an agrarian to an industrial society are emphasized as primarily responsible for the strain in modern Japanese life and for some forms of nationalism. From this viewpoint, nationalism provided "a symbolic outlet for emotional disturbances generated by social disequilibrium."

The most dramatic evidence of psychological strain in modern Japan was the rapidly rising suicide rate from the 1890's on. No one, so far as I have been able to discover, has studied the relation between Japan's suicide statistics and her ideological activity. Is it an accident that times of rapid rise in the suicide rate (the turn of the century, the immediate post-World War I period, and the early 1930's) coincide with times known for increased nationalist activity?

The relation between social strain and growth of nationalism has several times been alluded to in the writings of Dore. In his study of mobility aspirations in modern Japan, for example, he suggests that the growth of nationalism after the turn of the century fed on the frustrations of those who were unable to fulfill their ambitions. "Fervent nationalism," he writes, "took an easier grip on the nation in that it provided vicarious alternative satisfactions to those who had been disappointed in the struggle for success." He offers the example of the protagonist of Tayama Katai's *Inaka kyōshi*, who overcomes the bitterness of unfulfilled ambitions by identifying with his nation in its triumph in 1905. Nationalism in this view, is a catharsis or safety valve for "internal pressure caused by the excess of awakened aspirations."

Elsewhere, Dore elaborates on this interpretation. In contrast to the interest theory approach which argues that the groups dominating the country politically—the bureaucracy, the politicians, and the business elite—were the bearers of nationalism, he sees the less successful, the frustrated, and the resentful elements of society as its bearers. Rather than the bourgeoisie, which provided the real strength of nationalism in Europe and America, Dore contends that it was lower middle-class groups—

shopkeepers, small businessmen, grade school and secondary school teachers, clerical workers in government and business—which were the bearers of nationalism in Japan. Politically mobilized after the turn of the century, they provided the support for the leaders of the ultra-nationalist movement whom Maruyama calls pseudo-intellectuals: spokesmen for reservist associations, organizers of patriotic charities, etc.—men whose roots were in local communities and who became the opinion leaders of those communities. These lower middle-class groups "had enough causes," Dore points out, "for personal resentment against the dominant groups (there was only one educational ladder of success and they were the ones who had risen only halfway up it), and they were provided with enough moral grounds for expressing their resentment by the luxury and corruption of the business classes, the arrogance of the bureaucrats, the unpatriotic concern for sectional interests of the politicians, and the un-Japanese cosmopolitanism of them all."

He argues that the bourgeoisie in Western societies became the locus of nationalist strength in reaction to the cosmopolitan outlook of the aristocracy. In Japan, however, the new professional bureaucratic and business classes, of which the middle-upper groups in society were composed, were themselves cosmopolitan. Having received a Western-style education and owing their social position to the mastery of Western learning, they were afflicted by "an uncertain sense of cultural identity" that, in Dore's view, kept them from being the bearers of nationalism as opposed to cosmopolitanism.

Certainly the nationalist orthodoxy did find strong support from the lower-middle groups during the 1920's and 1930's, but it also should be pointed out that the middle-upper groups provided perhaps as much leadership of nationalist movements as the "pseudo-intellectuals." It could be argued that the uncertain sense of cultural identity among the middle-upper groups was no deterrent to nationalism, that instead the psychological need to resolve this uncertainty was one of the persistent motivating themes of Japanese nationalism, and that many of the leading nationalist ideologues came from among the middle-upper groups. One thinks of Inoue Tetsujirō, Uesugi Shinkichi, Tokutomi Sohō, Yokoi Jikei, and many others from the middle-upper groups who despite (or because of?) an early sense of cultural uncertainty became formulators and spokesmen for the nationalist orthodoxy.

Social discontent was doubtless one incitement to nationalism. The contribution of the strain approach, like the functional and interest approaches, lies primarily in its explanation of the dynamics of nationalist growth through elucidation of its social sources and psychological motivations. By firmly grounding their explanations in social structure and by seeing nationalism as the result of processes of social change, these approaches help us understand the springs of nationalism. Their difficulty lies in their short-circuiting the complex relationship between the activating social forces of nationalism and its ideological assertions. As Geertz writes, "the nature of the relationship between the sociopsychological stresses that incite ideological attitudes and the elaborate symbolic structures through which those attitudes are given a public existence" is often not adequately explained.

6. The problem of cultural uncertainty, just raised, suggests another method which I will call the cultural approach. It sees cultural disorientation as setting the stage and creating the need for the rise of modern nationalism; and it focuses analysis on Japanese cultural patterns and symbols as the shaping force in the formulation of nationalist ideology. Much of the recent interest in this approach has been stimulated by the writings of Bellah and Jansen. The former's study of Watsuji Tetsurō and other intellectual figures provided a new perspective on nationalism by relating it to the central value system and to the cultural tensions generated by Western ideas, industrialization, and bureaucratization. Jansen's writings, on the other hand, provided a different perspective by calling attention to a recurrent personality type in Japanese history, the *shishi*, who was active in proto-nationalist and nationalist movements.

Because definitions of culture are by nature inclusive, this approach tends to be pluralist and synthetic; and its comprehensiveness may allow it to subsume and integrate some of the diverse perspectives and insights of the other approaches we have considered. Cultural history occupies a mediating position somewhere between the domains of social and intellectual history. Kluckhohn and Kroeber identified the "essential core" of culture as historically derived ideas "and especially their attached values." The cultural historian is therefore interested, like the intellectual historian, in the derivation and influence of clearly articulated ideas; but he is also interested in "values, norms, tacit assumptions, ideologies, images, and myths." He shares with the social historian an interest in "the way the unstated presuppositions of society inform behavior and institutions and determine a society's style." He tries to recapture "the vital nuances of a state of mind and convey a sense of the functional interrelationship of beliefs, values, fears, aspirations, and emotional commitments." The cultural historian possesses a concern for the subtle interplay between social forces and processes of ideological formation that is essential for understanding modern nationalism.

Like the strain approach, the cultural approach recognizes the importance of rapid social change in the onset of nationalism, but it sees the focus of the impact as primarily cultural disruption and dislocation, rather than sociopsychological strain. Each exacerbates the other, of course, but it is above all a fundamental lack of surety, a pervasive sense of disorientation, about once axiomatic cultural values that creates the vacuum that nationalism fills. This approach also recognizes the importance of increased social communication and of the impingement of the international environment which are factors emphasized by the functional approach, but it stresses that these factors created cultural problems that nationalism emerged to resolve.

In this view, modern nationalism rises in response to a cultural crisis that occurs when a more highly differentiated polity (the modern nation-state) is developing and when the former central organizing principles of political life become discredited and outmoded. In the face of radically new problems, received images of the political process seem no longer adequate. This cultural confusion sets off an intense search for "a new symbolic framework in terms of which to formulate, think about, and react to political problems." To be successful, such a framework must be constructed from symbols and images that have meaning in the nation's cultural heritage, but that have been remolded to fit a new political environment.

Liquidation of the Tokugawa political order and borrowing of Western technology and institutions created a severe confusion of values by the mid-Meiji years. Traditional ways of organizing and viewing social and political life became problematic and controversial. My own study of the new generation of intellectuals is an attempt to understand this crisis by showing how cultural tensions and contradictions were internalized, struggled with and resolved through new nationalist formulations by articulate members of society. Tokutomi Soho's resolution of this crisis is perhaps representative of the way in which Japanese culture was reorienting itself at the end of the century. As Duus shows in his contribution to this symposium, the dilemma of trying to reconcile cultural borrowing and national pride, of striving to be both modern and Japanese continued to plague thoughtful people: it motivated Nagai Ryūtarō to seek a national mission that would prove Japan's cultural worth in the modern world.

This cultural disorientation, exacerbated by the strain of rapid social change and by intensification of international rivalries, set the stage for the rise of nationalist ideologies that would serve as an integrative social force by providing culturally acceptable answers to unprecedented political problems. "In Maruyama's perceptive comment, the atrophy of the Confucian values after the middle of the Meiji period and the failure to develop alternative transcendental ideals which might replace them—an agreed upon mandate of heaven or of history—made it difficult to restrain, and easy to promote, the ideologies of family state and divine nation." These ideologies sought to put an end to cultural confusion by reasserting traditional values and by defining a unique Japanese political order and social morality based on immutable principles. Notehelfer's essay on Kōtoku Shūsui in this symposium provides valuable clues to the cultural tensions that resulted when the social order began to harden and the dominant forms of nationalism became a distinctively conservative force.

As a consequence, Kōtoku, whose background had disposed him to regard nationalism as a progressive, transformational force, turned to socialism.

Eventually, after Kōtoku's time, one of the main streams of nationalist ideology developed this transformational potential. Wilson's study of Kita Ikki argues persuasively that radical nationalism in the Taisho period shared more in common with the socialists and the left-wing of the political spectrum than it did with the right-wing. Oftentimes, the revolutionary designs of nationalism were cloaked in adherence to traditionalistic symbols—such as the concept of "restoration." We have sometimes tended to dismiss the use of such symbols as simply backward looking and obscurantist without understanding the meanings they evoke in Japanese culture. From Najita's study of Yamagata Daini in this symposium we acquire an understanding of the roots of this mode of thought and of its peculiar meaning in Japanese culture. Moreover, his study suggests that we have a great deal to learn about other symbols, images, and modes of thought in the language of modern Japanese nationalism. Too often the possibility has been overlooked that nationalist ideology may draw its power, as Geertz says, "from its capacity to grasp, formulate, and communicate social realities that elude the tempered language of science, that it may mediate more complex meanings than its literal reading suggests." One deterrent to studying modern Japanese nationalism has been what Hasegawa Nyozekan called its apparent "intellectual vacuity." He was speaking of the seemingly rudimentary thought processes that characterized the nationalist writings of the 1920's and 1930's—their use of figurative language, primitive rhetoric, distorted metaphor, and their literal acceptance of Shinto mythology. Only when we succeed in putting these writings in their social and cultural context will their significance be more fully understood.

10

The Significance of Nationalism in Modern Japanese Thought

SANNOSUKE MATSUMOTO

A COMPARISON of Japanese and Western nationalism shows that each has derived from a vastly different intellectual-historical background. The European background is characterized by the universalism of Christianity which gave birth to "the conviction that mankind is one and has to form one community." Out of this medieval tradition, and through the testing of the Renaissance and the Reformation, there evolved a concept of the universal, abstract and rational individual. This individualism, in turn, provided for a universal concept of humanity. Modern European nationalism was born into such a universalistic culture, and because of that, despite its stress on the differences in nationality and national character, and despite its apparent conflict with individualism, it inherited a universalistic orientation. Thus, Hans Kohn has the following to say:

Nationalism is not . . . a harmonious natural growth qualitatively identical with the love for family and home. . . . [L]ove of home and family is a concrete feeling accessible to everyone in daily experience, while nationalism, and in an even higher degree cosmopolitanism, is a highly complex and originally an abstract feeling. . . . Nationalism—our identification with the life and aspirations of uncounted millions whom we shall never know, with a territory which we shall never visit in its entirety—is qualitatively different from the love of family or of home surroundings. It is qualitatively akin to the love of humanity or of the whole earth.

By contrast, Japanese nationalism had neither the kind of universalistic cultural tradition that the *corpus christianum* of medieval Europe nurtured, nor a history of the development of individualism. In Japan, the national consciousness came into being more as "a concrete feeling" than

Sannosuke Matsumoto, "The Significance of Nationalism in Modern Japanese Thought," *Journal of Asian Studies*, Vol. 31 (November 1971), pp. 50–54. Reprinted with permission of the publisher. Footnotes omitted.

as "an abstract feeling." It was distinctly *not* akin to "the love of humanity" as much as it was qualitatively identical with "the love of family or of
home surroundings." More specifically, Japanese nationalism took on the
following basic characteristics.

The first of these characteristics is related to the image of the international community. As a historical fact, Japan's national consciousness
was fostered indirectly by the knowledge of the situation in China following the Opium War and, more directly, through her own experience of
the foreign pressure for ending more than two centuries of isolation. Previous to this, Japanese had held to an extremely self-centered view of the
world based on Confucianism. Japan was regarded, along with China, as a
land of superior morality, while the West was considered "barbaric" for its
ignorance of proper moral concepts and manners. The Western encroachment on the Far East during the first half of the nineteenth century, however, quickly discredited the ethnocentric conception of the world order
and the sense of moral superiority among the Japanese. This experience
gave rise to a new image which saw the international community as being
governed by the law of the jungle. Hereupon, the Japanese began to re-
evaluate the West for its superior power, and conversely, saw themselves
as "backward" both politically and militarily. Taguchi Ukichi, in his celebrated *Nihon kaika shōshi*, claims that the national consciousness which
arose in the course of the "revere the Emperor, expel the barbarians" movement was a direct outcome of the Japanese fear of the Western powers. In
other words, nationalism in Japan was very much the result of the "external pressure" by which she was forced into the West-centered family of
nations and which in turn caused her people to harbor strong fears and
anxieties about their new contact with the alien world.

Thus, in contrast to the modern nation-states of the West which came
about as the result of fragmentation of the unified Christian world of
medieval Europe, Japan formed her national state through contact with,
and forced membership in, the alien world of "barbarians" from which she
had so rigidly distinguished herself. Because of this difference in the
formative process, Japanese nationalism was never able to encompass the
kind of universalism (i.e., internationalism) that the West continued to
cherish even after the respective countries had completed their nation-
building and national unification. Rather, Japanese nationalism was
doomed from its inception to be tormented by a constant awareness of the
qualitative difference between itself and Western nationalism-internation-
alism. And that awareness became an incurable source of the Japanese
sense of crisis and threat vis-à-vis the Western world in the subsequent
decades. It also provided one of the principal reasons why Japan's nationalism was always augmented by a call for "a militarily powerful Japan"
(*fukoku kyōhei*) and was inclined to tie itself with militarism.

The second characteristic of Japanese nationalism involves the pattern

of political integration in this country. The modern state is often characterized by the principle of "government by consent." What it means is that
the state's exercise of power is legitimized by the consent of the people,
and therefore that political integration in a modern state is possible only
through the attainment of popular consent. Needless to say, "government
by consent" presupposes the existence of free and independent individuals
(i.e., citizens) and is premised upon an individualistic-liberalist belief
that public will and public interest can be achieved only through free
exchange of opinions and rational persuasion among such private citizens.
Moreover, for political integration on the basis of the "government by
consent" principle, it is considered indispensable to guarantee both civil
liberty (freedom of thought, faith, conscience, expression, etc.) and political liberty, which involves the right of each citizen to take an equal
part in the making of the political will of the nation.

In the West, that principle continued to serve as the basic premise for
political integration even after the nation-state concept gained momentum
in the early nineteenth century and the unity of the nation, as opposed to
the liberty of citizens, began to receive an increased emphasis. This was
true despite the fact that "nationalism dominated the impulses and attitudes of the masses, and at the same time served as the justification for
the authority of the state and legitimization of its use of force, both against
its own citizens and against other states." It is perhaps safe to say that
modern European nationalism accompanied the idea of popular sovereignty
as an indispensable quality and developed hand in hand with democracy.

Such was not the case in Japan, however. From the very outset, Japan's
modern state pursued political integration along nationalistic rather than
democratic lines. The rational, dynamic approach which attempts political
integration through free expressions of divergent individual opinions and
through adjusting conflicting interests did not take firm root in practice.
Instead, the Japanese state relied more heavily on an emotional approach
which, in appealing to the national consciousness, dramatized the unique
character of the nation and the racial homogeneity of the people to effect
a national unity. The absoluteness of the emperor's personal authority and
the idea of imperial sovereignty were, of course, pivotal for the Japanese
pattern of national integration.

It may well be added here that throughout the modern period a small
minority of Japanese repeatedly made efforts to "democratize" the state's
approach to political integration. The early Meiji Enlightenment, the *jiyū
minken* movement of the 1880's, the *heiminshugi* (lit., plebeianism) of the
following decade, as well as the "Taishō democracy" movement, are the
best known and perhaps the most important of such efforts. But, none of
these went so far as to modify the basic pattern of political integration I
have described above. There were also consistent efforts made to enlarge
the scope of popular participation in politics as a way of consolidating na-

tional integration. This was in fact one of the basic trends in modern Japanese history which led to the adoption of universal manhood suffrage in 1925. But, here again, we must note an important limitation in the way in which the authorities rationalized popular political participation. That is to say, participation was encouraged not so much for private fulfillment —to allow individuals to pursue their private interest and happiness through exercise of their political rights—but more for a national purpose—to solicit greater service on the part of imperial subjects to the state for its continued independence and expansion. Quite symbolically, it was Uesugi Shinkichi, the ultranationalist scholar of constitutional law, who advocated as early as in the mid-Taishō period the implementation of universal manhood suffrage in this country. What is even more symbolic of the characteristically Japanese distortion of constitutionalism is Uesugi's rationale behind the proposal. He reasoned that universal suffrage would generate among the people a greater love of the nation and a heightened spirit of sacrifice for the good of the empire. For him, expanding the franchise was nothing but a means for expanding the empire! This episode attests to the disproportionate overgrowth of nationalism in Japan whereby even what appeared to be purely a constitutional action was in fact heavily influenced by nationalistic considerations. Under these circumstances, it was next to impossible for nationalism to harmonize itself with a more democratic pattern of political integration.

The third and final characteristic of Japanese nationalism is the particularistic idea of national mission it nurtured. As I have already pointed out, Western nationalism was at least latently akin to the love of humanity because of its reverence for the universalistic concept of the individual. Thus, the European nation-states were made aware at their inception of the existence of a universalistic value (humanity) that transcended themselves. The European national mission stemmed precisely from this awareness and warranted the dedication of each nation-state to the ultimate realization of that value. The American Declaration of Independence stipulated the founding spirit of the nation to be the guarantee, for all men, of their inalienable rights which included "life, liberty, and the pursuit of happiness." The French Revolution was carried out in the name of "liberty," "equality," and "fraternity." All this has been actually more of a myth than a reality, but it nevertheless provided later generations with a point of reference: the original principles to which one can go back and measure the extent of deviation on the part of the state.

On this point, too, Japan is different from the countries of the West. The Japanese nation-state never possessed a universal ideal that transcended itself. The ultimate end-value of this national state was nothing other than the preservation of its own national polity (*kokutai*). And that *kokutai* was to be preserved in the final analysis through the perpetuation of the Imperial Throne in an unbroken line. In a nutshell, Japan's national mission was the self-perpetuation and self-expansion of the nation-state itself. This unique feature of Japanese mission concept is, needless to say, closely related to the first characteristic mentioned above—that Japan's national consciousness was originally generated by her fears and anxieties of the outside world. The two characteristics are indeed opposite sides of the same coin.

The three principal characteristics that I have discussed here in their barest outlines are all contributing factors to the fusion of Japanese nationalism with militarism and their acceleration into ultranationalism during the 1930's. They represent but a few of the general tendencies that I find important in modern Japanese nationalism from an intellectual-historical point of view. It is necessary, of course, that our study of the basic constitution of Japanese nationalism be elaborated far beyond the sweeping generalizations that I have attempted here. Studies of nationalism in this direction will help us clarify in greater detail the complex of factors which made that fusion and that acceleration possible and even inevitable in prewar Japan. They will also be helpful in providing a historical perspective necessary to check the possibility of our postwar nationalism degenerating into the military-economic imperialism of the prewar type.

However, there is another direction in which we might pursue our study of Japanese nationalism. That is, we might attempt to dig out and shed light on those thoughts or thought trends in modern Japanese history that tried to challenge (or at least had some potential of challenging) the all-too-dominant nationalism of the past.

11 *A sense of the past is both an alienating and a provocative ex-*
perience. In the following selection I attempt to show why
alienation from the past stimulated many young men to turn
energetically to new ideas. Idealization of the past forced them
to seek success and new honors in the future.

FROM

Christian Converts and Social Protest in Meiji Japan

IRWIN SCHEINER

CONVERSION: MALAISE AND ALIENATION

C ONVERTS to a new faith glory in the electrifying effects of having found truth; apostates speak with rancor of their disappointment with the faith they left. Twenty years after his conversion to Christianity, Ebina Danjō, who exemplifies the feelings of many converts, located the source of his faith in the uncomfortable feeling of loss of status, order, and authority that overcame him with the Restoration.

Since I came from a *bushi* family I had to lose the person whom I had respected as a lord. Even my attitude toward my parents changed. The four classes became equal. The *bushi* felt that when farmers and merchants got equal power all good form had disappeared. Even art and music were destroyed.

Confucianism which had ruled the human spirit for many years was also destroyed. The Confucian classics lost their value. All this was a result of the Restoration. In such an age we were raised.

Ebina thus expressed his anxiety over the moral and social cataclysm that he feared the samurai faced. Besides sharing this same feeling, others also showed their resentment and hostility toward the Meiji government by directly opposing its formation and rationale. Although, for example, the authority of the emperor had now been confirmed by reference to tradition, some shogunate adherents, as well as many retainers of *fudai han*— domains allied to the Tokugawa—felt that however inevitable the over-

Irwin Scheiner, *Christian Converts and Social Protest in Meiji Japan*, 1970, pp. 48–61. Originally published by the University of California Press; reprinted by permission of The Regents of the University of California. Footnotes omitted.

throw of the Tokugawa might have been, to bow to the new government was degrading. As Uemura wrote a decade after the Restoration,

Changes of the age were unexpected when the Restoration began and the authority of the Tokugawa feudal government fell. . . . These changes were unavoidable; but both daimyo and samurai regretted the changes. It is said that those who know the current of the age and follow it are wise, those who resisted the emperor and fought the emperor's army . . . were those who did not know the relations of lord and retainer. . . . Those who assert such an opinion do not know the true relations of lord and retainer.

Not unexpectedly, Uemura, son of a *hatamoto* family, defended resistance to the emperor.

I think those who took the side of the Tokugawa and resisted the army of the emperor at the time of the Restoration did so out of a loyalty which Japanese had grown up with since olden times. [By resisting] they attacked the frivolous men who truckled to the currents of the age. If none had shed his blood [defending] the old feudal system, the Japanese conscience would have come to an end. . . . Therefore I cannot agree with those who felt that those who resisted the army of the emperor were traitors. When the fever of reverence for the emperor has died down, we can rewrite the modern history of Japan.

Uemura was only one among many samurai converts who vehemently opposed the Meiji order. Among his fellow students at Ballagh's Academy, Honda Yoichi had initially come up to Yokohama to oppose the Satsuma-Chōshū clique. Yamada Toronosuke of Hirosaki had for a time considered joining the Satsuma rebellion; and Ibuka Kajinosuke from Aizu domain had with his father fought against the imperial forces at the time of the Restoration. Also among the converts were adherents to Eto Shimpei's rebellion and samurai from Kōchi sympathetic to Itagaki's opposition to the government. Many leaders of Kumamoto and the students at the Yōgakkō also resented the assumption of powers of government by the new domain alliance.

Uemura's protest against the cavalier destruction of past loyalties was accompanied by a feeling of distress at the emptiness and chaos of the time. This feeling was undoubtedly heightened when, as Ebina so aptly pointed out, it was government policy in the early years of Meiji to destroy everything of the past one thousand years. "It was a destruction of morality, all former morality was destroyed." After his baptism Kozaki reflected on his impressions in early Meiji and noted that for him the Restoration had meant the extirpation of religious principles from education and the lack of any ethical-religious basis to politics.

Hostile and depressed, revengeful and confused, these young samurai who were to convert to Christianity were clearly opposed to the political trends of the time. Whereas some might have supported the Meiji governmental reforms had they been undertaken under *bakufu* (shogunate) leadership, they deeply resented these reforms of the new oligarchy. These young converts believed that so long as the Satsuma and Chōshū samurai monopolized high offices of the central government, they had no hope of joining the ruling elite. In this way, they felt estranged from the new political order in Japan. Furthermore, the Confucian moral order had given them authority and status. Moral chaos and the destruction of traditional lord-samurai relations destroyed proper Confucian relations and deprived loyalty and filial piety of any meaning. They were left alienated as well as estranged from the new political order.

Members of a political elite are expected to defend not only the political order they lead, but also the ideological foundations of it. But what could be expected in the case of these young samurai? The ideological foundation of their authority had been lost while the consciousness of their past status remained an important part of their psychological makeup. Moreover, they saw their traditional authority denied and apparently without any function.

Max Weber discusses the problem of conversion, asking who in society is most susceptible to conversion to a new religion. He examines the conditions under which conversion is possible—conditions which lead particular groups to make a break with an established order. He discusses various sensitivities to stimuli existing outside the established order. These sensitivities constitute what we now call alienation; they contain the elements which are more readily "available" to be stirred by prophetic movements.

Weber begins his study by analyzing those groups who are most deeply embedded in traditionalism, those who are least alienated. For one, the peasantry is firmly rooted in the traditional culture. In Japan, I would add, the peasants are tied to the primitive animism of the locality; moreover, they are burdened with the prejudices and fears that years of total subjugation to an authoritarian ruling order have left them. The unknown is feared; if it is made unlawful, as Christianity was, it is abhorred. The eye of the peasant is not turned outward, but inward to the community where years of experience of traditional cultivation teach what is best. Weber finds other groups that fit into the same category: "Those most heavily involved in secular responsibility are least susceptible to prophecy or alienation." Here he discusses those with institutionalized military functions, a feudal nobility, or a bureaucracy. Each of these groups has a heavy investment in maintaining the established order, simply to make it work. There is a dual character to the function of these groups: On the one hand, they need a realistic sense of their capacity to command resources to rule, on the other, they must have a sense of their "right" to do so. What is involved is the legitimization of their power. In all cases, Weber finds such groups conservative, not susceptible to "stimuli"; on the contrary, they need the past and its symbols to honor their rights in order to command the resources to rule.

Paradoxically, the samurai, the feudal nobility in Japan who staffed the bureaucracy, provided the leadership and most of the membership of the early Meiji Protestant Church. Yet this fact confirms rather than refutes Weber's example. The institutionalized order in Tokugawa Japan defined political rights and political order in moral terms. In this period all samurai were members of the ruling elite from the time of their birth. After the establishment of the Meiji government, they were ignored and cut off from power. Samurai from domains not active in the Restoration were made incapable of ruling. Many felt that no longer would have an opportunity to join the ranks of the new political elite, and for this reason they felt estranged. The Restoration also redefined the sociomoral-political order in such a way as to destroy hereditary relationships that had given all samurai rights to rule. For as Ebina Danjō said of his feelings following the Meiji Restoration: "I had to lose the person whom I respected as lord. . . . The four classes became equal. The *bushi* felt that when farmers and merchants got equal power all good form had disappeared." Now declassé, a tension existed between what the samurai thought they should be and what, in fact, they were. Convinced that they deserved high status, they despised the new order that offered a lowly one. Young men such as those at the Kumamoto Yōgakkō or those in the schools of Ballagh in Yokohama, were in the first instance more interested in the retention of a remembered status than in the definition of a total sociomoral system. Uemura's parents, for example, told him that since he was a samurai, he must be gallant, great, and successful. In Kumamoto, Kozaki entered the Yōgakkō in order to prepare himself to become a great leader. In this sense, Western ideas, notably those of Christianity, were thought helpful to this end while demonstrating what they already knew, that the ideology of the past could not help them retain their status. If there were tension between past status and declassé reality, there would be further tension between these young converts and their fathers and the authorities who continued as traditionalists.

The final resolution of the tension came through the direct rejection of the latter's authority by the acceptance of the new Christian synthesis of Western ideas and institutions. Rejection of the traditional was personal as well as intellectual. Acceptance of the new contained a personal transference of loyalty as well as an attachment to a new social order. Obviously not all samurai were estranged or alienated; and among those who were so affected by the Restoration, not all became Christians. It is clear, however, that a feeling of loss and distaste preceded conversion to Christianity rather than appearing as an apologetic for it.

For conversion the personal and intellectual relationship of missionary and young samurai was critical. The character of this relationship reveals even more about the loss of traditional authority and the search for a new one. Most missionaries were committed abolitionists, and all represented the stern puritanical cast of American Protestantism. Earnest moralists, they established schools that had rigid standards of learning and discipline. Like E. B. Clark and many other missionaries, Leroy Janes had served as an officer in the Union Army during the American Civil War. A West Point graduate, he took as his educational model for the Yōgakkō Dr. Thomas Arnold's Rugby School. Janes believed, as did Arnold, that the teacher must be a moral model and a moral preceptor, and that secondary-school education must instill within a youth a firm Protestant code. Like Arnold, he was primarily interested in character formation. Arnold's Rugby School aimed to shape boys who could serve a Christian state. Ultimately Janes sought to create Christian men who could shape a modern state.

Students at the Yōgakkō lived in dormitories, rose early, and led spartan, regimented lives. Academic standards were rigorous, and students who failed to meet the standards Janes set were immediately dismissed from the academy. Janes' academic philosophy and methods reflected Arnold's educational aims while representing the ethical considerations that led all Christian missionaries to offer Christianity as the basis of Western civilization. Clark and Ballagh taught Christian ethics, and when doing so, spoke of the character of the Christian man. Janes related all these elements noting that the basis of any modern strong nation was the ethical Christian man—a man of free conscience who combined social responsibility with firm individualism. He declared: "It is a fundamental undertaking to increase national power by encouraging industries, but it is even more necessary to make men." Men are made by "religion and education," and the small nation such as Switzerland "retains her independence among the world's powers because she is the most educated of nations. Those who wish to sacrifice their life for their country ought to take up either way [religion or education]."

For the moment let us ignore the implications of the philosophical relationship between ethics, the conscience of man, and national development, and concentrate on the relationships between the young former samurai and the missionary. In the previous chapter we saw how impressed samurai were with Christianity as a supplement to bushido. They also constantly spoke of the missionary's love of them. It was the intensity of missionary affections and their commitment to Japan as well as to Christianity that attracted the youth. Kanamori wrote of Janes: "Of course we were afraid of the Bible [i.e., Christianity], but we believed in our teacher and followed him." Kozaki wrote of his Kumamoto experience: "It was at his [Janes'] prayer meeting that I came to be impressed by him. With open eyes I gazed upon his attitude while praying and recognized that the tears that came from his eyes as he concluded prayer were for Japan and for the world. This was the beginning of my search for faith."

The missionaries with their stern moral rectitude, their fervor and commitment, were respected as teachers in the moral mold of the Confucian scholar. As we will see, they also brought new ethics and teachings that were more in line with the demands of Westernizing. Apparently, in many cases missionaries were not only figuratively referred to as parents by their students; they and their new ethics replaced parental as well as the Confucian mentor's authority. When they spoke of the creation of a new man for a new Japan, they could come by their convictions and education to symbolize this man. Converts at Sapporo and Yokohama were really living as students abroad. They were far from their home domain and lived in a foreign-dominated environment. Far from parents and home, they could regard the missionary as father and teacher without directly confronting their parents. Niijima, for example, could write his parents from the United States referring to his new Lord and parent, God, without having to challenge his parents face to face.

In Kumamoto none of the Yōgakkō were far from home and domain opinion could be easily affronted. Conflict between some students and their parents over proper behavior and filial piety preceded conversion. Ebina Danjō's father had angrily ordered him to cease his studies at the Yōgakkō, and when he refused his father began a hunger strike. With their conversion many of the band were recalled home. Yokoi's Tokio's mother threatened suicide unless her son recanted his faith. Yoshida Sakuya's father drew his sword, and Yoshida announced that he would be happy to die by his father's hand. Kanamori Tsurin was locked up in the house of a relative and lectured to by the leading Confucian scholar of the domain, Takizaki Sado, on the respect due family and domain.

Kanamori questioned the correctness of Takizaki's analysis and in fact repudiated his authority. Yoshida's father dropped his sword in disgust. One youth while apparently agreeing to follow family orders ran off to Kyoto to study at the Christian Dōshisha Academy. Ebina who had earlier waited out his father's hunger strike and returned to school, now offered his moral support and example to his friends, and finally joined the thirty who came back to the Yōgakkō without recanting.

When news of the conversion on Mount Hanaoka reached the Kumamoto community, some of the students believed that a large group of samurai would attack the school and kill the converts and Janes. Janes drew his pistol, and his students spent the evening preparing to defend themselves and their faith. No attack took place at that time; however, a revived *shimpuren,* a coterie of Kumamoto samurai violently opposed to Westernization, did attack only a few months after Janes and his students had left Kumamoto.

Kozaki, who at first was determined to resist conversion, lectured Janes on Confucian ethics. Confused by Janes' refusal to answer and the steadfastness of Janes's ethical commitment, he faltered in his convictions and began a rigorous study of Christianity. Unable to succeed in his new determination to find some resolution of his past ethics and his new belief that faith was needed, and further confused about Christian doctrine, he consulted Janes. Janes told him that study alone would not help, that "a fool can never know the mind of the wise. Similarly man can never know the Almighty God." Stirred by Janes, Kozaki said, "That night I earnestly prayed for the first time and finally decided to believe in Christianity."

Similarly, throughout Japan converts came to the faith and fought vigorously against parental authority, Buddhist attacks, and the general suspicion of the populace. Evidently resistance to these attacks by society was usually made easier by the beginning of emotional ties to a new authority —the transference of filial piety from parent to missionary—making easier the intellectual road to transference from feudal lordship to the lordship of God. It also appears that however emotionally difficult it was for the students to face their parents after conversion, the old ties had already begun to weaken.

Each case of conversion may have been prompted by a series of apparently different events, but in every case alienation was the result, and alienation was overcome by the transformation. Ebina Danjō's conversion reflects this transformation. His conversion came after a series of intellectual adventures which I shall discuss later, but his acceptance of God as Lord must first be seen as both psychological and social since conversion ended his apathy and resolved his agony at the loss of all past relationships.

Ebina first discussed his loss of a sense of personal mission because of the death of his lord. "Because the young lord was dead, there was no one to whom I could offer my life." Ebina felt a sense of loneliness and personal aimlessness.

When I first realized it was my duty to make God my lord, it was then for the first time that my conscience gained authority. I was exceedingly happy. This was the rebirth of my whole life. As for my faith, my conscience being bound to God, its power was restored. I dislike referring to this as being "saved," but I was drawn up to a very splendid place.

As Watase Tsunekichi has said, this experience was "the grasping of God as his father and himself as his beloved son. It was a noble transfer from one lordship [Confucianism] to another."

Ebina portrayed his conversion dramatically. His language is that of the theology student, the minister who has often reflected on the character of conversion. Others, probably no less estranged or alienated, made the move from traditional loyalties to Christianity under even more dramatic circumstances than Ebina; however, no detailed record of their feelings is available.

There is, for example, the case of thirty local samurai who were still in Fukuoka prison in 1879 for sympathizing with and joining Saigo's abortive revolt. Undoubtedly they had joined, as most of Saigo's adherents had, out of distaste for the government that had destroyed samurai status. With the revolt suppressed, they were imprisoned. Preachers from Dōshisha, American and Japanese, visited and preached at the prison for a number of months. When these samurai were about to be released, they all promised to help Niijima, president of Dōshisha, spread the gospel in Fukuoka. After returning home, one sold his house and land to raise money to help finance evangelical work in Fukuoka. Many others became peddlers and used their profits to help in the founding of a church. Most of the thirty sponsored the bringing of a Dōshisha-trained minister to Fukuoka, and all became leaders of the Fukuoka mission.

The pattern of revolt, imprisonment, and conversion illustrates the relationship of samurai estrangement to Christianity. Despair led these samurai to radicalism and revolt, but defeat did not lead them to a reconciliation with government policy; rather, their opposition to the government continued by the acceptance of a despised religion. The very radicalism of the samurai revolt and the abruptness of their acceptance of Christianity demonstrate the relationship of estrangement and conversion. In the absence of complete evidence, it is difficult to state in definitive terms whether their conversion carried with it an explicit recognition of a new lordship. But their defeat, the defeat of the samurai class in Satsuma, certainly carried with it a sense of loss of status. Their acceptance of a life of poverty in order to serve the church and the mission suggests the acceptance of a new ethic and service to God, the new lord, and the church.

Perhaps this story is overdramatic, but it indicates the relief found in a new belief when hostility to the new government had led to revolt and defeat. Certainly conversion and its accompanying relief are no more dramatic than Ibuka of Yokohama who was able to reconcile himself to the Restoration when he was told, "It was the providence of the Lord."

PART THREE
The Sense of Urgency

12

Neither classical nor Marxian economic theory offers a proper explanation of the economic development of Japan. What impulses, what urgencies, what kind of cultural and psychological background stimulated Japan's economic growth? In the following essay, George DeVos shows that behind Japan's responses to the West stands a perception of culture that has not been adequately described by standard "ethnic" theories of economic development.

Achievement Orientation, Social Self-Identity, and Japanese Economic Growth

GEORGE A. DeVOS

THE propositions set forth in this paper are two-fold. First, given Japanese culture, especially its expressive values related to the prevalent patterns of psychological organization found among Japanese of the late Tokugawa period, it is not surprising that Japan developed quickly into the first industrial power of Asia. Second, the ethno-economics and political theory developed by the Japanese themselves as an ideology directing their modernization is best understood from the standpoint of Japanese culture and personality variables, and a simplistic application of either Western classical economics or Marxian theory is not helpful to an understanding of the relative success of Japanese industrialization.

A CRITIQUE OF NINETEENTH-CENTURY ECONOMICS FROM A CROSS-CULTURAL PERSPECTIVE

One cannot develop a valid science of economics that holds for all societies without seeing man as a social-psychological animal as well as one governed by political or economic principles in the production and distribution of goods. Both Marxian economic theory and that of classical economics, creatures of 19th century social science, place too heavy emphasis on man as functioning rationally toward the achievement of instrumental

George A. DeVos, "Achievement Orientation, Social Self-Identity, and Japanese Economic Growth," *Asian Survey*, Vol. 5, No. 12, pp. 575–589. © 1965 by The Regents of the University of California. Reprinted by permission of The Regents. Footnotes omitted.

goals. The Marxian dictum that religion is an opiate would seem to refer to a vast spectrum of seemingly irrational behavior on the part of unenlightened or duped masses who refused to be motivated to a proper extension of their own interests through revolutionary self-assertion.

In similar fashion, in the vision of theorists of a free economy (related to the Protestant religious ethic of personal salvation and blended at the end of the 19th century with social Darwinism), economic success is equated not only with self-justification in religious terms, but is viewed as evidence of biological superiority in a competitive world where only the fit deserve to survive. With this later philosphy, it is entirely consistent to consider specific races and societies as relatively inferior, and sometimes requiring the guidance and supervision of those who have demonstrated their fitness to govern others.

In the latter half of the 20th century, such self-satisfied appraisals of social and intellectual superiority, among theoreticians at least, have given way to new philosophies. The communist revolutionary ideology is being countered by attempts at some form of evolutionary capitalism which seeks to find social means whereby human economic standards everywhere are raised, lest unregulated explosive population growth in many societies eventuates in irremediable political upheaval. Yet, proponents of both ideologies face considerable frustration when they seek to actualize programs to bring about economic betterment, whether their programs are based on the communist theory that people can be rationally motivated to act out of some totalitarian concept of altruistic social interest or the capitalist approach that seeks to induce individuals to benefit the general good by acting out of motives of enlightened self-interest. These difficulties are not only apparent in the application of these programs to economic-political satellites, but they are also manifest within the Soviet Union and the United States. Traditional rationalist economic theories, whether communist or capitalist, based as they are on the primacy of economic rationality and the application of political power as a means of implementing planning, tend to ignore determinants of human behavior related to specific cultural traditions and general psychological processes.

Direct concern with the difficulties experienced in actualizing economic goals has had some effect on recent theory. Modern economists, dealing increasingly with the non-western world, place greater value on the study of cultural traditions by historians and anthropologists as a basis for the understanding of the economic development of a particular country. Some even have come to realize that classical economics itself has been a product of Western culture. As such, it is what might be termed an "ethno-economics," rather than a science based on postulates that bear up well when examined cross-culturally.

THE ROLE OF PSYCHOLOGY IN ECONOMIC THEORY

But while the relevance of political science, history, anthropology, and sociology to understanding the course of economic development of a particular society is conceded, there is still a general reluctance to acknowledge the relevance of psychology as a social science—neglect which still leads to serious theoretical difficulties. Some knowledge of psychological processes adds another dimension to understanding the vicissitudes involved in economic development. An understanding of irrational motives as related to expressive behavior acts as a corrective to what might be termed the instrumental bias still found in most social science. Man, in creating a meaning for his existence, no matter in what culture, orients himself toward nature and his fellow men in terms of values not directly derived from "instrumental" activities or goals. He derives satisfaction from forms of behavior that are "expressive" of phychological processes, as well as being guided by rationally conceived goals that direct his behavior toward the realization of culturally defined ends. The study of psychology reveals why this is so. When psychological principles are applied to the understanding of the learning processes and means by which goals are internalized or activated in any particular culture, we gain clues to why people of this culture behave the way they do, and why it is difficult to modify their behavior to conform to some form of planned change, be it economic or political in nature.

Being socialized within a particular culture may in many subtle ways incapacitate as well as facilitate the actualization of goals set by the politically dominant element of the society. The degree of sustained effort that one puts into adult occupational roles, including the work role, is determined not only by immediate social inducements but by a complex series of prior experiences.

It is precisely the neglect of the expressive, persistently irrational, elements in man's social behavior, that often confounds economic programs based too heavily on abstract theories of economic and political behavior. Expressive behavior is found institutionalized not only in the religious life of the people or in its art, but also in the very patterns of social and sex relations in family life to which a group is heavily committed. To understand what motivates members of a particular culture, one must place political or economic motives within their proper social-psychological context. What gives man "meaning" are ideas and values imbedded in the symbols of social life. The economic system of the culture itself must be seen in expressive as well as instrumental terms. Some of the profundity in Max Weber's sociological analysis derives from his recognition of the role of what he terms "meaning" in social processes.

The sacred cow of India confutes Indian economic development. As an expressive symbol, however, it points up several of the anti-economic values of Hindu culture. From the standpoint of behavior recalcitrant to the rational programs of the economist, every culture has some form of sacred cow. It is from this vantage point that I would like to briefly examine in a psychological frame of reference, the achievement orientation of the Japanese as related to their economic growth.

For many economists viewing economic progress in Japan, the Japanese family system may seem to some degree to be analogous to the sacred cow of India. It has been seen by some as an impediment to a more rational form of modernization of the Japanese economy. But it can be demonstrated with some cogency that, looked at historically, particularized traditional Japanese social values as they were inculcated within the context of family life were to no small extent responsible for a prevailing type of personal motivation expressed both in government policy implementation and in social relationships around work that made possible the rapid industrial modernization in Japan. Both in its instrumental as well as its expressive aspects, socialization within the Japanese family inculcated in many Japanese a type of self-motivated achievement orientation which, present in a sufficiently numerous segment of the population, made it possible to adequately man the operation of the society that was being self-consciously guided toward gaining a position of eminence in a world that was then exclusively dominated by Western states.

This adventure in modernization was peopled by participants in government, in education, and in newly founded economic enterprises that were guided and organized by a quasi-religious paternalistic familism that united more than it divided into economic classes, created more harmony than dissension, more morale than alienation. Japanese familism in its psychological and attitudinal aspects has been a strong integrative force placing constraints toward cooperation on all segments of the society. For contrast, one might compare it to the type of familism reported for southern Italy. Banfield describes what he terms "Amoral Familism" as operative in the southern Italian family. The family is a fortress held against the outside society which is perceived with hostility and distrust. Life and social relationships are perceived as tragic and defeating—there is a general tone of pessimism, deprivation, and distrust of both man and nature. This type of familism is in direct contrast to that obtaining in Japan, where the community beyond the family is united by a network of interpenetrating obligations and expectations. The individual Japanese may be concerned with personal inadequacies and the difficulties of his environment, but he does not perceive himself as being defeated by the potential malevolence of his fellow men. He sustains himself by hard work and ultimately accomplishes some social goal—he remains optimistic through adversity and does not come to view society with distrust. He may fear standing out unduly with his fellow men, but he disguises such fear by emphasis on cooperation rather than defense or retreat. Above all, he is guided by a sense of self-dedication.

Many of the political and even economic leaders of Meiji Japan operated within a framework where such dedication as a consuming expressive need was not a rare quality. They could count on others—now not dedicated to feudal loyalties, but to advancing the totally conceived national interest. The Meiji period found the leaders and followers of the warriors and farming and mercantile classes joined in common enterprises, as well as educated toward the realization of common policies in the schools. The Japanese intellectuals, whatever their experience of strain suffered in the course of relating Westernized conceptions of science and economic rationality to their own country, or to their personal lives, were not overwhelmed. The Japanese values were not inundated but, during the Meiji period at least, crested this tide of new experiences.

Thus, the assimilation of aspects of Western culture did not alienate the leadership from the common people. The expressive ties of an intricately interwoven family society did not break. Also, from a psychological perspective, the new leadership in significant numbers learned to dedicate themselves to newly evolving social roles, the manner of dedication peculiarly derived from the previous Japanese culture. This sense of dedication did not become individualistically conceptualized as in Western entrepreneurial terms, but was permeated with a strong sense of social service. Not only the warrior gave his life, but also the bureaucrat, the educator, even the humble conductor running the railroad station—all derived "meaning" in Weber's terms from their occupational roles. They did not work only to earn their survival or to aggrandize themselves. Many worked out of a sense of self-realization, family and national justification.

This paternalistic structure of society in individual psychological terms was motivated from within. The early experiences of family life were sufficiently rewarding and gratifying to give life sufficient meaning without any transcending recourse to more universalistic roles and values of individuated purposes as occurred under a more universalist Western social philosophy.

In another article, in the context of Japanese suicide, I have discussed the extreme form of dedication to a particularistic social role that one found within Japanese culture. This dedication to social role was originally part of the samurai sense of self. With the abolition of the samurai class, the seeking of self-actualization was transmuted into the role of the Meiji government bureaucrat, into the role of teacher, or into the role of entrepreneur. This type of dedication stemming from the internalization of social values that occured within the family staffed the new bureaucracy as well as the economic and political parts of the social system with the type of individuals that had sufficient morale to make these parts work with a fair degree of success. There was a feeling of "we-ness" in the society, a sharing in which class divisions did not interfere with a sense of cooperativeness of purpose throughout the society. The former samurai, as a member of an educated class, became devoted to the total national polity, including the rural folk. A tremendous resource of human energy was directed into new channels. An important factor of the family system and the reorganization of the society in familial terms which cannot be overlooked is that it helped maintain a high morale and did not permit energies to be dissipated by an undue amount of social dissension or apathy in the face of economic change.

There was a dedication to role in all minor jobs which at times approached the ludicrous, but at other times kept the system working in a manner which was frequently not possible in European countries which were trying to reorganize in industrial terms. The paternalism within the system stressed obligations on the part of superiors as well as their subordinates. Occupational security was held dominant over efficiency of operation. But what looked inefficient on the surface from an impersonal economic standpoint on a day-by-day level, over the long period maintained concerted group action. Crippling dissension appeared only in rare instances.

For stable industries, Japanese modernization was aided by the fact that job security was considered more important than wages—where industries became stable they looked to the "fringe welfare benefits" of the workers, and would keep an uneconomic worker force rather than fire what were perceived to be faithful workers.

Conversely, in less stable industries, the rural family ties also provided an economic as well as emotional cushion in case of unemployment. Family members were readily reabsorbed within a rural village. They did not simply become unattached urban proletariats faced with the total consequences of particular economic reversals, as occurred under European conditions of industrialization.

Some of the major factors often referred to in purely economic analysis of the rapid industrialization and economic expansion of Meiji Japan, if more closely scrutinized, were in actuality derived from the psychologically satisfying familism permeating Japanese society. The above example of reabsorption of unemployed workers back into the village is often used simply as an economic explanation. A second explanation, usually discussed only in economic terms, is often related to governmental paternalism. The Meiji government sponsored and subsidized heavy industries that were subsequently taken over completely by private enterprises. This government paternalism prevented inefficient experimentation and possible loss by private entrepreneurs who could not immediately compete successfully in the international market. One can also see the characteristic of social trust in how the readiness to invest depended on trust in the government and its directives. Moreover, an appeal could be made to stoicism and frugality rather than to hedonistic qualifications in saving capital. In these factors and others, referred to by economists explaining Japan's rapid industrialization, one should point out the uniquely Japanese cultural psychological features found in their particularistic, paternalistic familism.

In another dimension one might cite Lockwood, who, not disagreeing with the theory which interprets the rapid industrialization of Meiji Japan in terms of the government's initiative and sponsoring of heavy industry which drew upon overpopulated farming villages for cheap labor, nevertheless emphasized the more important role played by thousands of small-scale Japanese entrepreneurs who often with their own family members as employees, worked hard and long, and also saved capital. Here too, Lockwood is pointing to the cultural psychology of the Japanese. The concerted effort was on the part of families, not simply individuals. The house, not the person, was being advanced by the small entrepreneur. Again, one had a strong sense of self-motivated achievement, but in the context of affiliative needs, as they are sometimes called in psychological research.

Briefly, the role of the Japanese family as a socializing agent, as a permanent recourse in times of stress, as well as a keystone of Japanese social values, must be considered in understanding both Japanese achievement motivation and the capacity for concerted group efforts which went into the rapid economic change witnessed in Japan. The point is that a sufficient percentage of the Japanese population was psychologically ready to make government directed modernization succeed.

This consideration must not be removed from context, however. We are not suggesting an entirely new theory of economic development ignoring other complex determinants already considered amply by the economic historian, but are simply attempting to bring into proper focus the type of motivational determinants that must be considered as an essential characteristic for any population to achieve social change. In the last analysis, *internally* induced and lasting social change in the economic sphere must be congruent, to some extent, with the psychological motivation of at least a good number of the participants in the economy.

CRITIQUE OF HAGEN'S THEORY OF SOCIAL CHANGE

What we have to say here in good part runs parallel to the arguments of Everett E. Hagen in his recent volume *On the Theory of Social Change,* but our contentions and propositions are somewhat different from his. His theory suggests innovation and creative behavior due to a tendency for elements of the population to retreat when they become alienated from traditional values as a result of the loss of expected status within the traditional society. While I would agree that some such process seems to be in ferment at the end of the Tokugawa period in Japan, Hagen's arguments still do not concern themselves with some unique features of Japanese psychology externally expressed in an ideological emphasis on future time orientation and the development of capacities for sustained application to tasks in the face of present frustrations toward future goals. The virtues of endurance and perseverance, as expressive of a personality orientation, characterize Japanese culture to a degree not readily paralleled elsewhere.

Nor is Japanese economic development to be explained simply in the sense that the Japanese were ready to accept foreign values more readily than other Asia societies, since it was part of their tradition to do so. My position would be more that the political leaders of the Meiji Restoration were able to call forth efforts on the part of the Japanese population related to a reinterpretation of the familial structure of the society on the basis of hierarchical system of loyalties which made deep emotional sense to the Japanese generally. It made emotional sense and was appealing to the Japanese because it was entirely consonant with learned behavior within the primary family that could be easily transmuted to the economic political plane in sustained work patterns phrased in social terms. The Japanese sense of accomplishment or achievement could only be satisfied ultimately by being defined as relevant to a sense of self as part of family, or part of something larger than the individualized self. The sense of self, for many Japanese, is realized only through repayment of deeply felt obligations. Should these not be fulfilled, a sense of intolerable guilt can arise. This sense of loyalty to authority and repayment of obligation stems from interactions of the child with parental behavior before there is any verbalization of an ideology of loyalty taking place beyond the primary family itself. Nevertheless, the emotional impact of life within the primary family sets the keystone to life's meaning. The traditional family system must be perceived as having maintained a quasi-religious connotation for the adult Japanese. In his very perceptive work, *Tokugawa Religion*, Robert Bellah demonstrates from a somewhat different perspective that it was not uncommon in Tokugawa time to find religious affirmation of the virtue of work and the diligent pursuit of one's occupation. Simplicity, frugality, and diligence were inseparably woven into the fabric on one's filial duty to family and society and thence to the supernatural extension of the family. Such feelings, however, were also an emotionally relevant part of personality integration, whether they were expressed secondarily in their religious system, or primarily as part of being a member of a Japanese family seeking continuity of the family through time. This sense of self-justification through work, as Bellah pointed out, is remarkably similar to what has been called the Protestant ethic in Western culture.

Hagen notes the similarity of a Puritan-like ethic in Japan, that of English non-conformism, and its doctrine that service to God lies in a diligent attempt to glorify him by making the earth fruitful. This doctrine in the English, Hagen points out, was associated with a deep pervasive sense of guilt that is central to Puritan psychology. While he sees the same ethic appearing in Japan, Hagen does not presume that in Japan it was related in a similar fashion to a sense of guilt, but rather, as he sees it, from some of the written literature, to a sense of inadequacy and shame. This position is an unwarranted dissimilarity as far as the point of view that I espouse is concerned, namely, whereas a sense of guilt in the West was very often associated with individualized problems related to sexuality, in Japan, there was a strong sense of potential guilt if one strayed from the path of work. Only through repayment of parental efforts could one find satisfaction in life and freedom from a sense of guilt. I have discussed Japanese guilt formation elsewhere in the context of achievement and arranged marriage.

To briefly recapitulate the argument here, in the paper on guilt and achievement, I cited evidence in detail that the continual concern of Japanese over questions of success and failure could not simply be explained in terms of concern with so-called "face" or social presence. Such explanations do not probe deeply enough into how the Japanese internalize their moral directives within the family setting. Guilt in Western man has been traditionally related to a universalistic moral system which governs the handling of sexual and aggressive urges. The sense of guilt was related to the self in universalistically conceived directives. In Japan, to the contrary, the moral structure was much more related to the consequences of behavior on the family or the nation or a feudal fief conceived in famialistic terms. There is a psychological analogue between the sense of responsibility to parents in Japan for social conformity and achievement, and the traditional relationship found in the Protestant West between work activity and a personal relationship to the deity holds fast. Concisely stated, my argument is as follows. Guilt in many Japanese is not only operative in respect to what is termed superego functions, but is also concerned with what has been internalized by an individual as a so-called ego ideal. Generally speaking, the psychological processes involved in resolving early identifications as well as assuming later adult social roles are never possible without some form of internalized guilt. The more expected of a child in defining ideal adult behavior, the more opportunity there is for ambivalence to develop toward the source of these difficult expectations. These social expectations need not put direct emphasis on prohibitive behavior as is done where there is a concern with punishment as a mode of training, very often found in the west. In Japan, rather than fear of punishment, there is more often a fear of rejection and abandonment on the part of those on whom the person places his ultimate dependence.

What is termed shame, as well as what is termed guilt, both undergo a process of internalization in the course of development. Both become operative in the individual relatively free from either external threats of punishment or overt concern with the opinion of others over one's behavior. Social behavior is automatically evaluated without the presence of others by an individual who has internalized the directives of his society.

Moreover, a simple dichotomy relating internalized shame only to ego ideal and internalized guilt to an automatically operative superego is one to be seriously questioned, although one finds such dichotomatization very often in psychological literature.

Whereas the formation of an internalized ego ideal in its earlier form is more or less related to social expectations and values of parents, the motivations which move a developing young adult toward a realization of these expectations can involve considerable guilt. Considering Japanese perception of social expectations concerning achievement behavior, there is ample evidence of the presence of such guilt. In fact, shame as a motive is much less in evidence in the psychological material to which I have had recourse.

Nullification of parental expectations is one way to "hurt a parent." Guilt in Japanese is essentially related to an impulse to hurt. Japanese children learn earlier that they have the potentiality of injuring a love object, usually the mother. That the mother very often suffers indicates to her children her vulnerability to their bad behavior.

There are other forms of guilt related to various internalization processes common in Japan, but generic to Japanese guilt seems to be some disavowal of an unconscious impulse to hurt. Only in some instances is there emphasis on fear of retributions resulting from this desire to hurt or to injure. In the fantasy stories of both rural and urbanized samples of men, tested by projective psychological test methods, guilt is often related to a possible rebellion against parental expectations. A potential way of rebelling is to dissipate one's energies in some form of profligate behavior rather than applying oneself to hard work or to dedication to an unexpected life goal.

Traditionally, guilt in women has been related to becoming selfish and unsubmissive in the duties involved in the maternal role. The principal adult role for the traditional woman was to bring up her child to be a success in the world and to have him realize his potentials so as to bring honor upon his family. Japanese mothers dedicated themselves to such a role with an intensity only equalled by similar extremes found in middle class parents in the United States who orient their entire behavior around the educational process of their children. This pattern of dedication continues today in Japan's new middle class. As Ezra Vogel has amply documented, such preoccupation on the part of mothers remains in the present-day white collar group in Japan, whatever its slow erosion in the society generally with the increased tempo of change now occurring.

FAMILY STRUCTURE—SELF IDENTITY IN ACHIEVEMENT ORIENTATION

In contrasting Japanese traditional cultural concepts of self and society with those prevalent in Western Europe in the 19th century during its industrial revolution, one finds that the Japanese placed little value on individualistic self realization in either the spiritual or the material realm. The

Western ideal of personal and self realization apart from family or social group has been, outside of a small group of intellectuals, entirely alien to the Japanese system of thought, up to very recently. The religious ideals of Buddhism emphasize the loss of self or selfish preoccupations as a means of release from worldly problems. Confucianist ideology which colored the thought of the governing classes throughout the Tokugawa period, as well as the subsequent innovators of modernization in the early Meiji period kept its central focus on the position of the family in the social system. The ultimate goals of life were non-instrumentally organized quasi-religious concepts of family continuity. Legally and morally an individual defined himself in the context of his family roles and their attendant obligations and expectations.

The state was defined not only in terms of a class or occupational hierarchy but also as a pyramid of social obligations in which all Japanese were somewhere interrelated in a hierarchical structure. It was within the context of this ideal social structure that the Meiji government defined its social and economic goals. Economic theory stressing individualized laissez-faire attitudes could make little sense as a mandate for modernization of development. Such individualized economic theory, even though it may have influenced Japanese theoretical economists, could not actually describe the Japanese atmosphere. The self concept under individualism, the economic man as instrumentally oriented, could not form the basis of a viable social or economic theory of direct pertinence to describe the course of events taking place in Japan.

The Western ideology sprang from a different tradition of seeking salvation or self realization. Personal freedom as a goal of human endeavor and creative individualism were at this time the paramount virtues in the West and especially in the newly emerging United States. The individuals internalized Christian conscience was given priority over the laws of the state and even over the traditional organized bureaucracy of the Roman church. The struggle for individual liberty became a source of religious and secular social conflict. It is not coincidental that this Western ideology appeared as a main feature of the economic theory of the 19th century. Adam Smith's theories gave reassurance that the individual was morally justified in seeking the maximization of his individual interests, since through the operation of the impersonal market they were ultimately entirely consistent with the social good and could lead to benefit for the total society. The illusion that rational self interest properly understood did away with any need for a controlling government apparatus, made sense emotionally to individuals reared consciously by parents who trained their children to feel guilt for unacceptable physical sexual urges, but also trained them to rely only on a direct dependent relationship with their deity. No other form of psychological dependency was considered mature. Assured of God's help, the individual could only attribute personal failure to moral flaws or to an incomplete conquest of internal evil propensities or lack of proper motivation. One learned not to turn too readily toward one's fellow men for social assistance since by doing so one demeaned oneself. With God's help, one could become sufficiently self reliant to overcome not only baser urges, but find sufficient strength to endure adversity and obtain long-range goals. Those too weak or incapable could be given alms, but for the righteously successful, the idea that poverty was a stigma of the intellectually and morally inferior lessened the feeling of together-ness with the under-privileged. In its later development the religious as-pects of this ideology was replaced with more secular arguments. Robert Lynd, in *Knowledge for What,* amply demonstrates how such thinking remains an essential aspect of American life.

The point being made here again is simply this, that the system of classi-cal economics developed in Britain and in the United States must be seen as ethno-economics. Its emphasis was very much on an instrumental view of human nature and its motivation. On the contrary, the type of economic social system envisioned by the Meiji government officials directing mod-ernization was much more expressively oriented and centered on the family and the nation as an extension of the family itself. To the Japanese, this type of integration made sense. Also, it made sense as a system under which there was a high degree of moral rather than class conflict. The feel-ings of mutual expectations between superior and subordinate were strongly operative in the motivation of those involved in economic pursuits. Whatever their goal with regard to the maximation of profit, they also felt a series of obligations to their subordinates which led to an emphasis upon fringe benefits and the retention of individuals once brought into the or-ganization. These particular features have been criticized by Western economists as showing an irrationality. But one could argue that they con-tributed to high morale, and prevented the significant appearance of con-flict in Japanese industrialization resulting from the alienation of the worker as had appeared with European capitalism.

Western economics is based on a commonly held assumption about the nature of achievement motivation as it relates to occupational self-justifi-cation among dominant social elements of the culture producing it. Ra-tional self-interest assumes the rationalization of the economy in accord with impersonal laws which, when they work, ideally demand lack of in-terference from government and state controls which parenthetically may be guided by non-economic considerations and hence prevent the maximi-zation of self interest. In the 20th century, considerable modification has occurred in attempting to make this system work better. Curiously, many of the modifications are in terms of a higher consideration of expressive elements in human motivation among workers. In contrast, in the Japanese system, one finds an increased recourse to instrumental concerns with the gradual dropping out of the family system as the major guiding ideology within Japanese thought.

From the 1920's on, Japanese intellectuals became more and more concerned with a Marxian interpretation of the social structure. The emotional climate of the Japanese, however, has not completely altered. The structure of Japanese feelings about self and class identity and social authority still makes class warfare of less appeal. The Japanese even more than the American identifies himself as middle class—an old tradition of the Japanese rural farmer which seemed to have been transmitted to the industrial worker. The company president, in the fantasy of many Japanese, has replaced the *daimyo* or feudal lord. Individuals are still motivated by feelings of loyalty to the organization. Such a feeling of loyalty would be considered by an individualistically organized middle class American to interfere with his achievement career which demands mobility of movement to a degree not possible within the Japanese system. To the ordinary American industrial worker, the idea of loyalty to a business or factory is an absurdity.

It is noteworthy that even today in the expressive fantasy of lower class Japanese, the status position of success very often depicted spontaneously in the stories, is not only that of the teacher as an advisor, but also the head of a company or entrepreneur who takes a paternal position and acts as advisor to his subordinates. This type of perception of paternalization is also helped by the fact that the individual who reaches this status position feels expected of him a type of protection and maintenance of his subordinates which is entirely in line with the familistic pseudo-kinship structures that were part of the old society. From the standpoint of some economists the system described by Abegglen in a Japanese factory looks uneconomical and inefficient; however, it is the very force of this system which helped the Japanese adapt to the modern age. The internalized type of personality structure, its concept of goals and the type of inter-connected relationships, the pattern of social expectations within the Japanese system, focused on the familial pattern was exactly the type of emotional and motivational force which helped maintain and direct Japanese society successfully in the new direction of industrialization.

SUMMARY

It is only recently that those social scientists concerned with problems of economic development have become cognizant of a need to consider psychological factors as relevant to the study of economic growth and change in particular cultures. Both classical economics and Marxist theory, in their heavy emphasis on man as a rational animal maximizing his political or economic power, tended to overlook or deprecate the influence of the expressive aspects of human behavior. Unless these culturally determined but psychologically structured expressive aspects are related in a facilitative manner to a sense of achievement and accomplishment relevant to economic productivity in the motivational structure of a sufficiently large segment of a particular population, political policy decisions and social planning, whatever their theoretical validity, cannot be adequately implemented.

The essay discusses some of the psychological structures prevalent in many Japanese which result in achievement motivated behavior. The socialization experiences in the context of Japanese society results in a strong need for self-realization through her work and a sense of accomplishment defined in social terms. These psychological features were common to a sufficient number of Japanese in a manner that made possible a relatively successful transmutation of a feudal society into a well functioning industrialized modern state.

Japanese achievement drive must be seen as motivated by irrational un-- common forces as well as socially defined goals. The system of familial obligation related to Japanese internalization of feelings of potential guilt and the lack of easy expression of hostility or aggression given the proper cultural-industrial context can result in self dedication to social role and to the maintenance of relatively high morale and lack of dissension in work situations.

The social climate occuring within the family was readily transmitted in particularistic terms to a larger social context.

This essay does not presume to formulate alternative theories of economic growth, but simply to supplement such theories with the insight afforded by the role of psychological variables in determining the relative rate of economic change found differentially among different cultures entering the modern industrial age. Psychological factors contribute both in respect to achievement motivation and in respect to the effectiveness of the social organization in bringing about commonly accepted new goals.

13　　*In the following selections from his autobiography Yūkichi Fukuzawa discusses the various crises that enveloped the world of both Tokugawa and Meiji Japan. He demonstrates the belief of many young men in the Tokugawa period that Japan could only deal successfully with the danger of the West by a thorough overhauling of its own system. Fukuzawa lived in a period that demanded both social revolution and political modernization. Through his reminiscences we see why and how some of the young responded so avidly.*

FROM

The Autobiography of Yūkichi Fukuzawa

YŪKICHI FUKUZAWA

"ALL the intercourse of life is governed by the rule of give and take. If the clan says, 'You should be grateful for the patronage given your family for many generations,' I shall have a word to say in reply: 'There is no occasion for you to demand gratitude, for my family has rendered honest service for a long time.' On the other hand, if the clan extends some appreciation to us, saying, 'We are glad to acknowledge the good service of a family like yours,' then I should feel like saying in return, 'I am deeply grateful for your constant employment. During our family's history, there have been some good-for-nothing men, also some weaklings. In spite of these, you have been good enough to give us our fixed salaries and enabled us to live comfortably. The benevolence of our clan is as exalted as the mountains and as deep as the sea.' So would I humble myself and return thanks. This is what I consider the law of give and take. I don't want to have gratitude demanded of me, or to be called disloyal without reason." In this way I dealt with the charge of my "disloyalty" to the clan.

I IGNORE THE CLAN'S CALL TO ARMS

A few years before the Restoration, the Chōshū clan was declared guilty of treason and the government had announced that the Shōgun himself would lead the combined forces of several clans against it. Accordingly,

From Yūkichi Fukuzawa, *The Autobiography of Yūkichi Fukuzawa*, 1968, E. Kiyooka (trans.), Columbia University Press. Reprinted with permission of the publisher. Footnotes omitted.

our Nakatsu clan sent orders recalling the students in my school for service. I think Obata Tokujirō and others were among them—about ten in all. But I said that it was too dangerous for the young men to go to war; they might be killed by stray bullets however carefully they went about in the battlefield. For this kind of absurd war, if they wanted figureheads in their ranks, they could as well hire farmers from the provinces. My students were too precious; even if they were not to be hit by the bullets, they might hurt their feet on thorns. So I had them answer that they were all too ill to carry arms. If we were to be punished, the worst would be dismissal from the clan. I did not consider the right or wrong of the conflict; I simply said it was not the kind of activity that students should take part in.

A REVEALING CONVERSATION ABOARD THE SHIP

Though I did not engage in politics, I was not entirely ignorant of the political world. On the voyage to Europe, I used to talk over the problems of the time with the other interpreters, Matsuki and Mitsukuri.

"What do you think of it?" I said one day. "The shogunate cannot hold the country together much longer. It seems to me that all the clans might get together and form a federation like Germany. What do you say to this idea?"

Matsuki and Mitsukuri agreed with me that this would be the most peaceful solution of the crisis.

Then going on to talk of our own careers, I said, "If I am to say what I'd like to do if I could, it would be to become tutor to the big chief (the Shōgun) with a salary of two hundred bales of rice a year and the chance of teaching him all the new ideas of civilization and bringing about a great reformation in the country."

Matsuki clapped his hands and exclaimed that that was just what he too would love to do. A salary of two hundred rice-bales and post of tutor to the Shōgun was the level of ambition for Matsuki at that time. This represented the average thoughts of all the foreign culture students of the age.

Later Matsuki, under his new name of Terajima, took high offices in the new imperial régime, even becoming a minister of foreign affairs. That seems to me a pretty wide departure from his early ambition, and rather a sad departure, knowing, as I do, his true personality.

But to return to the contemporary situation in the country, I noticed that all the ambitious adventurers and so-called patriots had collected in Kyōto around the imperial cause. The shogunate in Yedo, on the other hand, was trying to keep its own as the central government against this rising power. These two political forces had come to be called *Kinnō*, the supporters of the Emperor, and *Sabaku*, the supporters of the Shōgun. If I may sum up my position between those two sides:—

1. I disliked the bureaucratic, oppressive, conservative, anti-foreign policy of the shogunate, and I would not side with it.

2. Yet the followers of the imperial cause were still more anti-foreign and more violent in their action, so I had even less sympathy with them.

3. After all, troubled times are best for doing big things. An ambitious man might cast his lot with one or the other of the parties to win a place for himself. But there was no such desire in me.

To tell how I came to feel this way—ever since my first arrival in Yedo, I had not been impressed by the men in the Shōgun's government. At the first meeting they would appear to be genteel, well-mannered, and smooth in speech—so much finer than men in the provinces. But that was only superficial. Really they had no brains to think with, nor did they seem to have much physical vigor either. They were direct retainers of the Shōgun, however, and I was merely a retainer of a provincial clan. To them I had to bow most ceremoniously and use "sama" in mentioning their names whether the man was present or not. I was simply being officious to them as one would to *kuge,* the courtiers of the new culture. Now that I had the corroboration of the foreign statesman, I was truly discouraged.

Yet I was Japanese and I could not sit still. If I could do nothing toward improving the condition of politics, I could at least attempt something by teaching what I had learned of Western culture to the young men of my land, and by translating Western books and writing my own. Then perhaps through good fortune I might be able to lead my countrymen out of their present obscurity. So, helpless but resolute, I took my stand alone.

I have never told anyone of the dire, helpless state of my mind at that time. But I am going to confess it now. Watching the unfortunate condition of the country, I feared in reality that we might not be able to hold our own against foreign aggressiveness. Yet there was no one in all the land with whom I could talk over my anxiety—no one anywhere, east, west, north or south, as I searched. I seemed alone in my anxiety and I knew I did not have the power to save my country.

WHAT WILL BECOME OF MY CHILDREN?

If in the future there should come signs of foreign aggression and we were to be subjected to insult from foreigners, I would probably find some way to extricate myself. But when I thought of my children who had longer lives to live, again I was afraid. They must never be made slaves of the foreigners; I would save them with my own life first. At one time I thought even of having my sons enter the Christian priesthood. If in that calling they could be independent of others in their living, and if they could be accepted as Christian priests, I thought, my sons would be spared. So, in my anxiety, though I was not a believer in that religion, I once contemplated making priests of my boys.

As I look back today—over thirty years later—it all seems a dream. How advanced and secure the country is now! I can do nothing but bless with a full heart this glorious enlightenment of Japan today.

It was during the first year of Meiji, or the fourth year of Keiō (1868), that I moved my school from Teppōzu to Shinsenza in Shiba. Now that it had taken on somewhat the status of a regular school, I gave it the name Keiō-gijuku after the name of the era, this being a few months before the announcement of the change. Students who had scattered during the unsettled times were now returning, and the school again prospered. As the number of students increased, a more systematic supervision became necessary. So I drew up a book of regulations and, finding it impractical to have every student make a copy of it, I had the manual printed and distributed.

OUR INNOVATION—COLLECTING TUITION

Among other items, it included one on the collection of monthly fees which was an innovation in Keiō-gijuku. Until then in all the schools of Japan, probably in imitation of the Chinese custom, the students gave some gift of money on entering as a private formality. After this they revered the master as Sensei, and about twice a year, at the Bon festival in summer and at the end of the year, they brought presents to him. These gifts were sometimes money, sometimes articles, always presented in the old convention of wrappings and *noshi* (ceremonial seals). They represented tuitions, in quantity or value, according to the financial status of the students' families.

It seemed to us that no teacher would really give his best under such a system. For teaching is a man's work, too. Why then should not a man accept money for his work? We would openly charge a fixed amount for our instruction no matter what other people might say about it. We composed a new word *jugyōryō* for tuition and ordered each student to bring two *bu* every month. These collected fees were divided among my older pupils who had been appointed to do the teaching. At that time a teacher boarding in the school could live on four *ryō* a month; so if we had this amount for each from the tuition collected every month, we would have sufficient to keep ourselves alive. Any amount over and above that was to be used for the maintenance of the buildings.

Of course by now there is nothing unusual in this business of collecting tuition; every school follows it. But when we first announced it, such an innovation startled everybody.

We threw off all the dignity of the old master and simply told the students to bring the two *bu*—"Don't bring the money wrapped up or with the ceremonial labels on it. And if you don't have the exact amount, we will make the change for you." Yet some would, at first, hand in the tuition wrapped in paper, tied in *mizuhiki* (ceremonial cords). Then we would tell them the wrapping was inconvenient in examining the money, and we would purposely open it there and hand back the wrapping. Such were our rude ways, and no wonder they startled the good people around us. But now it is amusing to see that our "rude" manners have become the custom of the country and nobody gives a second thought to them.

In anything, large or small, it is difficult to be the pioneer. It requires an unusual recklessness. But on the other hand, when the innovation becomes generally accepted, its originator gets the utmost pleasure as if it were the attainment of his inner desires.

. . .

It is not only that I hold little regard for the Chinese teaching, but I have even been endeavoring to drive its degenerate influences from my country. It is not unusual for scholars in Western learning and for interpreters of languages to make this denunciation. But too often they lack the knowledge of Chinese to make their attacks effective. But I know a good deal of Chinese, for I have given real effort to its study under a strict teacher. And I am familiar with most of the references made to histories, ethics, and poetry. Even the peculiarly subtle philosophy of Lao-tzu and Chuang-tzu I have studied and heard my teacher lecture on them. All of this experience I owe to the great scholar of Nakatsu, Shiraishi. So, while I frequently pretend that I do not know much, I sometimes take advantage of the more delicate points for attack both in my writings and in my speeches. I realize I am a pretty disagreeable opponent of the Chinese scholars—"a worm in the lion's body."

The true reason of my opposing the Chinese teaching with such vigor is my belief that in this age of transition, if this retrogressive doctrine remains at all in our young men's minds, the new civilization cannot give its full benefit to this country. In my determination to save our coming generation, I was prepared even to face single-handed the Chinese scholars of the country as a whole.

Gradually the new education was showing its results among the younger generation; yet men of middle age or past, who held responsibile positions, were for the most part uninformed as to the true spirit of Western culture, and whenever they had to make decisions, they turned invariably to their Chinese sources for guidance. And so, again and again I had to rise up and denounce the all-important Chinese influence before this weighty opposition. It was not altogether a safe road for my reckless spirit to follow.

MY PUBLICATIONS ARE ALL AT MY OWN RISK

The years around the Restoration period were most active ones in my writing and translating. But as I have already written minutely of these in the preface to my collected works (Fukuzawa Zenshū), I need not now repeat. All of my books were done entirely on my own initiative without orders from or consultation with others. I never showed the manuscripts to any of my friends, to say nothing of asking prominent scholars for prefaces and inscriptions. They might be devoid of grace and form—I perhaps should have sought an old scholar for a graceful foreword—but I preferred, then, to have my books stand on their own merits. Naturally they remained unapproved by men of the old school, whether true or false. Still all my books proved very successful with the great tide of new culture sweeping the whole country.

.   .   .

Many a time a young man returning from abroad has come to me and asserted his belief in an independent career, saying he would not think of a government post. I usually listen to his proud declaration with half credulity. And sure enough, after a while I learn that the same young man has been appointed secretary in a certain department—sometimes he has been lucky enough to be placed in the higher office of a province.

Of course I have no business to be criticizing the choice of a man's career, but I have the feeling that this fallacy of the Japanese people is an evidence of the surviving influence of the Chinese teaching. To point out this fallacy to our people and lead them in the right way of modern civilization, someone must be an example. The independence of a nation springs from the independent spirit of its citizens. Our nation cannot hold its own if the old slavish spirit is so manifest among the people. I felt determined to make an example of myself whatever the consequences of my endeavor might be. If I should be the poorer for it, I should live poorer; if I chanced to make money, I should spend it as I wished. At least I would not depend upon the government or its officials.

In my intercourse with my friends, I do what I can to offer them hospitality, but if it is not sufficient for them, they need not continue my friendship. I am sincere in my efforts to share what I have according to the means of my household. When I have done my part, it remains with those friends to like me or hate me, praise me or denounce me. I should not lose my head from joy or anger.

All in all, I am determined to live independent of man or thing. I cannot think of government office while I hold this principle. Then again, I am not particularly anxious to prove that my principle is the right one for the rest of the world. If it proves good, very well; if bad, then that is unfortunate. I have no intention of bearing the responsibility of the result of my stand in the distant future.

From this very full analysis of the reasons for my not taking a government post, it may appear as if I had formulated them in the beginning and proceeded to live accordingly. But that is not so. Truly I have not been tying myself down with any theories. I made this analysis so that there may be some order in my presentation of this survey.

After all, in thinking over the whole of my attitude and my life, I may say that I am at best indifferent to politics. If we divide the world into two groups of men—old topers and teetotallers, the former having no interest in confectionary shops, the latter never entering a bar—I suppose I am a "teetotaller" in politics.

I AM A DIAGNOSTICIAN, NOT A PRACTICING PHYSICIAN

Not that I am wholly uninterested in that field, for I frequently discuss the subject and have written upon it, but for the daily wear and tear of its practice I have no taste. I am like the diagnostician in the medical field who can judge a disease but cannot care for a sick man. So people are not to take my diagnosis of politics as any evidence of personal ambition.

THE POLITICAL UPHEAVAL OF 1881

In the fourteenth year of Meiji (1881) there was an unusual disturbance in the political world of Japan, and in connection with it an amusing incident occurred to me. During the preceding winter I had had an interview with the three ministers—Ōkuma, Itō, and Inoue—who asked me to take charge of a newspaper, or official bulletin, which they were then planning to start. But at the time they did not reveal its purpose or anything about it. So I refused and left their presence.

After this, certain minor officials kept coming to induce me to consider the matter until finally they revealed to me the secret that the government was going to open a national diet and, by way of preparation, wanted a newspaper. That struck me as an interesting venture and I agreed to think the matter over. My tentative promise was given. But time went on without any definite move being made. The year passed; then the next year was nearly gone. Yet I was still waiting, and there was no particular hurry on my part.

Then it became evident that there was a rift between the principals in high places and subsequently Ōkuma resigned. The resignation of a minister is not a rare occurrence, but on this occasion the resignation had a wider and, I may say, ridiculous effect, reaching even myself. With the consequent shifting of many of the minor officials, many rumors were spread.

One of these stories had it that Ōkuma was a very wilful man, always scheming something, and that behind him had stood Fukuzawa supplying ideas. Moreover, it was said that Iwasaki Yatarō, the head of the Mitsubishi Company, was furnishing funds for us, that he had already given some three hundred thousand *yen*—fitting material for a cheap comedy.

After the resignation of Ōkuma, a general policy for the future was decided upon. Announcement was made for the calling of the national diet in the twenty-third year of Meiji. Many changes were brought about in other departments, notably in that of education. Here the Western systems were modified and the old Confucian teachings reinstated. Thus the department of education began to do some strange things. I am sure that by now, after more than ten years, the officials themselves are regretting this extremity.

It was really a temporary insanity among the men in office. It must have brought up some very difficult problems for the higher chiefs. I remember being called to Iwakura's residence many times, where he would converse with me in the seclusion of his "tea room" in the rear of the dwelling. He showed his anxiety and said that the present disturbance was even more difficult than the insurrection of the tenth year of Meiji.

To me the whole affair seemed farcical. The government had promised the diet to the people and the date was fixed for the twenty-third year of Meiji. That was the equivalent of an invitation to the people to participate in politics after ten years. But then the government proceeded to impose all sorts of harassing restrictions upon the people. Many persons were arrested and kept in prison; many were banished from Tōkyō. Furthermore, the officials were beginning to give themselves high-sounding titles in imitation of the ancient courtiers and feudal lords. Naturally, the common people were growing irritated, causing more troubles. The situation was as if the host and his expected guests were finding something to quarrel over before the party had really begun.

I took down a full account of the conditions, and have kept it among my private papers. But I have felt that I should not publish anything of so intimate a nature, revealing some very disagreeable circumstances of the time. Once I related the whole thing to my very good friend, Terajima, and added, "Suppose now I should go around telling people what I know. Don't you think a good many gentlemen in high offices would be embarrassed?"

Terajima, evidently surprised at this revalation, answered with some mischief, "Well, you are right. I always knew that politicians could show a pretty dark interior when it comes to hatching schemes, but this is too much. I think it might be a good lesson to them if you talk a little."

It was evident he would have enjoyed the results of some disclosures, but I said, "I am now over forty years old, and so are you. Let us remember this and beware of hurting other men."

I have really been looking on, in all this world of politics, erratic and loose as it is, with amusement. But from the other side, in the eyes of government officials, I must appear differently.

THE ORDINANCE OF PUBLIC PEACE AND SECURITY

One year when the Ordinance of Public Peace and Security was issued, it was rumored that I was to be condemned by this new law and banished from Tōkyō. Ono Tomojirō had heard of it from some close friend in the police department. The report was that Gotō Shōjirō was to be banished along with me. I did not take the story very seriously, for I said, "If I am to be banished, why, I shall just move to Kawasaki, or some other nearby town. After all, they are not going to execute me."

In a few days Ono turned up with another report that the idea of my banishment had been rescinded.

A few years later, some time in the twenties of Meiji, a former pupil of mine, Inoue Kakugorō, was involved in some affairs in Korea and was arrested. There followed a turmoil. The police even came to search my house. Then I was called to the court as a witness, and was asked a number of very odd questions. It seemed as if they were not unwilling to condemn me also.

All of these imputations have been the result of misjudgment on the part of the government officers. I have been simply amused in watching the reactions of other people on these occasions.

Yet on thinking it over, I can see that it is only natural that I should be suspected by the men in politics. First of all, I am conspicuous in avoiding office. Moreover, a man who has no political ambition would usually retreat to the country rather than remain in the capital. But there I was in the midst of the city, associating with all men, expressing myself in speech and articles. I must admit further that I have not been altogether without some experience in causing political movements. For instance, here is an episode which only a few know anything about.

A SINGLE EDITORIAL MOVES A WHOLE NATION

Shortly after the insurrection in the tenth year of Meiji, when the whole country had settled down to peace and people were rather suffering from lack of excitement, on a sudden inspiration I thought of writing an argument in favor of the opening of the national diet. Perhaps some would join in my advocacy and might even stir up some interesting movement.

I wrote an article and took it to the editors of the Hōchi—this was before I had my own newspaper. I said to them, "If you can use this piece as an editorial, do so. I am sure the readers will be interested. But, as it stands, it is too obviously my writing. So change some wording to hide my style. It will be fun to see how the public will take it."

The editors were Fujita Mokichi and Minoura Katsundo, both young men. They took my article at once and began a series of special editorials on the very next day. At that time all arguments in favor of the diet were still pretty feeble. We sat back and waited, curious to see the results of our challenge. For about a week, day by day, the subject occupied the editorial columns. And then Fujita and Minoura wrote further to challenge and agitate other papers.

In a little while an open discussion of the subject had developed in the Tōkyō papers. In two or three months it had spread throughout the country. Finally the bolder advocates of the diet were seen traveling to the capital to present petitions in favor of it. Of course it caused me no slight amusement to see what I had started, but at the same time I felt a little perturbed at the extent to which the movement had gone. For I must admit that my writing was chiefly for my own amusement as there was no personal gain I expected from it. And now that my amusement had brought about a national issue, I felt as if I had set fire to a field of grass and the fire was fast getting out of my control.

There had been anticipation of a national diet ever since the Restoration. I really cannot consider myself the originator of the whole movement. But my long article of several thousand words, which I wrote so carefully that any reader might understand, was the immediate forerunner of the widespread discussion; so I think I am right in believing that I set fire to the fuse that ignited the whole.

Not long ago I met Minoura, and as I could not recall the date of that series of editorials, I asked him about it. He remembered about it very well and lent me the old papers from his files. On looking through it, I found that the discussion ran from July 29th to August 10th in the twelfth year of Meiji (1879). It did not strike me as so badly written on this second reading; and I must confess to a certain glow of pride when I realize that this writing has been instrumental in promoting the Japanese National Diet.

Calling to mind these activities of mine, I must admit that it is not altogether unnatural that I should be suspected of having had some hand in various political disturbances. As my activity in behalf of the new representative government and many other innovations is of value to the country, it is all very well. But if it were to prove detrimental, I should, I fear, be liable to punishment in *Emma's* nether court of judgment even if I may escape the scourge of this world.

All in all, my activities with politics have been that of a "diagnostician." I have had no idea of curing the nation's "disease" with my own hands nor have I ever thought of politics in connection with my personal interest. But behind all I have done, there was a wish that this nation of ours might enjoy the benefit of the new civilization so that she might one day be a great nation, strong in the arts of both war and peace.

I have a number of acquaintances in the political field, but being content in doing what I can with my independent power, I never have a thing to request of them or consult with them. My quiet, contented life may look strange to those officials who have a different way of thinking. But I am without any ill feeling toward the present government or the men in it. Indeed, I feel a real obligation to the present government, for my living safely and comfortably at this old age is entirely due to its good administration. I can easily imagine what might have happened to me in the feudal time, had I persisted in living according to my own deas as I am now.

I ESTABLISH A NEWSPAPER

In the fifteenth year of Meiji (1882) I began to publish a newspaper which I called the Jiji-shimpō. It was the year following the political outbreak which had so stirred the country, and many of my senior pupils had urged me to start a paper.

I could see that our society was rapidly changing. The ever-increasing competition was bringing about more and more of bitter rivalry. Recently the government had experienced a very provoking quarrel inside itself. It was logical to expect similar reactions in subsequent economic and industrial rivalry. The greatest need in such a time is an instrument of nonpartisan, unbiased opinion. But it is easy to make satisfying theories about nonpartisan opinion and not so easy to realize it in practice, for the usual man, conscious of his own personal interests, cannot lightly throw off his partisanship As I looked about the country, I decided to myself that there were not many besides myself who were independent in living, and who had worth-while ideas in their heads, and who could yet be really free from political and business interests.

With this reasoning I set myself to the task of establishing a newspaper which became the Jiji-shimpō. After I had determined on this project, I paid no attention to certain friends who appeared to warn me of the difficulty. I decided that it should be entirely my own work, no help coming from outside whether the circulation be large or small. As I originated the paper, so could I destroy it. Even if I were to fail, I should not feel any regret or false shame; nor would my family suffer in the least. Thus forewarned and forearmed, I started publication with no regard for outside criticism. The journal has continued to be successful up to this day.

14

How could Japan maintain its international prestige and "achieve everlasting greatness?" Inoue Kowashi, a major bureaucrat of the Meiji government, was given the task of modernizing Japan's educational system and developing an ethical and educational code that would help create Japanese who would become disciplined servants of a modern state. In the following selection we see how Inoue used the Educational Rescript to help create such a citizenry.

Inoue Kowashi (1843-1895) and the Meiji Educational System

JOSEPH PITTAU

I F the Meiji Constitution fixed the framework of the political system of modern Japan, the Imperial Rescript on Education gave the country its moral foundation and fixed the norms and ideals for the generations to come. Inoue Kowashi took an active part in the formulation of both important documents. However, his role in education was not restricted to the imperial rescript but extended itself to many fields.

Already in 1878 at the request of Itō, Inoue Kowashi had written his *Kyōiku-gi* (Opinion on Education). It was an answer and criticism of *Kyōgaku taishi* (Fundamental Purpose of Education), a document written by Motoda Eifu, which purported to be the emperor's own sentiments and ideas on education. Motoda severely criticized the western-style ethics texts as responsible for the decline of public morals. The Japanese family system and loyalty to the state were being destroyed; students were being taught high-sounding academic theories and empty arguments. Motoda advocated a return to the teaching of the Chinese classics and the Confucian virtues.

Inoue accepted the descriptions of the evil customs of the day, but he stated that the evils in the educational system were more apparent than real. Educational methods stressing scientific and technical education were not invalid; adduced educational abuses were simply a reflection of the rapid changes stemming from the restoration itself. The changes had been too rapid, and the sphere of liberty in speech and action had been greatly increased. The former samurai found their new status not to their

Joseph Pittau, "Inoue Kowashi (1843-1895) and the Meiji Educational System," *Monumenta Nipponica*, Vol. 20 (1965), pp. 270–282. Reprinted with permission of the publisher. Footnotes omitted.

liking and were criticizing the new regime. To this discontent was added the new extreme ideological movement coming from Europe and spreading itself all over the nation.

It was too early to criticize the new system, said Inoue. This system had been established for the welfare of the country, and it would be a tragedy if it were changed without trial and were replaced by the old educational system. Inoue warned that if radical methods were used to try to extirpate these fleeting ills, the country might easily fall into the errors that had plagued Tokugawa Japan. Political moralizing and speeches were certainly not the need of the day.

Inoue did not deny the value of Confucianism in education, but he was also concerned with new technical knowledge and new educational methods. The western methods were to be adopted or condemned not out of prejudice, but according to the criterion of national utility. Inoue's Confucianism was closely tied to Yokoi's real and practical learning. While Inoue was one mind with Motoda in upholding Confucianism, he was also very close to Mori Arinori who advocated strong nationalistic principles of a predominantly utilitarian trend. From the manuscripts preserved in Goin Bunko of Kokugakuin University, it is clear that Inoue prepared drafts for the educational ordinances and reforms promulgated by Mori Arinori, then the Minister of Education.

The fundamental principle of the new ordinances and reforms was this, that education should serve purposes of state. What was done in the administration of all schools was not for the sake of pupils but for the sake of the country. The regulations creating the new university opened with an article stating that the purpose of the university was to teach the arts and sciences essential to the state, and the educational system was conceived throughout not in a spirit of free inquiry but in conformity with nationalistic ideals. Mori's educational reforms expanded the Meiji educational system and succeeded in taking firm root. But on the other hand, they were also responsible for an ultranationalistic tendency in education. In a speech delivered by Mori Arinori we find the nationalistic tendency at the base of Meiji education.

"If we want to maintain the prestige of Japan among the powers and achieve everlasting greatness, we must cultivate and develop our national spirit and morale. This is possible only through education. Now, in the wake of civilization, our daily life is improving in many ways. But is the spirit of our people well trained, so that it can stand hardships and carry out the heavy responsibility in the future? Has the progress of these twenty years taken true and firm roots in the people's mind so as to stabilize the foundation of the country? Besides, since the feudal period, the *shizoku* (ex-samurai) have monopolized the civil and military affairs, taking all responsibility themselves in an emergency. But at present, it is only a small portion of the population that supports and promotes the campaign for enlightenment and progress, while the majority stand in a daze without being able to understand the significance of the founding of the country. . . . The spirit of defense of the motherland by the people and the custom of loyalty, courage and obedience, which have been cultivated and handed down by our ancestors, still exist among us. This is a priceless capital and the most precious treasure for enriching and strengthening the country. . . .

"If people learn and take into their heart loyalty and patriotism, have stability and purity of character, are ashamed of cowardice and have hatred toward insult, they will be able to withstand any hardships, cooperate with others and launch an enterprise, make efforts to learn without being urged and promote civilization in this spirit and energy. It is this spirit that cultivates wealth in industry. It remove all of the obstacles and promotes the fast development of the nation's power. When the elders teach this spirit to the young, parents impart it to children, people inherit it, families assimilate it, then the spirit of the nation is stabilized forever, and she will firmly establish herself as a strong power."

According to Mori Arinori the most important point of education lay neither in mastering piecemeal the crust of western civilization, nor in regulating the educational system and provisions, but in pointing the direction toward which the whole nation should march. This was the goal of education. This reform was executed on the assumption that education at that time lacked this most important point. Inoue agreed completely with Mori Arinori's educational aims. He closely worked with Mori for the establishment of the system of previous inspection of textbooks, determining in this way the official line of thought and morality for the whole nation. After Mori's assassination, Inoue described Mori's principles which were also his own:

"The fundamental principle of Mori's educational policy was education based on the *kokutai*. Education does not mean merely to collect and explain the materials of textbooks. The most important thing in education is to build up the character and give orientation to the students by showing them the spiritual way. This is an extremely difficult task. The education which was practiced 2,000 years ago in the reign of Shun cannot be used today. In Europe there is a religion which serves to confirm the spirit of the young. There is no such creed in our country. I think that it is very difficult to achieve a sense of unity among the people through education. Fortunately in our country we have one beautiful treasure which is incomparable with that of any other country. This is the *kokutai* based on the imperial line unbroken for ages eternal. Nothing but the *kokutai* can be the keynote of education. No other country has a history like ours: our people have been loyal to the emperors of an unbroken line from the beginning of the country and they will be loyal to all future emperors as long as the national land continues to exist. Therefore we should make the *kokutai* the first principle of our education. Nothing else can be the basis of our educational system, and this was the first principle of the late Mori."

As in the constitution the cornerstone had to be the *kokutai* because Japan did not have a religion which could unite the hearts and minds of the people, so also in education Inoue was convinced that the only principle to give unity and orientation to the pupils was to be found in the *kokutai*. Loyalty to the emperor as the living symbol of the *kokutai* was supposed to be instilled into the minds of the children as the first value. The main purpose of education was to foment the spirit of nationalism. Thus the state became the only absolute in education as well as in politics.

It was precisely on this point that Inoue and Yamagata both made their stand when the time came for the formulation of the *Kyōiku chokugo* (Imperial Rescript on Education.) Yamagata Aritomo was Prime Minister when the First Diet convened in 1890. In a famous speech about the need for military preparedness, Yamagata used the two concepts of "sphere of soverignty" and "sphere of national interest," saying that though the sphere of sovereignty was restricted to Japan proper, the sphere of national interest extended itself also to Korea and other Asian territories. This famous speech had been drafted by Inoue Kowashi as can be proved by the existing manuscripts. The title of this draft is "Plan to Defend the Sphere of National Interest." In it Inoue writes:

"There are two indispensable elements in the field of foreign policy: the armed forces first and education second. If the Japanese people are not imbued with patriotic spirit, the nation cannot be strong, no matter how many laws are issued. . . . Patriotism can be instilled only through education. Every powerful nation in Europe strives to foster through compulsory education a deep sense of patriotism together with the knowledge of the national language, history, and other subjects. Patriotism becomes a second nature. Because of such an education the minds of the people become one in the defense of the national interest even if they have different opinions in other matters. Therefore I think it is of vital importance to improve the patriotic spirit among the Japanese people, because the very survival of the nation depends on it. The two things mentioned above are indispensable to make a nation fully independent.

"I feel it is unfortunate that Japan should be isolated by the sea, because there is the danger that the people might feel overconfident caring only about territorial sovereignty without thinking of the sphere of national interest. If people make patient efforts to protect the line of national interest and make Japan a fully independent nation, in about twenty years our policy will reach splendid successes."

Inoue wrote this draft when he was already aware of possible military confrontations between Japan and other Far Eastern countries, especially Korea. He supported a positive diplomacy backed by a strong military force, and at the same time he considered education an indispensable condition for Japan's full independence.

In May 1890 Yoshikawa Akimasa (1841–1920) became Minister of Education. Immediately after his appointment, Yoshikawa was told by the emperor to stress moral training as the fundamental policy and to edit proverbs suitable as a basis of moral education. The drafting process of the rescript on education started almost immediately. The people directly involved in this process were Yamagata Aritomo, Prime Minister, Yoshikawa Akimasa, Minister of Education, Nakamura Masanao, Professor at the Imperial University in Tokyo and advisor at the Ministry of Education, Motoda Eifu, advisor to the emperor, and Inoue Kowashi, then director of the Legislation Bureau.

The first draft was prepared by Nakamura Masanao and was submitted to Yamagata by Yoshikawa in June 1890. Nakamura's thought was essentially based on Confucianism, but there were also strong western elements derived from Christianity and the English utilitarians. In a letter to Yamagata dated June 20, 1890, Inoue strongly criticized Nakamura's draft inasmuch as it was based on philosophical and theological principles. According to Inoue, philosophical and theological reasoning should be avoided, because this kind of thing was not subject to the ruler's decree and somehow aroused violent reactions among the people. Inoue attacked especially the statement by Nakamura that loyalty and filial piety derived from a religious attitude of respect to the teachings of the Lord of Heaven. Inoue, however, later used a few points from Nakamura's document when making his own draft.

Motoda prepared three different private drafts, in which a very narrow exposition of traditional Confucianism accompanied the explanation of *kokutai*. The five relations (ruler-subject, parent-child, elder brother-younger brother, husband-wife, friend-friend) and the three virtues (wisdom, benevolence, courage) are made the base of all education. While Motoda was preparing his drafts, Inoue was asked by Yamagata to prepare an official draft for the imperial rescript. On June 20, 1890, Inoue submitted his plan to Yamagata. On June 28, Inoue visited Motoda and asked his opinion on the draft. After this visit he revised his draft and resubmitted it to Yamagata on July 23. This draft was examined and somewhat revised in the cabinet and in the Ministry of Education and later it became the text of the Imperial Rescript on Education. From this summary exposition of the vicissitudes of the drafting process of the rescript it is clear that Inoue played an important role, and probably the most important, in determining the educational and moral policies of the Japanese school system up to 1945.

In the preparation of the rescript we find the manifold trends of thought which influenced the emergence of modern Japan. Assembled in an attempt to achieve a synthesis these trends were mainly three: that represented by Yamagata who wanted to base the national unity and progress mainly on military strength. The second was represented by Motoda who wanted to go back to traditional Confucianism and identify ethics and politics. And finally the trend urged by Inoue, who though accepting both

Yamagata's principle of military strength and Motoda's respect for Confucian principles, was convinced that Japan would prosper only through modern constitutionalism.

Inoue was opposed to Motoda's idea of making Confusianism both the moral basis of education and the state religion in the sense that it would be the unique aim of political life. According to Motoda, Confucian morality was above politics: politics and politicians should be judged according to Confucian ethics. Moreover, Motoda wanted to uphold a feudalistic Confucianism with anticapitalistic and antiutilitarian tendencies, which were in clear opposition to the new trends of modernization and industrialization in Meiji Japan. Inoue accepted Confucianism without, however, rejecting modernization.

During the political crisis of 1881 Inoue had written that after the Meiji Restoration a revolutionary atmosphere had been brought about by English and French literature. Inoue suggested that the only possible way to redirect such a trend was to promote the study of the Chinese classics in which loyalty and the traditional virtues were taught.

This common attitude toward Confucianism made it possible for Motoda and Inoue to collaborate in the preparation of the Imperial Rescript on Education. Motoda's traditional Confucianism and Yamagata's militaristic nationalism were blended together with Inoue's constitutionalism and other modern elements. Therefore, the character of the imperial rescript can be defined as the sum of Yamagata-Inoue militaristic nationalism (education and military power are the elements of national strength), Motoda-Inoue Confucianism (the traditional virtues are the center of instruction), and Inoue's modern elements of constitutional government, of utilitarianism and practical learning to improve society.

Inoue accepted the ideas of both Yamagata and Motoda, but in order to give the rescript as much universality as possible he opposed both Yamagata and Motoda on a few points. He objected to Yamagata's plan to have the rescript published as a political ordinance of the government; he said group politics ought not interfere with the content and promulgation of the rescript. Inoue stated that the rescript should be always considered as a document above politics making it the universal principle of morality in the nation. He also mitigated Motoda's literal and narrow approach to Confucianism by the insertion of new principles.

Against Motoda's attempt to remove the phrase "respect the constitution and observe the laws," as an undesirable element weakening allegiance to the person of the emperor, Inoue insisted that the constitutional principle had to be inculcated in the hearts of the young students. In the end the words "respect the constitution" were left in the rescript through the direct intervention of the emperor. The final result of the imperial rescript was the inculcation of the three principles represented by Yamagata, Motoda, and Inoue. Inoue's main contribution was in bringing into the rescript the constitutional principle which was certainly not thoroughly understood either by Yamagata or Motoda. Inoue was able to collaborate with both Yamagata and Motoda because he had something in common with both of them: the idea of a militaristic and Confucian nationalism. Thus the three ideas: militaristic, Confucanism, and constitutionalism can be found in the imperial rescript.

"Our Imperial Ancestors have founded Our Empire on a basis broad and everlasting, and have deeply and firmly implanted virtue. Our subjects ever united in loyalty and filial piety have from generation to generation illustrated the beauty thereof. This is the glory of the fundamental character of Our Empire, and herein also lies the source of Our education. Ye, our subjects, be filial to your parents, affectionate to your brothers and sisters; as husbands and wives be harmonious, as friends true; bear yourself in modesty and moderation; extend your benevolence to all; pursue earning and cultivate arts, and thereby intellectual faculties and perfect moral powers; furthermore, advance public good and promote common interests; always respect the Constitution and observe the laws; should emergency arise, offer yourselves courageously to the State; and thus guard and maintain the prosperity of Our Imperial Throne coeval with heaven and earth. So shall ye not only be Our good and faithful subjects, but render illustrious the best traditions of your forefathers. . . ."

The traditional Confucian virtues of loyalty and filial piety are clearly stated, so also the respect for the constitution and the military service in a courageous dedication to the state. The moral code of the "Admonition to Soldiers" became in a certain way also the code of civil society. The draft for the Admonition to Soldiers had been prepared by Nishi Amane at the request of Yamagata. Inoue, too, had participated in the writing of this important document. The admonition enjoined soldiers to be guided by the ideals of loyalty, bravery and obedience and warned against criticizing regulations or any government policy, insulting the emperor or even expressing private opinions on important laws. If the admonition defined the ideals of the modern soldier, the rescript on education defined the ideals of both civil and military society. In this way the dualism between civil and military society which appeared in Nishi's thought was destroyed by the unty of the rescript on education.

INOUE KOWASHI AS MINISTER OF EDUCATION

In 1893, Inoue was appointed Minister of Education in the second Itō Cabinet. He was Minister for only one year and five months but his influence on the educational system of Japan was greater than the short term of his service would suggest. His influence reached all fields, and his drafts of laws, speeches, memos, and other papers of the period when he was in office show his deep knowledge and thoroughness in approaching educational problems. These documents are now preserved in the Goin Bunko of Kokugakuin University in Tokyo.

Inoue was all in favor of Confucian moral education. In this he was at one with Motoda Eifu, but this aspect was only one side of his educational program. Besides this, he was in favor of an education that would help the development of industry and the modernization of Japan. His Confucianism was intimately connected with practical learning. Inoue's fundamental contributions in educational matters can be summed up in two principles: offer equal educational opportunities to all and foment technical industrial education.

The reforms he induced into the primary school system, in the middle schools and girls' schools stem from the first principle. From this standpoint, too, he was strongly opposed to an over-centralization of educational facilities in Tokyo, a phenomenon emerging already in Meiji Japan. He wanted the diffusion not only of primary schools but also of high schools and universities all over the country. In order to give all children the opportunity to attend school Inoue strongly backed the plan for establishing an "Elementary Education Fund" out of the government budget. However, because of his conviction that education was merely one of several ways to enrich and strengthen the country, he felt that this establishment of the fund had to be balanced with other expenditures, especially in view of military needs for the Sino-Japanese war of 1894–95.

Diffusion of education was not enough for Inoue; he also insisted on the contents of education. He wanted *practical* learning. Education was intended not as an end in itself, but as a means toward the ultimate value of the state. The educational system was supposed to prepare the future soldiers and the future leaders of business and industry in Japan. From this conviction arose his eagerness to make people aware of technical and industrial subjects. He was also responsible for the establishment of the Institute for Technical School Teachers.

Inoue saw a changing world in which technology and industrialization were going to play the leading role in the shaping of political affairs. In this he was probably one of the most influential leaders in the building of the new Japan. To Inoue is due a large share of the credit for constructing the base which enabled the newly emerging nation to achieve such phenomenal progress in industry, technology and science.

During his short term as Minister of Education Inoue issued a series of orders concerning industrial, technical and agricultural education. While modern industry was rapidly developing, Inoue thought that the four years of compulsory education were not sufficient for the new needs. What Inoue planned was a system of education adequate to the daily needs of young workers and to the needs of modern industry. He defined the aims and curricula of the already existing industrial and technical schools and apprentices' schools which had nothing technical or vocational about them except their name. The regulations issued on November 20, 1893, for industrial continuation schools and related instructions of November 22 were decided by Inoue as well as the regulations for apprentices' schools (July 1894), the enactment of the Government Subsidy Act for Industrial Education (1894) and many other directives. Vocational training and knowledge which lead to improved methods of production and help the modernization of the country were to be at the center of the technical and industrial education. In a revealing passage Inoue wrote:

"The national strength and wealth of all countries in the world are growing larger year after year. This is simply because, in these countries, scientific study is encouraged, new inventions are applied to practical purposes and the production is greatly increased by their insistent effort in improving technical schools. Japan has not become fuly civilized yet and scientific knowledge and the ability of the nation has not improved. Education and labor have no influence upon each other. . . . Under these circumstances, it is earnestly desired that for national prosperity we should establish the scientific and technical education which is most necessary for the industrial development of Japan."

Inoue considered education the foundation of independence and prosperity; hence it was incumbent on teachers to develop the spirit of patriotism among the students. Vocational training and guidance were considered all important. For this Inoue wanted specialization in courses and curricula. Teachers must be skilled and equipped to meet the demands of various regions and situations.

Inoue makes mention of Okinawa: teachers going there should know about the cultivation and production methods of the sugar industry. Teachers working in other regions should study the best ways to improve the peculiar products of their special area. Inoue insisted also on physical education and the last ordinance he signed before resigning might be called "the ordinance about physical fitness."

Never in good health himself, Inoue had to resign his post as the Minister of Education because of sickness on August 29, 1894. He then retired to his villa in Hayama but he never recovered.

The title of Viscount was conferred on Inoue in January of 1895. He died on March 15, 1895.

INOUE KOWASHI'S THOUGHT

So far we have examined Inoue's contributions in the framing of the Meiji Constitution and the organization of the Meiji educational system. Now we want to attempt a general description of Inoue's ideological principles. It is hard, though, to find a system in Inoue's thought. His published books and writings are very few. Many of his manuscripts are political, legal or educational opinions prepared as answers to particular questions from Iwakura or Itō or Mori; these answers emerged from concrete, well defined situations. Although these documents may not express the whole range of his thought, yet they give us an outline.

A very important document is the letter he wrote to Ikebe Yoshitaka on September 28, 1886, entitled *Fukyō wo sonsu* (To Preserve Confucianism). This letter is extremely important because it was written when Inoue was already working on the drafting of the constitution. It has been often stated that Inoue's thought was in opposition to that of Motoda Eifu and that the principle stressed in the Meiji Constitution were very different from the principles of the *Kyōiku chokugo*. An analysis of the *Fukyō wo sonsu* will help us to decide whether these oppositions were as deep as some authors have described or whether they were minor differences which did not destroy the fundamental identity.

From *Fukyō wo sonsu*, it is evident that Confucianism was an essential element of Inoue's thought. This long letter starts with a general description of the origin of both the western and eastern civilizations. In the West, Egyptian culture constituted the basis of Judaism and Christianity. In China the moral ideas of Yao and Shun were transmitted from generation to generation through the teachings of Confucius and Mencius. While the doctrines of Judaism and Christianity were artificial and based on supernatural notions and myths, the moral ideas of the East were based on nature and on common sense.

Inoue found the reasons for the decline of Chinese power not in Confucianism itself but in the ritualistic and formalistic approach to the Confucian doctrines of the Chinese scholars. The Chinese had adhered to the letter without grasping the spirit of Confucianism. The West on the other hand had tried with great success to develop mechanical civilization, raise the standard of living and increase the wealth of their countries. At first, the reason for this contrast between China's decline and the West's progress might appear to be in that the West had accepted Christianity whereas China was non-Christian. But on deeper analysis of the Bible and the life of Christ, Inoue said, one comes to realize that Christianity was not the source of the West's progress. Christianity, on the contrary, was very inimical to the well-being of the political community, especially because Christian dogma believed in one God above all human authority, a God who gives reward and punishment after this world. Thus Christians were inclined to obey divine laws and respect the judgment of the next world rather than obey the human laws and respect the judgment of the political authorities. Christians considered the propagation of their doctrine an obligation, and death for their faith was esteemed as the supreme act of loyalty and a great honor. Christianity had been the cause of many a revolt against the political authorities and the origin of many a war and many a tyranny.

Religion which proclaimed itself as based on a revelation from God had in most cases led only to bloodshed and aggression. Confucius and Mencius, on the contrary, based their doctrines not on some theological principle or divination but on moral principles common to the whole world. In Confucianism there was neither dualism which separated politics from religion nor a clergy which imposed its authority in opposition to the political powers. Confucianism was the best ethical system because it did not base its teachings on revelation but on nature. Thus Japan ought to adopt from the West the ideas of civil law, the techniques of agriculture and industry, but in ethical problems it should follow the Chinese teachings and the Chinese classics.

Inoue's strong objection against Christianity was mainly due to the Christian dualism in the principle of loyalty: a Christian, he understood, is supposed to be loyal first and foremost to God and the Church; only a secondary obedience is due to political rulers and leaders as the recipients of limited powers from God. Moreover Inoue thought that Christianity dealt only with the relation between the individual and God; it did not care, according to his interpretation, about the social relations among men. These ideas expressed by Inoue were close to those upheld by Motoda Eifu.

The difference between the two was in this, that Motoda advocated the idea of the unity of religion and politics; thus he wanted the emperor to be both the political ruler and the high priest of the Japanese nation. Motoda's political and religious system was essentially *Ōdōron* (imperial way), involving the direct participation of the emperor in the determination of moral ideals and political decisions. The emperor and the court advisers were supposed to join the cabinet in the decision-making process in order to carry out the realization of a system of moral politics. Inoue, on the contrary, accepted constitutionalism as the first principle of a modern form of government; he wanted a clear separation of the fields of thought and politics. Government could not be involved in the determination of moral principles deriving from a religious point of view. There was also another fundamental difference between the Confucianism of Motoda and that of Inoue. For Motoda the Confucian principles were eternal, not susceptible to change, and the Chinese classics were the only source of moral education and political behavior.

Inoue's Confucianism, however, was never so narrow. If Confucianism was the "teacher," the Japanese classics and the *kokutai* were the "father." Motoda thought that Confucianism represented a universal morality with unique absoluteness and that the Japanese political and social system had to be adapted to such a universal norm. Inoue considered the Japanese *kokutai* as unique and absolute, and Confucianism was just a means to maintain the *kokutai* in its purity. The *kokutai* was for Inoue the only absolute: Confucianism and western civilization—legal system, technology and general culture—were the supporting elements of the wealth and power of the Japanese nation. Practical learning, in Inoue's scheme, was combined with the study of the Japanese language and literature and the Chinese classics. Motoda, in a word, was a moral scholar; Inoue was mainly concerned with problems of political power. Motoda was more of a Chinese Confucianist, whereas Inoue was primarily an advocate of the principle of *kokutai*.

Thus although Confucianism was a very important element of Inoue's ideological system, it cannot be considered the main characteristic of his thought. Foremost in his system was the principle of the *kokutai*. This principle gave unity to his whole career, especially to his work in the framing of the Meiji Constitution and in the drafting of the Imperial Rescript on Education. Both the preamble to the constitution and the rescript began with the fundamental statement of the uniqueness of the Japanese nation based on the imperial line unbroken for ages eternal. The same principle was stated also in the rescript promising the establishment of the diet in 1881 and in the imperial oath at the proclamation of the Meiji Constitution. The notion of the *kokutai* applied to political thought, implied the absolute sovereignty of the emperor. The emperor became the only repository of sovereign power, and this power apparently came from the divine ancestors.

One might ask the question why Inoue accepted such mythological notions. The answer is probably found in an important speech by Itō Hirobumi on June 18, 1888, at the first meeting of the Privy Council before starting the discussions on the draft constitution. On this occasion Itō spoke about the principles that had guided the framers of the constitution. Itō said that every system of government, especially a constitutional form of government, required the rationalization of a set of fundamental beliefs of religious or quasi-religious character into a political way of life. According to Itō and also according to Inoue, in Japan there was no religion nor tradition of responsible participation of the people in the affairs of state. Only the Imperial House and the ideology of the *kokutai* could become the foundation of the new constitutional system.

The third principle of Inoue's system was transcendentalism, that is, the conviction that the cabinet should be above political parties and free from the interference of the diet in executive matters. This principle was stated openly in the documents Inoue wrote during the political crisis of 1881. In these documents Inoue strongly attacked the English form of constitutional government. Also, because he was under the influence of Roesler, Inoue defended the principle of monarchic constitutionalism with strong conservative implications. The administration had to be above all political division and struggle. The cabinet could not be a party cabinet, because by definition a party cabinet would represent only the interests of one part of the state.

Behind this theory of political transcendentalism was the Hegelian ideology of the role of the state. This ideology had influenced Lorenz von Stein and through Stein had been accepted by Roesler and Inoue. Society was essentially class society, and class struggle was the true content of society. The general and inalterable condition of society was the struggle between a dominant and a dependent class. The social order was necessarily a class order; its prime feature was self-seeking, that is, the general inclination of each to acquire the means for his own independence and the means for making others dependent. In contrast to the principle of society, the principle of the state was the development, progress, wealth, power and intelligence of all the individuals without distinction, positing all individuals as free and equal. The state preserved the common interest, impartiality, and freedom from the conflicting private interests of society. Only the state could give a superior spiritual and moral sense.

Inoue's opposition to the party-cabinet principle was based on this ideology. He asked Roesler what the basis of a true form of constitutional government had to be. Roesler turned in a long and detailed description of his sociopolitical system. Roesler saw that the development of society would lead necessarily to a democratic form of government. He predicted that the bourgeoisie would become the dominant class in Japan. It should be checked lest it undermine the security of other classes: both the landowners and the proletariat. Roesler said that the state's most urgent task was a harmonious social balance through social legislation and an active administrative policy that worked for the physical and cultural welfare of the lower classes. To overcome class conflict and to maintain an ethical political attitude that placed the welfare of the whole above class interest, the institution of hereditary monarchy was necessary. This monarchy, possessing the loyal allegiance of the people, would care for the common welfare and would become the custodian of the weak. Inoue applied this theory to the Imperial House and to the cabinet. The cabinet as the executive branch of government had to be independent in carrying out the policy of the common welfare.

The last but not the least element of Inoue's thought was adaptation to modern trends. This adaptation started from his formative days in Kumamoto: *jitsugaku* or practical learning meant matters of taxation, judicial administration, irrigation, land reclamation, welfare policy and so on. Adaptation led Inoue to study modern languages and the legal and political system of other countries. He was not a narrow minded *laudator temporis acti*. If the *kokutai* remained his fundamental principle, and Confucianism gave him the mental attitude to solve moral political problems, he also saw that many techniques and principles had to be adopted from western countries. Constitutionalism was among these modern elements. Inoue again and again stressed the point that the constitution had to be a *modern* one, according to the principles of western tradition. This was of essential importance. The aim of a modern constitution was to limit the powers of the monarch and to defend the rights of the citizens. This modern element appears also in Inoue's insistence on technical instruction in his educational policies.

. . .

Inoue Kowashi in his ambivalent attitudes and principles represents the ambiguous commitments and solutions of the early Meiji period. The leaders of Meiji Japan firmly believed that they had achieved a synthesis between traditional Japanese elements and modern western aspects. They thought that *kokutai,* transcendentalism, constitutionalism, freedom of thought, Confucianism, scientific spirit and traditional ethics could be mingled into one system always preserving the equilibrium among these conflicting aspects. History proved them wrong; but the historical result does not alter the fact that theirs was a serious attempt to achieve for Japan a suitable compromise between the modern and traditional aspects, between continuity and change.

15

Much as American historians of the New Left have sought a radical American tradition, post-world War II Japanese historians have searched for an indigenous democratic past. Daikichi Irokawa is one of the most original and persuasive of these writers. In the following essay he argues that many of the Meiji period popular rights activists in eastern Japan came from among the sons of gōnō (wealthy peasant elite). Gōnō fathers, Irokawa further argues, had been well tutored in the classics and they became bold assimilators of the new Western learning. In local areas, among the peasantry and their traditional village leaders, can be found a major source for the incitement and development of the Meiji Popular Rights Movement.

Freedom and the Concept of People's Rights

DAIKICHI IROKAWA

"THE Meiji era was a splendid age which is a worthy object of our nostalgia. It was thanks to the energies latent in the Japanese people, cultivated during and since the Meiji era, that Japan could make such an astonishing recovery after World War II. This period, during which Japan absorbed the civilization of the advanced countries of the world and rapidly carried through the process of modernization, was an age in which the leaders and indeed the whole nation were filled with progressive spirit. It was also an age in which Western civilization and traditional Japanese society came into contact with each other, and the alien civilization gave rise to severe stresses. However, during this process of modernization, instead of being entirely Westernized, Japan's traditional ways of thinking and faith were carried through from first to last. Let us search out the significance of this age, let us sing its praises!"

Such is the call which is being made at the present time by the government and the press in Japan.

In the face of all this high-pitched publicity, Japanese historical scientists have on the whole been calm and even cautious. Nevertheless,

Daikichi Irokawa, "Freedom and the Concept of People's Rights," *Japan Quarterly*, Vol. XIV, No. 2 (April–June 1967), pp. 175–183. Reprinted by permission of the author. Footnotes omitted.

in the present year, exactly one hundred years after the Meiji Restoration, the historians have seemed to be interested in drawing up a balance-sheet for the past century of their country's history. For this purpose a variety of balance-sheets—such as those dealing with problems between race and race, and between state and people—are being prepared.

My task in the present article is that of making clear how much was achieved on the side of "politics" in this history of modern Japan. The political history of Japan in these one hundred years comprises four periods, the politics of which differ completely in nature. The first period extended from the Meiji Restoration to the opening of the Diet (1868–90); the second from the opening of the Diet to the collapse of the Taishō democracy movement (1890–1930); the third comprised the subsequent fascist period of the Shōwa era (1930–45); and the fourth the period following the defeat in the Pacific War. Consequently we cannot give an account of the political history of these times under the simple heading of "The Hundred Years Since the Restoration." I have, therefore, confined the subject of this article to a discussion of under what conditions, and by what efforts on the part of the people, the modernization of Japan was formed, particularly in the political field. In particular, I wish to place the main emphasis in my account on the first period, the process leading up to the opening of the Diet.

One of the questions is whether modernization of Japan in the field of politics was carried out as a mere imitation of the West or not. In other words, the question concerns just what reactions were exhibited by Japanese traditional society and what changes of aspect became apparent in the long-established traditional ways of thinking. It is here that we may be able to find the intrinsic conditions which contributed to the modernization of Japan in the political sphere.

The Meiji Restoration, which in 1868 overthrew the Tokugawa Shogunate, the longest-reigning power in feudal Japan, was not a modern democratic revolution analogous to the French Revolution, but was an epoch-making change which transformed a feudal state into an absolutist, centralized and unified state. On this point the opinions of a large number of scholars are in agreement. Because of this fact, the Meiji Restoration is considered as the first step toward the modernization of Japan. But inasmuch as democratic participation in politics by the people was not achieved by the Restoration, just such participation was strongly demanded and was fiercely gained in the course of the Freedom and People's Rights movement which arose about ten years later.

This Freedom and People's Rights movement, which involved millions of the Japanese people, was develolped between 1874 and 1887. It was entirely because of the occurrence of this struggle against the Meiji government that Japan was able somehow to become a country possessing a national Diet, and to set out on the road leading to a modern constitutional state. The fact that it was possible for a great democratic movement to arise about the time of World War I, and for a sudden democratization movement to arise after the Second World War, was also due to the continued vitality of this tradition.

The movement which possessed so great a significance began as an anti-government movement by a very small number of intellectuals of samurai origin, and it earned the name of "the ex-Military Class Freedom and People's Rights Movement." But when Saigō Takamori, the greatest representative and hero of the military class, was induced by some tens of thousands of discontented members of that class to rise in revolt (the Satsuma Rebellion of 1877), and when this revolt was thoroughly suppressed by the Meiji government, the power of the military class declined decisively and the mainstream of the movement gradually shifted into the hands of the members of the upper stratum of the peasantry known as the *"gōnō"* (wealthy farmers). Thereafter, the movement went on to become nationwide, involving peasants and townspeople, with the *gōnō* stratum cooperating with a certain section of the military class intellectuals.

It was after the beginning of this stage that the *Kokkai Kisei Dōmei*, a nationwide organization devoted to the cause of establishing a national assembly, was formed, and in the 1880's the number of signatories to petitions for a national assembly organized by the Kisei Dōmei exceeded 240,000. Political societies were also formed in all parts of the country and those political societies, which were well known, numbered more than 150 at this period. Political meetings and debating or study societies flourished in the agricultural villages in the provinces, and there followed an unprecedented period of enthusiasm for learning among the peasantry. There have been scholars who have described this upsurge from below as a development from "the military-class People's Rights movement" to "the *gōnō* People's Rights movement." We, too, have been able to confirm this rise of the People's Rights movement in our surveys of agricultural villages in eastern Japan. I wish to present a part of this evidence and to make clear how the people themselves struggled for political modernization.

It was after the "equality of all classes of the people" had been declared by the Meiji government and the various reforms got under way that a strong demand for participation in politics arose among the Japanese people. In particular, what may be called the four great reforms carried out by the new government—the replacement of the fiefs by prefectures, the introduction of the educational system, conscription, and the reform of the land tax—awakened the people to politics to a marked degree. Some among them were awakened to the realities of the outside world out of the necessities of their business undertakings. Some sought participation in politics as a result of their ideological studies. Some came to recognize the necessity of a national assembly as a result of their experience in the struggle for people's assemblies or in the struggle in opposition to the reform of the land tax.

Among these reforms the implementation of the new system of education on a national scale from 1872 was of great significance. It is said that in response to this call from the government approximately 20,000 primary schools had been opened by 1877. (Modern Japan's primary schools now number more than 26,000.) This feat could not, of course, be realized merely by a proclamation by the government. According to Professor Shōji Kichinosuke of Fukushima University, in the last years of the Tokugawa Shogunate 521 temple schools were in existence within the area covered by modern Fukushima Prefecture in the northern part of Japan, and that the greater part of them were run by *gōnō* or village headmen (only 6.3 per cent of them by members of the military class). Since it is said that there were 386 scholars of the Japanese classics in Inadani in the Province of Shinano, an area in the center of the Japanese archipelago enclosed by the Japanese Alps, we have reason to believe that there was a considerable spread of education in the last years of the Tokugawa Shogunate. This would have been all the more so in the great cities: the number of temple schools located in Edo is said to have been more than a 1000, and those in Osaka more than 2500.

By "temple schools" is meant irregular, privately established schools for members of the common people, excluding the military class. The appellation came into use because it was common for a part of a temple building to be used as a classroom and for instruction to be given by Buddhist or Shintō priests, but this does not mean that all the private schools were of this kind. In the agricultural villages, cultured village headmen and village officials opened part of their own houses and undertook the instruction of the children of the village.

About a hundred kilometers from Edo there was a hilly rural area called Tama. Among the small villages located in the valleys between these hills there is one called Ogawa-mura. Hosono Kiyoshirō, the eldest son of a *gōnō* who was hereditary headman of Ogawa-mura, was one of the commoners who went to such a temple school to study.

He was born in 1854 and was 15 when the Restoration took place. In those days he devoted himself to the study of Confucian teaching at the village school in his native place and, when he was a little older, went to a nearby town and attended a private school for the Chinese classics. From 1874 on, he assisted his father, then the village headman, and by grappling with the great work of the land tax reform he came into contact with the new policies of the government. It was also about this time that his eyes were opened to new forms of political thought. Among the contents of the family's old storehouse we find a fair number of works translated from foreign languages dealing with political matters. Among the older works are Katō Hiroyuki's *Kokutai Shinron* (*New Theory of the National Policy*) 1874, and Biedelmann's *Kakkoku Rikkenseitai Kiri-tsu-shi* (*History of the Origins of Constitutional Government in the Various Nations*) 1875, and there is also a copy of J. S. Mill's *On Liberty* as well as works by Rousseau, Spencer, Bentham, and others.

In 1877, after the Satsuma Rebellion when the Freedom and People's Rights movement was gradually spreading to all parts of the country, Hosono Kiyoshirō also presented a petition to the government on behalf of Ogawa-mura calling for the opening of a national assembly. At the same time he combined with like-minded peasants in nearby villages to organize a study society called the Takumakai and began an enthusiastic studies of politics. At first they learned from articles by Japanese popular educators such as Fukuzawa Yukichi and Nakamura Masanao, eventually took up Rousseau, Mill, and Spencer and, when these studies had reached a certain level, they invited noted Tokyo journalists of the Freedom and People's Rights-group to visit them and held public political meetings during which they received direct instruction from them.

On the whole these study societies usually comprised between 20 and 30 members, but there were some such as the Hakuaikai in a neighboring village that had more than 100 members. As regards the mode of study, two methods were employed alongside each other. In one method each member in turn undertook the study of some newly published work and presented a report on it before a meeting of the society after which questions were asked. In the second method a topic for debate was fixed for each meeting of the society and members were asked to present reports for and against, after which these were debated by all the members of the society. Once they had attained a certain level we even find the study societies inviting city intellectuals so that they might benefit from their criticism of the society's debates or might listen to the models of public speaking and debate provided by their lecturers.

These study societies met their own expenses with the help of *gōnō* such as Hosono. In practically all cases their meetings were open to the public and they welcomed the participation of the masses at large. Societies which began as book-reading groups, made up of a small number of *gōnō* came to have the appearance of schools of politics for all the adult members of the village, and at length, by declaring for some kind of political belief, they developed in the direction of provincial political societies.

The national movement for the opening of a national assembly which swept over the whole of rural Japan in 1880–81 was backed by village political societies such as these. At this time study societies or political societies with such names as Yūkansha, Ryōsōkan, Yōeisha, Shinyūkai, Hakuaisha, Kōgakukai, Yūbunkai, and Sōaisha were being formed one after another in the villages near Hosono's village, and under their auspices political meetings were frequently held.

More than 260 local meetings by journalists of the People's Rights advocates are recorded as having been held in the Kantō region between January 1881 and June 1882 (according to statistics for the whole of Japan there were 1,817 meetings and 7,675 speakers in the year 1882 alone), and the local political societies which received these speakers may be numbered at approximately 150 over Japan as a whole, to mention only those which are well known. The government resisted these attempts to make a direct approach to the masses and these political meetings by instituting all manner of repressive legal regulations, notably the Regulations Relating to Public Meetings and the Regulations for the Press, and subjected them to fierce pressure, but the movement became more and more fanatical and for a time was of such intensity as to penetrate deeply into the people of the provinces. The *Tōsui Minkenshi* (1900), written by Sekido Kakuzō, who was active in the actual Liberty and Popular Rights movement in Ibaragi Prefecture at this time, describes the flourishing conditions of these political societies as follows.

"In February 1880 the representatives of more then ten societies in Ibaraki Prefecture met together and decided to raise a petition for the opening of a national assembly. They divided among themselves the areas in which each was to address meetings and swore to fight furiously day and night with the aim of winning over the 800,000 and more people living in the 18 counties of the prefecture.

"These 40 or 50 organizers, carrying their lunch boxes and wearing straw sandals, visited not only the headmen and notables in each area and village but every member of the population without exception, they explained Japan's situation at home and abroad and the urgent necessity for opening a national assembly and obtained signatures from all those who were in agreement with them. They applied themselves to soliciting large numbers of people from early morning until late at night, sometimes braving wind and rain and walking along muddy roads, leaving no mountain village or isolated spot unvisited. For approximately three months several thousand members of these societies were traveling about the countryside looking in every conceivable spot for people who would agree with them. Because of this, they obtained the signatures of 11,814 men of the influential stratum in the agricultural villages in the Prefecture and presented a petition."

If this form of organizing work of the Ibaraki type which aimed at penetrating the remotest communities of the people had been repeated in a thoroughgoing manner over the whole country, the Meiji government might well have found that the basis of its existence had been completely undermined. This was because these organizers were not city intellectuals with little connection with the soil, but were in many cases members of respectable families resident in the country for generations, or *gōnō* and able, by making effective use of the discipline of the traditional communities cultivated over many years, to draw the whole population of the villages into the antigovernment movement.

Hosono Kiyoshirō was one of them. He left some notes in diary form on the subject of the development of his political thought, and from it we learn how one who first applied himself to the acquisition of the new knowledge under the strong influence of city intellectuals and others came at length to stand alongside the city intellectuals and even to address audiences. After 1882 he stood on his own feet as a *gōnō* advocate of People's Rights and a peasant public speaker, independently carrying his political work to the people of neighboring villages and other countries in the Prefecture. In sum he performed a very fine transition from an acceptor to a functioner within the ideology of People's Rights.

We may divide the history of the Freedom and People's Rights movement into an early period, before 1881, during which it was a movement petitioning for the opening of a national assembly, and a late period after that date during which it formed political parties and had repeated fierce clashes with the Meiji government. In the course of this development some truly remarkable political growth was evinced by the core of the movement, the *gōnō* stratum of the peasantry. Thus the Freedom and People's Rights movement possessed an important significance as an ideological movement and not only as a political movement demanding changes in the form of the State. If this movement had not occurred it would have been unthinkable that the motive power for the modernization of Japan in the first half of the Meiji era should have come forth from the people with such strength. It would also have been impossible from the nationalist point of view which sought to break through the feudal provincialism of the peasantry and grasp the nature of one's country's fate in world terms, to become a possession of the nation at large.

Yet what is actually meant by the *"gōnō"* in whom I have found the key to Japan's leap forward in the Meiji era? To describe them briefly as "the middle stratum" loses sight of their historical nature. Since *gōnō* was originally a concept of the peasants of the Edo period (the feudal period) this concept would naturally disintegrate if and when capitalism developed, but it has survived because the transition to capitalism in Japan was delayed until as late as 1887–96. Nevertheless we would seem to be obliged to distinguish between the *gōnō*, who owed their existence to the *hombyakushō* system of land tenure of the Edo period, and those of the Meiji era, who lived at a time when the process of transplanting modern large-scale industry from a higher level and the stage of petty bourgeois production were proceeding in parallel.

The *gōnō* of the Meiji era are transitional and precede the disintegration of their social stratum into parasitic landlords or merchant bourgeoisie, and consequently they display some complicated aspects. For example, at the same time as being landlords levying rent they were also cultivating their own farms. (The area of land owned by them was frequently on the order of 10–20 hectares.) They also displayed a mercantile aspect as sideline pawnbrokers or wholesale dealers, as well as the aspect of the small factory owner carrying on business which included processing work involving raw silk, textiles, tea, brewing, etc. In particular, since raw silk and tea were the chief export articles of this period, the acute historical consciousness of this age was felt with especial poignancy by these *gōnō* who were connected with the production and sale of these goods.

These men were also the repository and transmitters of the tradition of popular culture. The traditional natural science which was the business of the group of agricultural improvers called the *rōnō* ("old peasants")— the studies of the Chinese pharmacopoeia, of the calendar, of mathematics, astronomy, and agronomy—formed a rich basis for development as indigenous modern science. The Japanese Inō Tadataka (1745–1818) a world figure in the history of the science of geography, appeared as a *gōnō* who had inherited this tradition of science; Makino Tomitarō (1862–1957), who occupied a similar position in the history of botany, came from the same class and could be described as a child of *honzōgaku* (traditional medical botany); while Funazu Denjibei (1832–98), one of the "Three Great *Rōnō*" of the Meiji era, was able to cultivate his scientific spirit at a private school in the Seki tradition of mathematics located in a nearby village.

Of the early Meiji era in eastern Japan, the majority of the *gōnō* of whom I have found evidence were also cultured in studies of classical Chinese literature, Japanese classics, and Japanese poetry and there were also many who were lovers of *ongyoku* (music), *jōruri* (ballad drama), and the drama. While living in such forms of traditional culture these men were also avid assimilators of new learning during the early Meiji era, and we may see vivid testimony to their vitality in their sending the majority of their children to join the ranks of activists in such positive endeavors as the Freedom and People's Rights movement.

When considering the motive power behind social development in the Meiji era I always direct attention to the connections between three dimensions in such motive power. The energies of the leaders among the ruling stratum of the new regime for one of these three dimensions. However, these energies were not the decisive factor. It was only when the creative powers latent in our Japanese masses succeeded in winning a certain degree of historical liberation in the period of the Restoration and the Freedom and People's Rights movement that these creative powers became possessed of the fundamental conditions required by them. I shall call these powers "basic energies" in contradistinction to the "leading energies." The combining of these two, however, would have proved impossible without the existence of the third motive power or awareness in the two social strata which were the media for these energies. The special characteristics of the Meiji era is to be found in this point.

We may say that as the intermediary social stratum which performed a central role in national unification, the *gōnō* stratum came on to the stage of history in the principal role in the period between the Restoration and the rise of the Freedom and People's Rights movement, displayed an enthusiasm for learning and an awareness that were astonishing, and brought about a sublimation of the basic energies, making them into the motive power for a new leap forward. In addition I should like to think that they possessed the secret of infinite vitality in that they carried out the internal interconnection and structuring of the powers latent in these several dimensions, and made them into a dynamo powering social development.

Even so, in what way did this *gōnō* stratum receive its modern political theory? May we, as Western readers will expect, interpret the situation as meaning that the constitutionalism of the advanced countries of Europe and America had flowed into one of the backward countries of Asia like water finding its own level, and had provoked the Restoration and the Freedom and People's Rights movement? What manner of reactions had been exhibited by Asian society, with its long traditions, before the influx of Euro-American ideology? The reader will no doubt be interested in these matters. But in the case of Japan there were no violent reactions on the part of traditional society as occurred in Ch'ing dynasty China. What was characteristic is to be found in the fact that moves in this direction (such as the movement for expelling foreigners) were suppressed and the formula of "adopting what is advantageous and supplementing what is deficient" under the principle of a dichotomy between "Japanese spirit and Western art" was adopted. Conversely, the fact that Japan was able to adopt a sovereign attitude in her acceptance of the advanced culture of Europe and America may be considered to have been due to the strength deriving from spiritual accumulation which had taken place within the Japanese consciousness since the beginning of the Edo period.

Let us consider the occasions for intellectual awakening in regard to modern political thought in the inner life of Hosono Kiyoshirō, the typical *gōnō* village activist. We have already noted how Hosono had acquired an education in Confucian learning in the first years of the Meiji era and at length, after carrying into effect such new policies as the reform of the land tax, made his approach to the political ideology of Europe and America. Analyzing the original text of Hosono's first political speech in 1882, the contents of his speech entitled "The Origins of Inequality" in the following year, and the Chinese poems and prose which he wrote at that time, we find that his ideal image of politics was still that of the ancient Chinese figures Yao and Shun (the embodiments of sagacity) and it is clear that it was still non-Western European in character.

Expressing ourselves somewhat boldly, we may say that in Hosono at the height of the Freedom and People's Rights ideology the theory of revolution of "primitive Confucianism" and the Sung rationalism of "nature' 'and "the ideal forms of moral obligation" are reproduced, and are restored, transformed, in such manners as to meet the requirements of political change in the new age. In speaking here of "primitive Confucianism" we have taken the expression "primitive Christianity" as our model. The reforming vitality of the old Confucianism born out of the troubled times of the Ch'un Ch'iu and Chan Kuo periods in ancient China had been brought to life again in the midst of the violent social changes of the Meiji Restoration, and had been assimilated by Hosono and his like. The *gōnō* advocates of Freedom and People's Rights took the ideal of primitive Confucianism to consist in the ideology of the love of Emperors Yao and Shun for the people—the ideology of "dynastic change" which stated that incompetent emperors should abdicate or be replaced, and that the absolutism of the sovereign was not the natural "will of heaven," and also the utopian vision of the simple society in which people live in happy contentment, as "the will of Heaven." The *gōnō* then, by joining this ideology with the revolutionary ideology of Europe and America (the modern doctrine of natural rights) and the doctrine of joint rule by sovereign and people, formed the ideology of Freedom and People's Rights. Thus we may say that the Way of the Sages of Yao and Shun was conceived, with certain limitations, as something which transcended the authority of the Emperor of Japan, and that it was even posited as the norm in matters of morality and the ideal basal axis for a democratic system.

Examples of traditions of ideology among the *gōnō* and the peasantry which, although dating from the Edo period and surviving in the ideology of the Freedom and People's Rights movement, are considered as a modern form of political thought and are by no means confined to the case of the Confucian tradition. Mori Tahei, *gōnō* advocate of Freedom and People's Rights from Inadani in Nagona Prefecture, was produced by the nationalist school of scholarship and advocated the policy of "revering the Emperor and overthrowing the Shogunate," and at length, after directing the great struggle against the reform of the land tax, was suddenly awakened to the ideology of Freedom and People's Rights. Again there is no small number of examples of the revolutionary idea *yonaoshi* (reformation) which appeared in peasant revolts, etc., in the last years of the Shogunate having made its way into the ideology of the Freedom and People's Rights movement. Sunaga Renzō, the leader of Komminto in

Kanagawa Prefecture, was originally an undistinguished *gōnō* living in
Yanomura in South Tama County, the county in which Hosono lived,
but at the request of the people of his village he took his place at the
head of the peasant struggle. In a document written by this Sunaga shortly
before he was arrested, we find words to the effect that although something
might be the law of the land, if it threatened the survival of the people
it meant that the law itself was devoid of validity. We have reason for
supposing that this idea of *yonaoshi,* combined with the doctrine of
natural rights of the Freedom and People's Rights movement, was the
ideology of resistance which inspired such bodies as the Kommintō of
Chichibu. The piece of Meiji-era printed matter entitled "Gimin Sugoroku," which I discovered in the house of the Sunaga family, traces in
pictures the story of the peasant hero of the Edo period, Sakura Sōgo,
showing him leading a peasant revolt and being condemned, and the
attainment of the peasants' demands is depicted in the winning position
in the game of *sugoroku.* It was because the revolutionary spirit was alive
in this variety of traditional forms that the political modernization of
Japan, in turn, was capable of rapid advance.

When in July, 1879, less than two years after the miiltary-class rebellion,
Sakurai Shizuka, a member of a village council in Chiba Prefecture,
published on his own initiative an appeal to all members of prefectural
councils to unite in demanding a national assembly, and distributed some
thousands of copies of a prospectus explaining his design to addresses all
over Japan, he at once got more than three hundred responses from all
parts of the country. That his action proved to be the beginning of the
national movement which swept the country in the 1880's testifies to the
fact that the social base provided by the *gōnō* stratum, the stratum which
produced such men as Sakurai, had already come to maturity. Looking at
the newspapers of those days we see that as early as 1878 the following
counting-song was in popular circulation. A certain important personality
in the government asserts that the song started in the Province of Tosa
in Shikoku and was being sung by all the women and children in the
villages and towns.

Diary of Sasaki Takayuki:
No one is set over another. We all have equal rights, since we are all men.
My life of which I have not two—if I were not to have Liberty I would
throw it away without regret.
Divided into five are the Five Continents. Among them Asia is semi-
civilized. How shameful this is!
To think of times past, America's independence, too, was won under the
flag of revolt. How brave this is!

In these words like Fukuzawa Yukichi's *Gakumon no Susume* and the
feelings of nationalism in the people. Further, the Province of Tosa

(modern Kōchi Prefecture) which produced this song also produced the finest thinkers of Japanese democracy, such men as Nakae Chōmin, Ueki Emori, and Baba Tatsui. In May 1881, the Tosa society named the Risshisha, set up a bureau for the study of constitutional law, and with Ueki and others as delegates they set about producing a draft constitution devised by the people themselves. It was about the same time that Naitō Roichi, Muramatsu Aizō and othrs of the Jiyūsha, a society in the Province of Mikawa, published an "Anticipated Draft Constitution of Japan." With this as a model, local political societies all over Japan began to produce draft constitutions. Among them the Draft Constitution of Japan devised by Ueki Emori in August includes the following astonishing article as being "the right of liberty for members of the Japanese nation":

Article 72. If the government willfully breaks the provisions of the Constitution or willfully acts to the detriment of the rights of liberty of the people, and stands in the way of the aims embodied in the foundation of the State, the Japanese people may overthrow it and set up a new government.

Only 14 years after the overthrow of the Tokugawa Shogunate the Japanese Freedom and People's Rights movement had attained such a level of democracy as this. It of course goes without saying that one of the reasons for Japan being able to attain this level at so early a date is to be found in the international pressure to which Japan was subject at this time, the juncture presented by world history. But it is undeniable that a deeper cause of Japan's success in turning this external situation into a source of power for internal development lay in the energies for political growth stored within the Japanese people, and especially in the *gōnō* stratum.

In October 1884, the Liberal Party, which had been the core of the Freedom and People's Rights movement, dissolved itself as a result of government oppression and internal dissension. But that this did not mean the total disappearance of the voice of Freedom and People's Rights is shown by a second upsurge of the mass movement in 1886 and 1887 over three great questions—freedom of speech, the reduction of the land tax, and the termination of a foreign policy humiliating to Japan—and by the Daidō Danketsu (coalition) movement which extended into 1889. Further, the end result of these forces led to Japan taking her first historical step in the direction of a "modern state" possessing a Constitution and a Diet which were the first in Asia, even if the Diet was so closely hedged about with restrictions that it was described as "Constitutionalism for Show."

Thus was the motive power for the modernization of Japan accumulated in the midst of the struggle of several millions of Japanese in the period following the Meiji Restoration.

16

Modern states need intellectuals. But from what social stratum and with what backgrounds can we expect to find such men? In the following two essays by two outstanding modern Japanese intellectuals, Chie Nakane and Masao Maruyama, we can see the various roles that traditional thought and Japanese intellectuals played in Japan's response to the urgencies of the Western threat and of sudden political and social change.

Characteristics of Japanese Intellectuals

CHIE NAKANE

THIS essay will deal with certain characteristic features of modern Japanese intellectuals with particular reference to their role in society and how that role has been conditioned by Japanese history. The outstanding characteristics of Japanese intellectuals are their weakness in the face of political authority combined with their apathetic attitude toward that authority, and, at the same time, their feeling that they constitute an elite group in Japanese society. These characteristics seem to be closely related to the way in which intellectuals group together and to the traditions which they have inherited from their predecessors of the Tokugawa feudal period (1600–1868). Specifically, their predecessors were the *bushi,* or warriors, who, because of their status, were the principal political and intellectual leaders of the time.

The modernization of Japan was started with the Meiji Restoration, and with the Restoration the recruitment of intellectuals to be both the rulers and the civil servants was no longer restricted to the *bushi* class. Recruitment was opened wide to all strata of society and was greatly facilitated by the rapid establishment of modern institutions of higher learning. A great number of the people who were educated in this modern educational system joined with the descendants of the *bushi* class to form the new intellectual stratum of modern Japan. Year by year the number of people who graduated from the new system of higher education increased to the point where they overwhelmed the traditional intellectual class. Today a very

Chie Nakane, "Characteristics of Japanese Intellectuals," *Journal of Social and Political Ideas in Japan,* Vol. 2 (April 1964), pp. 24–28. Reprinted with permission of the publisher.

high percentage of these new intellectuals derive from rural and small urban areas. The majority of the intellectuals of rural origin are the second or third, rather than the eldest, sons in their families. Instead of helping them to set up an independent family unit by furnishing them with houses and land in their home villages, their families give them a university education or the equivalent. Once they finish their education and find employment in the city they must depend entirely on their salaries; only very few of them continue to receive financial assistance from their families. In this respect, these people who have been incorporated into the new intellectual stratum are like the retainers in the retinues of the old feudal lords of the Tokugawa period because they have neither land nor other private assets. The *bushi's* livelihood in Tokugawa times was guaranteed by stipends in kind awarded to him by his overlord. Only the great feudal barons (*daimyō*) who were the direct vassals of the *Shōgun* received and held allotments of land in fief. Since the *bushi* below the status of the *daimyō* depended entirely upon stipends rather than upon land for his livelihood, he always faced possible impoverishment should he be expelled from the domain of his overlord. So much economic dependence quite naturally influenced the ways in which he thought and acted; it disposed him to be weak in the face of authority. This situation that characterized the Tokugawa intellectuals still characterizes the modern intellectuals. They are today drawn into a mammoth, modern system of which they are only a helpless part; their lives are forced into a state of economic dependence on the system. They differ fundamentally from the English intellectual in the past who either derived from the gentry class whose members managed their own land or other private assets or from the merchants who accumulated wealth through their own efforts and initiative. The lack of self-conviction and self-assertion of Japanese intellectuals today seems to be related to the fact they are not accustomed to relying on their own resources. Japanese intellectuals continue to display the same weakness toward authority that is characteristic of people who must depend entirely on stipends for a livelihood. The exceptions were the intellectuals of the Meiji period who, by reason of their own efforts and capabilities, became the political elite.

During both the Tokugawa and the Meiji periods, intellectuals and politicians formed an integrated community. But then, as the modern political, economic and social systems became more stabilized and as the intellectual community became more fragmented, there developed more differentiation between the politicians (including the bureaucrats) who formed the power elite, and the intellectuals (in the restricted meaning of the term) who limited themselves entirely to intellectual occupations. The result was that these two groups developed an unhappy tension between themselves and adopted mutually hostile attitudes. The former succeeded in holding the advantage of authority but their standard of intellectual performance lowered, and the latter developed a fundamental dislike of political authority. The intellectuals' apathy and cynicism and their unsuccessful ventures against political authority have caused them to be labeled the "pale intellectuals" and the "literary sycophants." The ineffective feeling of hostility that the intellectuals have had toward political authority, together with their lack of independent economic resources as described above, have prevented intellectuals from participating in political and economic activities. I cannot point to a single case in any other society where the gap between politicians and intellectuals is as wide as it is in Japan. It is almost as though our political and intellectual leaders were of different races.

The intellectuals, who at once are powerless and are antipathetic to political authority, find their role largely limited to educating and enlightening the public, a role which satisfies their elite feelings. The feeling of moral superiority which the intellectuals have inherited from their *bushi* traditions, and the snobbishness which characterizes the intellectuals of rural origin, cause modern intellectuals to act as though they are a special, privileged class in Japanese society. But actually, the intellectual stratum of Japan might better be classified as just a hodge-podge of people who subjectively and erroneously believe that they constitute a privileged class. It is because it is such a hodge-podge of people that it does not have a common forum in which its members can communicate with one another. Certain magazines (but none of the daily newspapers) in Japan are supposed to aim at the intellectual, but, actually, intellectuals do not discuss things with one another in these magazines. Instead, the intellectuals who write articles for these magazines attempt to educate the general public. In doing so they frequently assume a very superior attitude. These articles are not discussions: figuratively speaking, they are one-way sermons. Because the intellectuals assume that their task is to educate the public, they usually write like school teachers rather than specialists. The intellectuals seem to be intoxicated by their feeling of mission to enlighten the public. One result is that the majority of the readers of these magazines are not intellectuals: either they are university students who are accustomed to looking to their superiors for guidance and instruction, or teachers who live in rural areas and want to keep up with the current trends in the principal cultural centers of the country.

Even though the intellectuals feel very strongly that they are the elite members of the public, the fact remains that they are not qualified to be a true elite because they have never been able to acquire economic and political influence. A true elite is normally composed of a minority of intellectuals who have power and influence. Although this self-designated, intellectual elite of contemporary Japan has been able to exert considerable influence by reason of the teaching role it has assumed, it has been situated intellectually too far from the scene to acquire, or to even make an approach to, real power. This is, I think, the inescapable tragedy of Japanese intellectuals.

It is all very good and democratic that the intellectual stratum in Japan has been recruited from many different segments of society, but the unfortunate result of this process has been a general lowering of the quality and a lessening of the homogeneity of the stratum. Because so-called intellectuals have always been active as mentors who address themselves to a relatively less-educated public, they have been able to enhance somewhat the educational and cultural levels of their audience. But at the same time it remains unfortunately true that Japanese intellectuals, being preoccupied as they are with educating the public, tend to forget to cultivate themselves.

Whatever the quality of intellectuals may actually be, the fact is that the feeling intellectuals have that they are an elite group is accepted in Japanese society. It is also interesting to note that people in Japan are too prone to believe that intellectuals and farmers are completely polarized. One reason for this current belief is the system of feudal status in the Tokugawa period which divided the people into *bushi,* farmers, artisans and merchants. It was the policy of the Tokugawa authorities to keep the *bushi* (the intellectuals) and the farmers (the tillers) geographically and socially separated. Rural areas were places where only farmers lived. This Tokugawa policy led to the development of a type of agricultural community that is unique in world history and to the very special connotation of the word "village" (*nōson*) as used by Japanese. The view still prevails in Japan today that a village is culturally and economically inferior to a city. It is still commonly believed that the social status of people who live in villages is low and that the farmer receives only meager remuneration for his labor.

The situation is very different in the old, well-established societies of India and China and in the countries of Europe. In those countries, an intellectual usually stands at the social apex of the rural community. Even though a hierarchical relationship exists between the great landowners and the peasants (or serfs) in these countries, the peasants usually feel a certain closeness to the landowners who are the intellectuals. To say this in another way, each rural community is structured in such a way that at its apex there stands an intellectual who possesses both economic and political influence. In addition, each rural community has its own unique culture which commands the respect of its residents. Thus, in their relations with other rural communities and cities, the villagers of a given community proudly assert themselves as small but organically independent social units. It is not at all unusual to find college-educated intellectuals residing in such rural communities.

In Japan, both city intellectuals and villagers generally think of villages as being places of impoverishment and of farmers as being socially and economically handicapped. But this belief does not coincide with present realities. Today the life of the independent farmer who owns two and a half acres of single-crop land compares very favorably with that of a university professor who lives on his salary. In fact, the farmer is better off because he owns his own land and house and because farming is no more demanding than work in a city.

The work and economic status of the farmer have often been unfavorably compared with those of the city intellectual, but the differences really are not very great. The intellectual stratum and the typical agricultural community function along very similar lines. If having a university education and engaging in mental work are the only criteria for being an intellectual in the broad meaning of the term, then an intellectual stratum does indeed exist in Japan. But since the intellectual stratum of Japan is just a hodge-podge of people who have no common grounds for communication, miscellaneous groups of intellectuals (in the broad meaning of the term) are mushrooming everywhere. In such a situation there is a tendency for intellectuals (in the restricted meaning of the term) to form little scattered groups similar to small agricultural communities, each with its own peculiar temperament and snobbery. Just like a rural village that has its own dialect, each group of intellectuals has its own exclusive pattern of thought and mode of in-group communication that are not understood by outsiders. Each is concerned with its own "village" problems. While all of these groups stress the importance of freedom of speech, the surprising thing is that all members of a given intellectual "village" think exactly alike because of their special mode of in-group communication. Depending on the current intellectual fad, members of a group change their way of thinking. It is interesting to note that when such a change does occur, all members of a given intellectual group follow the leader and change accordingly. This is similar to what happens in a communist or totalitarian country. The members of these groups do not seem to see any contradiction between freedom of speech and their private rules which are binding on the group.

Even though the formation of numerous intellectual "villages" has been a very effective way to protect the intellectuals who are socially and intellectually insecure and unstable and who lack private financial resources, it has also had the negative effect of limiting their perspective and giving them a peasant-like mentality. True intellectuals are people who are international both in knowledge and personality. Despite the fact that intellectuals do acquire a certain amount of knowledge and understanding, they lack the experience and cultural breadth necessary for the development of rich, refined personalities. This is largely because their lives are so restricted to their own respective "villages." The results are that, first, the knowledge they do acquire is not effectively used and that, second, there is a large and widening gap between their knowledge and their conduct. It seems to me that their peculiar ways of life, at both the real and the intellectual levels, causes them to be too easily swayed by their emotions and excessively prone to theorize.

Times are changing. The appearance of new intellectuals during the post-World War II period and the increasingly frequent exposure of Japanese to foreign intellectuals have been very influential factors in demolishing some of the traditional "village" relationships of Japanese intellectuals. One direct manifestation has been the disintegration of the exclusive literary cliques, called *bundan*, in the postwar period. There is now less *raison d'être* for the premodern "traditional community relationships" that have been a typical feature of Japan's intellectual groups. I anticipate that the victors who emerge from the present period of disintegration will, by reason of their own abilities, play very active roles in the future of Japan as truly modern intellectuals.

17

Japanese Thought

MASAO MARUYAMA

A REVIEW of the development of Japanese thought reveals that there have indeed been thinkers in each period of Japanese history who were distinguished by their profound philosophic speculation and originality. Nevertheless, great difficulty is encountered when one attempts to relate the system of thought of any particular thinker to any over-all system of thought that has persisted throughout Japanese history. In other words, it is extremely difficult to grasp clearly what organic relationship existed between a specific idea of a particular thinker and other ideas current during the period in which that thinker lived. It is likewise difficult to determine how specific ideas of a given period in history were integrated with the ideas of a subsequent period. These problems arise from the special way in which Japanese adopt, explain and make use of ideas. There has never developed in our intellectual tradition an axis with which to co-ordinate the various ideas of a given period and place them in proper historical perspective. This particular lack is reflected in "modern" Japan in which supermodern and premodern elements are uniquely intertwined. In the absence of such a coordinating axis, it is not possible to detect what fundamental differences exist between the "traditional," non-Western thought of Japan of the periods before the Meiji Restoration and the "foreign" thought which was adopted by Japan after the Restoration. We know that the two have existed side by side in "modern" Japan but they have never been historically integrated to form an aggregate of Japanese thought. After the Meiji Restoration the traditional ideas of Japan became even more disjointed. They could provide a basis neither for resolute opposition to foreign ideas nor for the orderly integration of these new ideas into traditional thought patterns.

The facts that ideas did not aggregate in Japanese intellectual tradition and that traditional ideas became disjointed and immersed in the new ideas were really two manifestations of the same problem. Hideo Kobay-

Masao Maruyama, "Japanese Thought," *Journal of Social and Political Ideas of Japan*, Vol. 2 (April 1964), pp. 41–48. Reprinted with permission of the publisher.

ashi (b. 1902), one of Japan's foremost literary critics, has frequently
stated that history is memories. This proposition contains a kernel of truth
as far as it relates to the "succession" of ideas in the typical intellectual
development of Japanese thinkers. By and large, Japanese intellectuals
adopt new domestic, as well as new alien, ideas one after another without
giving adequate reflection to their own past ideological convictions. Because of this lack of reflection, new ideas of whatever origin win extremely
quick victory over the intellectuals. Intellectuals place their past beliefs
and convictions to one side and make no conscious effort to confront the
new ideas with their established convictions. This is the reason why a Japanese intellectual will suddenly spout ideas which he conceives of as being
something new but which are really reminiscent of convictions he has held
sometime in the past. Sohō Tokutomi (1863–1957), Chogyū Takayama
(1871–1902) and Riichi Yokomitsu (1898–1947) all shifted their respective intellectual positions in support of Japanism (*Nihonshugi*) despite
the fact that each man had been culturally oriented to the West. Each of
these mutations can be interpreted as a reversion to intellectual expressions
that were reminiscent of the convictions each man had held previously.
This same kind of mutation can take place on a national level during political crises. We have examples of this in the destruction of Buddhist
statues during struggles at the time of the Meiji Restoration, in the revival
of Confucianism around 1881, and in the constitutional controversy in
1935 over Tatsukichi Minobe's (1873–1948) "organ" theory on the role
of the Emperor.

The special traits of Japanese thinking which I have described above
have conditioned the particular way in which foreign ideas have been
received in Japan. In many instances, European philosophy and thought
were first dismantled from their European historical contexts, severed
from their original intellectual premises, and then adopted in Japan piece
by piece. Only fragments of highly abstract, Western theories attracted
certain Japanese because they appealed in some unexpected way to a
particular Japanese custom or traditional sentiment. Many of these ideas
in their European countries of origin had been expressions of desperate
opposition to tradition. When the ideas were transplanted to Japan, however, they dovetailed perfectly with certain already accepted, traditional
Japanese concepts. Some Japanese intellectuals preached, for example,
that certain ethical principles found in German idealism were in full
accord with the precepts of the Chu Hsi school of Confucian philosophy.
Other Japanese intellectuals believed that there was a spiritual affinity of
sorts between the symbolic poetry of Stéphane Mallarmé (1842–1898)
and the *haiku* poetry of Bashō (1644–1694); others felt that there was a
certain identity in the modes of thought of Western pragmatism and the
kind of pragmatic philosophy developed by townsmen during the Tokugawa period.

The intellectual tradition of Japan may be characterized as "tolerant." In evolving intellectually, a Japanese may embrace and adopt a limitless variety of ideas and academic propositions, even when some of them are contradictory. Ever since the Meiji Restoration, Japanese intellectuals have rejected only the Western thought and academic approaches that would not yield to the kind of tolerant embrace required by Japanese tradition. They rejected those systems of thought that contained logic or value systems in terms of which all human experience must be explained. Christianity during the Meiji period and Marxism in the early 1920's were two cases in point. Even though as systems they were diametric opposites, they both experienced marked intolerance at the hands of Japanese "tradition" which required "tolerance" irrespective of the principles involved. Both Christianity and Marxism in Japan had to decide whether or not to compromise themselves: compromise would have meant the loss of their unique reforming vitalities; intransigence would have beckoned intolerance. Only the former course would have satisfied Japanese intellectual requirements.

The special way in which Japanese intellectuals have evaluated and criticized the ideas of their opponents requires our attention. Japanese intellectuals have usually pointed to the role played in society by the system of thought to which they were opposed; they have then indirectly criticized the system by revealing the hidden intellectual motives and intentions of their rivals who support the opposing system. It is important to note that this type of approach has been a "traditional" mode of criticism which developed very early in the intellectual evolution of modern Japan. The arguments used toward the end of the Tokugawa period by those who advocated the expulsion of foreigners from Japan illustrate this point. These xenophobic arguments criticized European thought for its possible destructive effects on the traditional value system and social order of Japan.

Another special feature of Japanese intellectual criticism has been the role played by the idea of "evolution." The intellectual tradition of Japan does not provide the means for assessing ideas and concepts in terms of eternal values. Since the Meiji Restoration, Japanese intellectuals have always considered superior those Western ideas and philosophic systems appearing most recently in European history. This tendency resulted from two facts that are related. The first fact is that ever since the Meiji Restoration Japanese thinkers have felt that Japan is inferior to the "advanced" countries of Europe. The second fact is that the idea of historical evolution was introduced to Japanese intellectuals after the Meiji Restoration. As a result of the conjunction of this attitude and this idea Japanese intellectuals considered the relative historical newness of a Western idea to be more important than the idea's practical implication for Japan. The way in which reactionary factions criticized the progressives in the Meiji period illustrates this point. The reactionaries used the "traditional" Japanese argument that the ideology of the progressives was outmoded for Japan because it was already outmoded in Europe and America.

When Hirobumi Itō drafted the Meiji Constitution, he considered the prerogative of the Emperor to be the very core of political authority and the throne to be the spiritual axis for the nation. There was built on these considerations the quasi-religious idea of "national polity" (*kokutai*), an idea which wielded magic-like power to induce Imperial subjects to undertake an infinite amount of responsibility for the sake of the state. Inevitably, the state used this idea of national polity as a substitute for the deficiencies in our Japanese intellectual tradition. Because the idea of national polity was a vague sort of ideological system, it conformed very well to the traditional Japanese intellectual approach of embracing all sorts of other ideas irrespective of principles. When the idea of national polity was expressed in the form of state policies, it became a stern power mechanism directed against all of the supposed enemies of the state. Through this power mechanism the state was able to create an extremely effective thought-control system that advanced beyond the limitations normally placed on a constitutional government.

It has often been pointed out that Japan in its modern period has been "Westernized" only in so far as its system of government is concerned. However, some very important questions remain to be answered: To what degree did the system of government created in Japan reflect the spirit that was responsible for the development of modern systems of government in the West? Also, how did this "modern" system of government work in Japan and what were the attitudes of the individuals who functioned within that system? It is with these questions in mind that I must now examine the Japanese state as it has functioned under the Emperor system.

The Meiji Constitution declared itself to have been based on the Imperial prerogative and bestowed on the people by the Emperor. The Constitution made no provision for raising any questions about who originally had the authority to write and promulgate the Constitution. The supreme prerogative of the Emperor combined with the Meiji Constitution to produce a gigantic state mechanism. Before the end of World War II, Japanese intellectuals often discussed the Meiji Constitution and the legal and political systems based on it. However, these intellectuals discussed this Constitution and these systems as though they were completely isolated from the basic question of who had authority in the first place to create them. The sole concentration of political authority in the hands of the absolute, transcendent Emperor made it difficult for the political system established by the Constitution to function effectively. For the system to function effectively, the policies of state had to be formulated by extralegal and extraconstitutional groups of elder statesmen clustered about the Emperor. At no level in the political system did one know clearly who had the authority to make decisions and who had the ultimate responsibility for them. An uncertain sharing of responsibility was preferred so that no one person could be pointed out as bearing the ultimate responsibility for decisions. It is obvious that the mechanism of the Emperor-system state had inherent within it the danger of developing into a colossal system of irresponsibility.

From the time of the Meiji Restoration the Japanese system of government was seemingly "modern." On deeper inquiry, however, we find that the political power at the upper echelons of the system was neither unified nor rationalized. We also find that the intransigence of the traditional social organization at the village level prevented the development of a people possessing truly modern individuality. Only at the middle stratum of society was it possible to effect speedy "modernization," and then only through the preservation and use of the premodern institutional and ideological traits of the top and bottom strata of society. The particular brand of local political "autonomy" favored by Aritomo Yamagata (1880–1922) made it legally possible for the state both to preserve intact the kind of community relationships that were traditional of the lower strata of society and to link these lower strata directly to the Imperial bureaucratic system. These traditional community relationships made possible the link between the so-called system of local "autonomy" and the positions of authority of the influential landlords at the local level where they headed old, well-established families of considerable wealth.

The concept of the family state (*kazoku kokka*) was an ideological manifestation of the linking together of traditional community relationships and the Imperial bureaucratic system. The way in which the Imperial system was symbolized, expressed, and maintained at each level of society provided for the required balance and subtle interdependence between the functional rationalization of the state (i.e., bureaucratization) and the traditional patriarchal social structure. Such functional rationalization is required by modern states to balance the factionalism, mutual obligation and personal considerations of a traditional patriarchal social structure. Modern rules and systems are first set up to standardize and regulate the infinitely diverse, complex factors that are involved in social realities. However, when such rules and systems are first set up it is essential that the leaders be aware of the limitations in the degree to which they may be standardized and applied. The mechanism of Japanese society from the Meiji Restoration until World War II represented an irrational union of political power and the traditional norms which governed interpersonal relationships and mutual obligations. Consequently, that mechanism tended in every way imaginable to enter and regulate the daily lives of all individuals. The bureaucratic thinking of the time held that the system and its rules were absolute and had unlimited applicability. Such thinking prevailed because too few people were aware of the distinction and sharp tension between the system's artificiality and the way in which it actually worked. The traditional web of interpersonal relationships which were characteristic at the level of the rural community made up the "natural order" of Japanese society. These relationships provided the lowest level of society with a model to be followed in developing a traditional Japanese type of "resistance" to the modernization (i.e., bureaucratization) that was being instituted by the highest levels of society. This resistance to modernization grew out of the feelings of the people based on day-to-day experiences at the lowest level of society rather than out of universally applicable norms. Because this resistance was just an expression of such feelings, it was incapable of conceiving new social norms with which to establish a new social order. It was a resistance which expressed itself only in sporadic outburts that were unrelated to the daily, normal activities of the people themselves.

The patterns of thought of the common man (as distinguished from citizens who have an awareness of their function and rights in a modern society) and the bureaucrats became incompatible and unbridgeable. This occurred because the system and its rules became static and absolute in themselves and because the behavior of the people was largely regulated by their feelings derived from real-life experiences and remained so influential in the social structure. In the final analysis, there also sprang from this same situation the parallel but unbridgeable patterns of thought between Japanese social scientists and men of letters. The social scientists employed "traditional" thought patterns, but the thought patterns of the men of letters were even more traditional because of their excessive reliance on feelings and intuitive realization. We can find in Japanese literary traditions some of the reasons why men of letters developed their own characteristic thought patterns. First, the Japanese language has a rich vocabulary for expressing subjective nuances, but it has a poor vocabulary for expressing logical processes and universal concepts. Second, classical Japanese literature has always tended to phrase subtleties in a highly-polished style framed in terms of nature and the seasons. Third, Western literary realism, as introduced into Japan after the Meiji Restoration, was understood only as the antithesis of the traditional moralism found in Japanese literature of the Tokugawa and early Meiji periods. Japanese literary realism lacked a rational, scientific background, a background which was an essential part of the realism found in modern European literature. The approaches used in Japanese literary realism were easily linked by many men of letters with the traditional approach used by the scholars of Japanese classical studies (*kokugaku*). In this traditional approach, Japanese scholars selected specific facts from reality and laid primary emphasis on the importance of these facts in themselves. In their analyses of these facts, they relied heavily on intuition rather than on a scientific methodology.

Most men of letters in the post-Meiji Restoration period felt themselves to be superfluous in Japanese society because they had strayed from the norms usually followed by Imperial subjects. These literary men had strayed from the usual norms because of some unfortunate experience. They had stumbled in their climb up the ladder of bureaucratic advancement, or they had been disappointed in political activities or for one reason or another, they had fled from their families and home towns. They felt antipathy against the bureaucracy and the established order. They had an almost pathological dislike of abstraction and conceptualization; their antiworldliness, in the background of which was a kind of Buddhist pessimism, increasingly "traditionalized" their antagonism for rational, scientific modes of thought. These various subjective factors combined to produce in Japanese men of letters a reliance on intuitive realization or faith in their own powers to perceive "truth" intuitively in their daily experiences.

Next I would like to take up the question of the degree to which our social scientists rely upon theoretical conceptualization, particularly as it relates to Marxism. By discussing this question I shall be able to summarize a few of the important intellectual problems of modern Japan. Before World War II, Marxism was the sole representative of the social sciences in Japan. Our intellectuals first acquired from Marxism a methodology for analyzing social phenomena in comprehensive terms. Marxism aroused intellectuals to study the many diverse elements that have gone into the historical background of Japan and to seek the fundamental causative factors which generated them. Marxism also taught Japanese certain things about the logic which has been an inherent part of Western intellectual development from the time of Bacon and Descartes. It taught them that one can use theories as levers, so to speak, for generating changes in realities only when one manages to divorce oneself intellectually from the realities of one's existence. Theories can be used as levers when one becomes aware of the sharp tension that exists between oneself and objective reality. Marxism taught intellectuals that they must use logic to reorganize the realities of their environment. It taught many Japanese intellectuals that the ideas they produce must not be just intellectual playthings but must be practical for application to social problems. It taught them that they must be willing to assume a real and vital responsibility for the social ideas they did express.

It was a tragedy for Marxism that it assumed such importance in the modern intellectual development of Japan. First, Marxism had to face singlehandedly all of the resistance and antagonism which traditional Japanese sentiment has against that which is theoretical, conceptual or abstract. Second, when I mentioned earlier that Japanese Marxist social scientists are prone to place faith in theoretical conceptualization, I was referring specifically to the fact that they tend to attach more importance to the result of an abstraction than to the process by which an abstraction is derived from reality. Consequently, the theories are often mistakenly identified with reality itself. This peculiar Japanese tendency to place faith in theoretical conceptualization cannot be isolated from the marked tendency in modern Japan of thinking that institutions and law are absolute and unlimited in their applicability. Marxism was not alone responsible for the development of such a faith. A similar faith comes into play whenever any doctrine, ism, or world view is devoutly adopted by Japanese intellectuals. Because Marxism is a highly systematized intellectual doctrine, in Japan it has suffered particularly from the overtheoretical tendencies of its followers.

The fundamental task of the theoretician is not to identify reality; it is to provide, in the light of certain criteria, a methodological framework in which to arrange the complex factors of reality. However methodologically perfect a theoretician's arrangement and cognition of facts may be, his arrangement and cognition can neither completely explain all of the infinitely complex factors of reality nor be used as substitutes for these factors. In forming his understanding of reality, a theoretician can select and arrange, on his own responsibility, only a few of the infinite number of factors involved in reality. Japanese theoreticians tends to believe that their theoretical perception of some of the factors involved in reality can and does encompass the totality of reality itself. Because of the peculiar intellectual climate of Japan, in which theory is accepted independent of existing reality and is not constantly challenged by reality, Japanese theoreticians claim they bear an unlimited responsibility for understanding reality. This claim induces them to equate irresponsibly their academic theses with the totality of reality.

The reader will see from what I have written that there are certain common denominators in the faith which Japanese men of letters have in intuitive realization and the faith which Japanese social scientists have in theories. Both kinds of faith are the products of a schism between the theories which have been made objects in themselves and the indigenous, interpersonal relationships which function in the foreground of theory. In Japan, the former is of Western, or European, origin, and the latter is "traditional." Only when the men of letters and the social scientists of Japan become aware of this schismatic duality in Japanese "modernity" will they have some common ground for communication with one another. Only when there is such a common ground will it be possible for the men of letters and the social scientists of Japan to develop a truly modern system of Japanese thought formed through an inward fusion of varying and even conflicting ideas.

18

All Japanese were faced with the necessity of change and the urgencies of adaptation to a new world. The effects of the crisis were traumatic, as major Japanese novelists repeatedly showed. In the following essay by Howard Hibbet we can see the result of this trauma on modern Japanese sensibility.

Tradition and Trauma in the Contemporary Japanese Novel

HOWARD HIBBETT

VIEWED from abroad, the really "novel" characteristics of modern Japanese fiction seem to derive from the venerable literary tradition linking an age of Peace and Tranquillity, that of the Heian court a millennium ago, with the age of anxiety of the present reign. But it is a long way indeed from the serene world of Prince Genji, whose accomplishments included incense-judging and performing Chinese dances, to the traffic-choked Tokyo of a novel dominated by the *noirōze* ("neurosis," now a household word) of its antihero. It is no wonder that younger writers in Japan sometimes assert that any meaningful link with the past has been broken. Most Japanese novelists, especially in the early stages of their careers, have rebelled against their native literary tradition. Writers and public alike are familiar with a vast range of Western thought and literature, extending from Greek mythology to American Zen; the Tokyo avant-garde in all the arts is seldom outdistanced by New York or Paris. Yet the comparatively few novels that have been translated from the Japanese retain a special flavor unaccountable except for the lingering, pervasive influence of the traditional culture.

The literary themes and techniques imported so eagerly since the Meiji Restoration of 1868 were often successfully grafted onto the ancient stock, and soon seemed indistinguishable from it. Often the attempt was made to transplant whole genres or ideologies, as if they could be expected to survive without modification. Innumerable hybrid and variant forms began to flourish in the Meiji era, to be labeled romanticism, realism,

Howard Hibbett, "Tradition and Trauma in the Contemporary Japanese Novel," *Daedalus* (Fall 1966). Reprinted with permission of *Daedalus,* Journal of the American Academy of Arts and Sciences, Boston, Mass., *Fiction in Several Languages.* Footnotes omitted.

naturalism, neo-idealism, or whatever, with a fine enthusiasm for each new exotic bloom. But there was always a more or less traumatic process of change, as intellectuals discovered and defined their *Angst,* as writers adopted alien conventions of fiction, and as a newly revitalized literature began to influence as well as to reflect one of the most rapidly developing societies of modern times. Despite the extraordinary growth and prosperity of the literary profession, its wounds have been undeniably severe. Many novelists have suffered from the stresses of an uneasy individualism, and from a related compulsion to confess, if not to sin for the sake of confessing. Among their standard themes is the disgraceful vacillation or anguished choice between family duty and personal freedom of a character who appears to be a self-portrait of the author. Suicide is a frequent solution to such dilemmas, and novelists have been among the notable suicides of every generation since Meiji. Even the themes and tone of popular fiction, with its hopeless marriages, inevitably parted lovers, and conventional unhappy endings, create an atmosphere of gloom almost as impenetrable as that of the serious novel. Naturally these literary and social patterns often recall old configurations. It is not coincidental that the mid-Meiji enthusiasm for *Werther* was accompanied by renewed interest in the seventeenth-century suicide plays of Chikamatsu, nor that Japanese fictional counterparts of the frustrated heroes of Goncharov and Turgenev lapse into moods colored by the Buddhist melancholy of the theme of the medieval *Tale of the Heike:* "The temple bell echoes the impermanence of all things." That epic of defeat was to inspire many popular historical novels, first among them a sad, lyrical tale by Takayama Chogyū, who had already studied Chikamatsu and translated *Werther.* But most writers thought of their private or public agonies, their sense of impermanence and destructive change, as wholly modern phenonemena. The literature of their own past represented a burden rather than a store of accumulated wealth.

To be sure, such leading contemporary novelists as Kawabata Yasunari and the late Tanizaki Junichirō have used the resources of their own tradition to advantage. Among younger writers none has done so more skillfully than Mishima Yukio, now in his early forties and the single new postwar novelist to have made an international reputation. Certainly Mishima owes much of his success to the enrichment of his otherwise unexceptionably up-to-date psychological fiction and drama by elements of traditional Japanese art. His "modern Nō plays," for example, brilliantly exploit the possession theme of the Nō, the dramatic inner conflict of a person haunted by the past. The ghosts may be only of the recent past, perhaps of the Meiji era, and may be evoked in a downtown Tokyo park, an antique dealer's showroom, or a mental hospital. But their power has its source in clusters of association that were time-honored long before Zeami used them, with a mastery of literary and dramatic techniques that were also the product of long tradition, in fashioning the classic Nō plays of the fourteenth century.

Unlike Tanizaki or Kawabata, Mishima seems to be drawn toward a theatrically self-conscious art. A discerning critic as well as novelist and playwright, he has stated that the heart of his method is to rely on the unconscious—and has explained in some detail how he controls it. Indispensable to the ritual of writing is a visit to a suitable setting for a work: paradoxically, in view of his skill at manipulating dramatic situations, Mishima says that he is more deeply moved by landscapes than by people. But these expressive landscapes, like the ones Kawabata has mentioned as the origin of many of his stories, are seen as symbolic metaphors of emotion in a manner already well established in Heian literature. Thus *Death in Midsummer* (*Manatsu no shi*) is a detached study in the French analytic vein of a woman mourning her two drowned children. What one remembers most vividly, however, is the ominous beauty of the setting—the "anger in the rays of the sun"—and the tragic irony of death in such a season. The epigraph is from Baudelaire (*La mort . . . nous affecte plus profondément sous le regne pompeux de l'été*"), and possibly the images of the sea have a glint of the Aegean or the Mediterranean. But the sensibility is of a kind that has been cultivated in Japanese literature in every age.

Touches of this sort enhance even the somber last novels of Natsume Sōseki, those in which he portrays with intense poignancy, but also with wit, drama, and profound psychological insight, a sense of loneliness and hopeless failure in human relationships. His memorably unhappy characters are realized through superb dialogue, dialogue heightened by analysis and by the delicately controlled tension of each scene; and they exist in a world that has its own sensuous reality rather than against a flat theatrical backdrop or in abstract detachment from their surroundings. As a novelist of alienation Sōseki has the Chekovian gift of depicting boredom and depression without being boring or depressing, but he has also the sensitivity to nature, the awareness of the changing seasons, of a *haiku* poet. (He took his literary name "Sōseki" when he began studying *haiku*, and he wrote distinguished poetry in Chinese as well as in Japanese.) Still, even this master, surely the greatest novelist of modern Japan, has been criticized both for insufficient skill at natural description (by the extremely high Japanese standards) and for undue skill in creating "fiction"—that is, imaginative writing that has a clearly defined structure and cannot be readily interpreted as autobiographical.

To purist critics in Japan, Western concepts of the novel have often seemed incompatible with the transcendent virtue of sincerity, a virtue that is thought to sanction both meandering reminiscence and confessionalist self-exposure. Insistent on the frank identification of author and protagonist, advocates of what is called the I-novel (*shi-shōsetsu*) have tended to equate fiction with falsehood, a Confucian prejudice, rather than with a means toward poetic truth. Novelists who disclaim auto-biographical intent risk the charge of frivolity. Mishima and Tanizaki, among others, have been similarly criticized for their inventive talents, particularly after their novels began to attract attention abroad. Un-fortunately, only a few of Sōseki's many novels have been translated, and only one of these (Edwin McClellan's version of *Kokoro*) into English of appropriate literary merit. But Japanese critics are inclined to regard with suspicion any novelist whose work has been admired in the West. Perhaps it is to be expected that writers in the discursive reminiscent vein of the I-novel should strike Western readers as so many wayward essayists, and that, conversely, novelists whose techniques are closest to those of the West are more likely to be read merely from an interest in their exotic subject matter. Yet in fact much of the appeal of modern Japanese novels abroad lies in the treatment of familiar themes—however unfamiliar their cultural setting. These themes have been explored most effectively by writers of verve and daring whose methods are in part traditional but who are also alert to the innovations that have transformed the literature of Japan since Meiji.

By far the most vigorous of the older Japanese masters whose careers survived the shattering Greater East Asia War was Tanizaki Junichirō, a novelist so prolific that one learns with surprise from his memoirs that he wrote very slowly. He envied Natsume Sōseki's capacity to dash off an installment for a newspaper serial in the morning, leaving the after-noon free for more lofty pursuits; he also regretted that his work had allowed him inadequate leisure for such pastimes as reading, travel, and love. Still, after more than half a century of dazzling successful industry, with all the rewards and honors due a pre-eminent literary elder states-man, Tanizaki remained as devoted as ever to his craft. His chief pleasure was writing, a pleasure which, along with his predilection for reading his own works, he modestly ascribed to weakening eyesight. But he also wanted to entertain, to enlighten, and to shock. In his flamboyant early stories Tanizaki seemed to be trying to naturalize the more outrageous literary ideas of Wilde and Baudelaire, but his later work makes it clear that these themes were indeed his own, and that the traditional elements in their expression—the Kabuki-like settings and atmosphere—were also important to him. Neither as a Westernizing bohemian nor, in the thirties, as a writer of beautifully finished tales in Heian, medieval, or Meiji styles did he use his virtuoso techniques merely to disguise the alarming impli-cations of his art. From his debut in a literary magazine in 1910—he must have been chagrined that the issue was banned because of someone else's contribution—until his death in the summer of 1965 at the age of seventy-nine, he continued to devise new ways to reveal disturbing truths to a wide reading public.

Perhaps the most disturbing of all his novels, indeed of all post-war Japanese novels, was *The Key* (*Kagi*), a spare, claustrophobic study of middle-aged depravity which appeared in 1956 when Tanizaki was seventy. The very style of *The Key* seems as shamefully naked as Ikuko, the professor's wife, in the scenes of bath and bedroom where she lies drugged with brandy, exposed under glaring lights to her husband's voyeurist scrutiny. The book opens with the New Year's Day diary entry of the aging professor (the reader never learns his name, and has only a hint of his apparently neglected occupation) and goes on with alternating extracts from the diary of his somewhat younger wife. Their diaries and their energies are concentrated on the stimulation of sexual passion, by whatever means and at whatever cost. For the husband, like the author a victim of high blood pressure, the ultimate cost is death. But his demure, respectable wife becomes an insatiable *femme fatale,* quite ready to destroy Kimura, the young man who is by then her lover and who is to marry her daughter. That her husband has carefully arranged the liaison, if not the engagement, seems a reasonable stratagem in this desperate battle. The two "secret" diaries, used as a deceptively guarded means of communications between husband and wife, permit candid though confusing glimpses of the process by which a cultivated, tormented man, presumably trying to recapture sexual vitality, sacrifices all the less exacting pleasures of his highly civilized world in a blind effort to enact his persistent fantasies.

The two diaries stand in antagonistic contrast, different even as printed in their external form—the husband's written by fountain pen in the square syllabary used for official documents, the wife's by the traditional (and soundless) writing brush on thin rice paper in a feminine cursive script. Both diarists are wily, deceitful, intent on the life-and-death erotic struggle that culminates their two decades of unhappy marriage. We never know how far to believe these confessions, nor do we learn much, except indirectly, about the thought of the people who write them. At first Ikuko declares that she has no intention of reading her husband's diary, in spite of having been allowed to find the key to the locked drawer in which he keeps it: "I haven't the faintest desire to penetrate his psychology, beyond the limits I've set for myself. I don't like to let others know what is in my own mind, and I don't care to pry into theirs." Later she observes that most of that passage—all but the part about not liking to let others know her own thoughts—is untrue. Thus the reader has the privilege of enjoying intimate but suspicious revelations. The narrative method only hints at characterization; a few quoted snatches of dialogue delineate the student-accomplice Kimura and the disgusted, jealous, but conspiratorial daughter. The minds of the characters hold as many secrets as does the shadowy, silent old Kyoto house, the faintly sketched background against which the drama is played.

Rarely has there been such dramatic intensity in the modern Japanese novel as there is in *The Key*. The diary form, stemming from an ancient literary tradition in Japan, is usually a quasi-fictional genre, hardly differentiated from the novel. The novel itself is often considered "pure" only in the vein of autobiographical fiction of the I-novel, disguised very thinly if at all. The I-novel recommends itself as literature partly by stylistic beauty but mainly by the sincerity—whether of contemplative earnestness or confessional daring—of the author. Self-analysis is a frequent aim, though the results are seldom rigorously analytical. A mist of romantic or sentimental self-deception often clouds the supposedly pure I-novel. Tanizaki, however, was one of the few major novelists who used a wide range of Western fictional techniques without a trace of anxiety. He willingly defended the importance of fabrication, of plot, the "lie" that many Japanese writers have considered an obstacle in their search for truth. But Tanizaki also took whatever he needed from traditional literature. He adapted the style of the leisurely essay to a dramatic narrative, for instance, or blended the conventions of the diffuse, elegant *monogatari*—the "tale" in the sophisticated lineage of the eleventh-century *Tale of Genji*—with those of modern fiction.

In his last novel, *Diary of a Mad Old Man* (*Fūten rōjin nikki*, published in 1962), he used the diary form to create a sharp satirical portrait of an unruly though severely ill old gentleman whose tantrums and perversities belie the stock character of the elderly connoisseur of the arts. A man with tastes similar to those of the bland narrator of earlier novels (who revealed himself only discreetly, quoting a bit of poetry here or commenting there) has confided to this singular diary his most secret and ignoble thoughts, his curious remaining lusts, his childishness, his ill temper, his bitter humiliations and the perverse satisfaction derived from them, together with the richly orchestrated suffering and obsessive self-regard of a man whose sensibilities have for decades been attuned to art, to the nuances of sexuality, and to death.

Utsugi Tokusuke, the shrewd, Sybaritic Mad Old Man, seems to be a diarist with remarkable self-analytic insight, to say nothing of frankness, a model of psychological perspicacity in the service of a sincere desire for self-knowledge. He knows that he has a weakness for women with bad character and beautiful feet. When he observes his growing interest in the young Kabuki actors who play feminine roles, he calmly speculates on the relation of a youthful homosexual experiment to the sexual impulses that persist, at seventy-seven, now that he is impotent. He tends to dwell on his physical deterioration and other disagreeable qualities, much as he insists on removing his false teeth in order to show his daughter-in-law Satsuko exactly how ugly he is. He recognizes the masochism in his costly infatuation with Satsuko—a girl with a doubtful past who likes imported luxuries and who enjoys boxing matches, the bloodier the better. He is quite aware that his efforts to provide her with a lover have a selfish motive. Yet Utsugi is not merely shown to us in the unflattering glare of satirical illumination, nor as a more realistic (because more fully human) variant of the self-portrait of the I-novelist. Although there is no male-female counterpoint between diaries after the fashion of *The Key,* the comic, querulous, touching monologue ends abruptly and is followed by a quick succession of accounts from other points of view as the reader awaits with suspense the outcome of the gravest of the old man's attacks. All that is revealed of it, and of later events, is what is set forth in the nurse's slightly vulgar report, the doctor's formidable clinical records, and the notes by a daughter, sullen or shrewish in the diary, who is seen in an unexpectedly sympathetic light. Once again Tanizaki concludes his novel on a tentative note, the future in doubt and the characters somewhat more ambiguous than the reader had at times taken them to be.

Again the underlying themes are the relationship between love and cruelty, the necessary antagonism between Eros and Thanatos, between sexuality and the dark forces of decay symbolized by the medicines and appliances meant to combat them. The embodiment of these themes in character, action, and atmosphere is as spontaneously vital as ever. Utsugi's dream of his mother, recalled in all her classic Bodhisattvaesque beauty when he was a small child, is immediately associated with thoughts of the utterly different (though equally beautiful) modern temptress Satsuko. Far from shaving off her eyebrows and dyeing her teeth black in proper early Meiji style, Satsuko "has her hair set in a permanent wave, wears earrings, paints her lips coral pink or pearl pink or coffee brown, pencils her eyebrows, uses eye shadow on her eyelids, glues on false eyelashes and then, as if that isn't enough, brushes on mascara to try to make them look still longer." Utsugi's schemes to apotheosize Satsuko as a Bodhisattva engraved on his tombstone, or, better yet, to have Buddha's Footprints carved to the pattern of rubbings of her feet, supply a further, doubtless unconscious link between the usually isolated and antithetical images of woman as madonna or harlot, the sexually "pure" mother or the degraded, degrading seductress. In *The Key,* Ikuko, a respectable woman with an old-fashioned Kyoto upbringing whose body has "the gently swelling lines of the Bodhisattva in the Chuguji Temple," is corrupted from her stubborn feminine modesty as she takes to wearing earrings, lace gloves, and Western-style dresses that reveal her voluptuously curved legs. In *The Bridge of Dreams (Yume no ukihashi)* the images of mother and mistress are again fused, and the aura of incestuous guilt is particularly noticeable. Yet these mysteries, too, elude easy translation into pathological terminology. Such a tale may well be interpreted as a male fantasy of the sort described as "the most prevalent form of degradation" in Freud's first and second "Contributions to the Psychology of Love." But the novel's narrative subtlety, its indefinably complex characters, its nostalgic setting of a secluded Kyoto house and garden all suggest the atmosphere of *The Tale of Genji* (to which the title, the opening poem, and the plot itself allude) darkened by the influence of modern psychological fiction.

The cruel but irresistible temptress appears as the heroine of Tanizaki's first short story, and reappears, along with her willing victims, in nearly everything else he wrote. Sometimes she is set off against women of contrasting temperament, sometimes against a background from the lost world of the past. In *Whirlpool (Manji)*, the *femme fatale* is a beautiful young art student whose features are the model for a drawing of a Bodhisattva but whose actual character is perverse, deceptive, and destructive in the extreme, as she demonstrates in her seduction of a mild-mannered lawyer as well as of his rather aggressive wife. But the setting is Osaka, a city heavy with memories of the old Japan, in contrast to the shallow modernity of Tokyo. The entire novel is narrated in a lush feminine Osaka dialect, symbolic of the langorous charm of the traditional culture, a charm that softens the harsh outlines of this bizarre confession. Later the same year (1928) Tanizaki began serial publication of *Some Prefer Nettles (Tade kuu mushi)*, in which the protagonist's romantic interest is divided between Louise, an expensive Eurasian prostitute in Yokohama, and the doll-like, solicitous O-hisa, his father-in-law's mistress, who has been meticulously groomed to suit the refined tastes of a conservative Kyoto gentleman. These two women provide alternative attractions to Kaname, a young man whose wife has long ceased to interest him. The rival claims of flashy Western-style Yokohama sensuality and the subdued, enduring appeal of an idealized Japanese beauty imply the cultural conflict between Western influence and the native tradition, betwen the new and the old, which has been such an engrossing problem in modern Japan.

As in *Some Prefer Nettles* the conflict is always sexualized in Tanizaki's fiction—one aspect of a single-minded devotion, unparalleled in Japanese literature, to the myth of the idolized fatal woman. Everywhere he stresses the sinister role of feminine adornment in working this transformation. Women have been drastically changed, corrupted but freed by those alluring Western garments that encase them in a glowing, resplendent skin, and yet, unlike the constricting trousers, coat, and tie (with stickpin) of European-style men, release their vital powers. And cultural change in general, while less absorbing, has for Tanizaki a considerable degree of morbid fascination. Of course such attitudes are not unknown among other Japanese authors, although most of them have a consuming interest in the predominantly masculine society in which they live. Relations between father and son, between brothers, between friends whose wives stay quietly at home, seldom visible, are at the core of most Japanese novels. Even the usual triangle consists of two men and, somewhere in the middle distance, a woman. But cultural conflict may be sensed in almost every modern Japanese novel—not because Japan has failed to assimilate any significant elements of Western culture, but because the process of Westernization (and modernization) has intensified a national self-awareness, a feeling of radical difference, ambivalently superior and inferior, from the intrusive civilization of the remote, inscrutable "foreigners."

In his longest novel *The Makioka Sisters* (*Sasameyuki*—literally, and more poetically, a term for thinly falling snow) Tanizaki depicts with nostalgic affection for detail the life of a once-prosperous Osaka merchant family between the years 1939 and 1941, when it was still possible to believe that suitably arranged marriages could preserve the heritage of the past intact. Most of the book was written during the war; the ironic ending (it appears that the family's future has at last been settled) is the final note of an elegy to a vanished era. A stable former generation has already disappeared by the time the novel opens, and the family continues to disregard even the few conspicuous signs of changing times, such as the austerity edicts and rationing of rice that are mentioned toward the end of the book. Yet within this narrow, decreasingly privileged circle there is still a tension between the old and the new: between the tastes and loyalties of all the sisters, and especially between the conflicting styles of the two unmarried ones, the elder of whom, so reserved as to seem inarticulate, resists marriage by conventionally genteel tactics, while the other, given to elopements and dangerous liaisons, has the independent spirit of a thoroughly modern young woman. Except in reference to some chance foreign neighbors, however, the ominous public events of the day seem unreal, hardly worth mentioning at all. They lack even the briefly noted reality of the student demonstrations (the 1960 Security Pact demonstrations, it may be assumed) in *Diary of a Mad Old Man,* where the blocked streets cause some inconvenience in driving downtown to a restaurant after the theater. And such an atmosphere of isolation from all but personal matters is not peculiar to Tanizaki's novels. Disillusionment and retreat from involvement with public issues have been important tendencies in Japanese literature since Meiji; they reflect a widespread anxiety, especially acute among intellectuals, over the political and social problems of modern Japan. Withdrawal into the world of the past or into the preoccupations of private life is not only a novelist's stratagem and a response to unsettling change, but a long-established mode of minimizing the pressures of a tightly organized society.

In his essays and memoirs Tanizaki often writes movingly of the past, and of the losses suffered in the course of Japan's headlong modernization. Through his own work he has done much to preserve traditional values, notably by his twice-revised modern version of *The Tale of Genji* and by his various stories and novels in a limpid classical vein. But he has no sentimental illusions about turning back from the doubtful, if not disastrous, path of Western-style progress, only a regret for what has been lost along the way. It is in the arts and in surviving customs and manners that one may hope to find some benefit from cultural continuity. Thus Tanizaki's historical tales are far from romantic escapism, just as those with contemporary settings always imply a living connection with the past. Throughout his fiction, problems of technique are solved with the restrained, sure taste of a craftsman in a well-defined tradition.

In characterization, for instance, Tanizaki's art has a closer affinity with traditional life and letters than with the practices of the Western novelists who have influenced him. Even *Some Prefer Nettles,* written in his more naturalistic manner, discloses its meaning delicately and tentatively, with a certain reticent decorum. Faithful to the texture of the life he deals with, Tanizaki shows a well-bred preference for hinting at feelings rather than seeking to penetrate the innermost mysteries of his characters. That is also true of *The Key,* and of such a massive realist novel as *The Makioka Sisters,* in which he might have been expected to use the privilege of omniscience to tell us far more than he does about the motives and reflections of his principal characters. After witnessing many incidents, being told of still others, and overhearing endless conversations, we may yet feel that we are only superficially acquainted with the declining Osaka family: the shadowy, idealized Yukiko, her scandalously impulsive younger sister, the ineffectual men, and even the central figure, Sachiko, who is portrayed without the tinge of fantasy that makes the others seem at home in Tanizaki's larger fictional world.

Perhaps, it has been suggested, so much attention to the surfaces of life results from the characters' own unawareness of any deeper feelings, their inner lives being governed by the same oppressive forces as their social behavior. Yet there is no lack of evidence, not least in literature and the drama, of the frequent Japanese failure to dam up "the spontaneous overflow of powerful feelings." What seems more likely is that such techniques of characterization reflect a preference for intuitive ways of knowing, whether in solitary thought or in interpersonal relations. From a slight gesture, a fleeting expression, a change in tone, or a verbal hint there may come a sudden revelation more significant than an overt act or declaration of sentiment. Once, in criticizing a novel by Nagai Kafū, Tanizaki commented wistfully: "Such things as psychological description, the expression of emotions and states of consciousness, the attempt to penetrate deep into the interior of a character, have come into fashion only very recently." Often in his own novels Tanizaki preferred to rely on the reader's intuition to fill out a seemingly inadequate characterization. And other major novelists have used similar techniques.

In Kawabata Yasunari's *Snow Country (Yukiguni)* the climactic scene between Shimamura and the geisha Komako turns on a single word: after having affectionately called her "a good girl," and having been obliquely reminded that he once asked her to bring a prostitute for him, Shimamura feels a wave of sensual attraction and calls her "a good woman," which she

correctly and despairingly interprets as marking the limit of his commitment to their love affair. As self-centered as he is, Shimamura soon comes
to realize why his innocent remark provoked an outburst from her, but the
Western reader may well find this a puzzling nuance. Even the Japanese,
though finely attuned to just such faint implications, are often enough
betrayed by their trust in intuitive understanding. For Kawabata, however,
sensitivity to emotional nuance, the frequent misunderstandings that
nevertheless occur, and the resulting possibilities for literary expression—
all this fragile network of communication is at once an invaluable technical resource and a subject that illustrates his recurrent theme of loneliness and human isolation. Instead of analyzing his characters at length, he
prefers to hint at their inner life by noting gestures, fragments of dialogue,
momentary feelings. Thus, in revising the beginning chapter of *Snow
Country* for book publication, Kawabata deleted several paragraphs describing Komako's first impression of Shimamura, her past experience with
men, her present uncertainty—and replaced the whole passage (following
the sentence "She opened his hand, and pressed her cheek against it") by
the single phrase: " 'This remembered me?' " In its context, it is sufficient.

To be sure, such economies are offset by a tendency to extend the context, to add more and more episodes, each brilliantly elliptical and evoca-
tive but joined to the others by the suggestive illogicalities of Japanese
poetry rather than as parts of an architectonic whole. Kawabata's novels
rarely come to a decisive ending—he has the habit of adding episodes
from time to time over the years—and their slow growth often seems to
occur by a process of natural accretion. Like several of his other novels,
Snow Country was originally intended to be a short story. The material
stretched over into a second installment, published the same month (January, 1935) but in a magazine with a slightly later deadline. Further chapters were added—two more toward the end of the year, two in 1936, and
so on—until after numerous extensions and revisions a presumably final
version was published in 1947. This is doubtless an extreme case of dila-
tory lyricism, but even under the journalistic pressure of producing serial
fiction for magazines or newspapers, most Japanese novelists write without
a plan or with only the sketchiest of notes to indicate the way ahead.
Mishima Kukio, though unusual for his careful advance preparation of
materials, has remarked on the pleasurable spontaneity of a serial novel
which has proceeded without plan and has been enriched by unforeseen
complications. In his own work, once he has finished the preliminary
stages and written a novel straight through, he makes it a point to eschew
revision. If few novelists are as close to the traditional *haiku* aesthetic as
Kawabata, or as loath to revise as Mishima, many more share a preference
for lyrical improvisation as a working method.

Early in his career Kawabata wrote a number of very brief tales—minia-
ture *contes* were then in vogue—which he hoped to make the prose equiv-

alent of the Japanese poetic forms. He later called them his "youthful poetry." But he continued to write occasional three- or four-page stories after others had abandoned the genre; some of these remain among his favorite works. Often they recount dreams, hallucinatory fables, curiously enigmatic anecdotes, but even the slightest of his sketches and vignettes convey an emotional state with extraordinary vividness. Imagery of the sort found in *haiku* may provide an essential element. Thus, the "Pomegranates" (*Zakuro*) of the title of a story written in 1943 suggest the complex feelings of a girl toward her mother, her dead father, and her lover who is going off to war. Overnight the pomegranate leaves have fallen, dislodged in a strangely neat circle by a cold late autumn wind, and the suddenly revealed ripe fruit calls to mind the time of year her father had died, as other memories associated with pomegranates awaken a sense of guilt over her mother's empty life and her own secret joy. A tree in the garden or a wide, lonely landscape may be equally effective in expressing the awareness of time, place, and human feelings that is indispensable to the *haiku*.

Again, in *Snow Country* the natural setting not only creates mood and atmosphere but helps to define character. The mountain background, freshly green in spring, darkening in late autumn, then bright in snow, adds to the emotional significance of the work. Sometimes by poignant contrast, it heightens Shimamura's half-bored erotic longing, even his pleasure in Komako and his interest in her friend Yoko, but it also echoes the varying kinds of loneliness that afflict them all. Natural imagery in the *haiku* manner vivifies the foreground as well, with a symbolic relevance to the human situation that goes beyond fragmentary visual metaphor to help compose a harmonious world in which nature is neither adversary nor merely the setting for an unrelated drama. A sensuous, intuitive response to people and places may at times incline the Japanese novelist to create a series of beautiful but static pictures, like the *tableaux vivants* at moments of dramatic tension in the Nō and Kabuki, and to show various facets of his characters as if they had "suddenly and briefly caught his attention, not because of any personal quality they possessed in their own right, but because they seemed at the moment to be such an integral part of the mood of the scene around them." Kawabata in particular often seems to construct even his more dramatic novels by linking one impressionistic scene to the next in the associative manner of *renga* ("linked verse"), the historical precursor of the *haiku*. Lyrical and imagistic, where Tanizaki would be drawn rather to the manner of the mellifluous discursive essay, Kawabata is another of the major Japanese novelists who have mastered Western fictional techniques without abandoning the resources of the native tradition.

Kawabata's career began in the early 1920's, and his writings are often directly influenced by experimental Western fiction. But his most obvious importations—of a "stream of consciousness" style, for instance—are his least successful. Only when an exotic technique has been fully assimilated to the needs of his essentially Japanese art is it adequate to express his own haunting themes of loneliness, the fragility of love, the cold, interstellar distances of withdrawal from human involvements. In the exquisite opening passage of *Snow Country* when Shimamura sees a girl's face reflected against the evening landscape in the window of the train, there is a cinematic movement to the scene—the heart of the passage is a flashback, and the novel advances by moving back and forth in time. But there is also a vision which accommodates surrealist imagery, pointillist detail, unusual camera angles, and the laws of optics to the familiar natural symbolism of the *haiku*:

The light inside the train was not particularly strong, and the reflection was not as clear as it would have been in a mirror. Since there was no glare, Shimamura came to forget that it was a mirror he was looking at. The girl's face seemed to be out in the flow of the evening mountains.

It was then that a light shone in the face. The reflection in the mirror was not strong enough to blot out the light outside, nor was the light strong enough to dim the reflection. The light moved across the face, though not to light it up. It was a distant, cold light. As it sent its small ray through the pupil of the girl's eye, as the eye and light were superimposed one on the other, the eye became a weirdly beautiful bit of phosphorescence on the sea of evening mountains.

Somehow the effect is closer to the vision of a *haiku* poet (such as Issa, who observed "the distant hills mirrored in the eye of the dragonfly") than to Bunuel or Breton.

If Shimamura is a cold, withdrawn figure, one who prefers to witness life through an estranging window, Komako is depicted with all the empathy and mastery of feminine psychology that is characteristic of Kawabata's art. Frustrated women, subtly corrupted or disfigured women, especially very young girls who are destined to unhappiness—these are among the unforgettable portraits in his work. Youth is associated with lost love, with parting, with death. No doubt his elegiac themes may be traced back to his own childhood experience of the early loss of both his parents, followed not long after by the deaths of his grandmother, his only sister, and then the grandfather with whom he lived alone from the age of seven till fourteen. Funerals and separations occur in many of his earliest stories. Yet even his darkest fiction suggests a strongly sensuous response to life. Kawabata's eroticism is as much at conflict with death and decay as Tanizaki's, despite all the differences between them. In *Sleeping Beauty* (*Nemureru bijo*) and other recent works, these related themes become as explicit as in the late novels of Tanizaki. But Kawabata's "sleeping beauties" never awaken—they are heavily drugged young girls placed at the disposal of the old men who visit a special club. The single developed character, a man painfully sensitive to the anomalies of this sad pleasure, is left alone with his sensuous impressions of the girl, with his memories of other women, his dreams and nightmares, and, finally, with death. The novel offers a striking example of severe reduction in fictional paraphernalia, of poetic economy which increases the value of every glimpse into the interior world of a character.

For Kawabata, and also for Tanizaki and other perceptive Japanese novelists, even the microcosm of the family is no longer a secure refuge either from the menacing outer world beyond private experience or from the sorrows, frustrations, and bad dreams of the lonely, labyrinthine inner world. Like most serious novelists since Meiji, they have tried to explore that inner world; they have followed any path, old or new, which promised to lead into it. Gifted younger writers such as Abe Kōbō and Oe Kenzaburō are finding still newer paths, paths that often resemble those of their contemporaries abroad. These novelists are also interested in the larger world of political and social change, if not in the changing conditions of family life. Their journeys into the interior seem rapid, purposeful, and comparatively well-organized—perhaps at the sacrifice of random insight as well as of leisurely grace. But in their work, too, it is possible to discern traditional qualities that mark it unmistakably as Japanese. Fortunately, like the Nō and the *haiku,* the novel in Japan has been strengthened by a long literary tradition of economy, restraint, and poetic sensitivity. Without that source of strength, modern Japanese literature might well have been overrun rather than regenerated to new and vigorous growth by the aimless luxuriant tangle of Western-influenced writing which once seemed likely to obliterate the past.

PART FOUR
The Sense of the Future

19

From the Meiji period on, all Japanese intellectuals were dominated by thoughts of the future. Would Japan adapt with sufficient quickness to the West, avoid the dangers of colonization, keep a sense of its own identity? In the following essay Masao Maruyama analyzes the different responses of three major and representative Japanese intellectuals to the thought of the future.

Fukuzawa, Uchimura, and Okakura: Meiji Intellectuals and Westernization

MASAO MARUYAMA

I

W HEN the names of the three thinkers, Fukuzawa Yukichi 福澤 諭吉, Uchimura Kanzō 內村鑑三 and Okakura Tenshin 岡倉 天心, are cited together, it is difficult to call to mind by direct association some keynote common to them all. For those who know something about them, it may even be natural to sense discord before anything else. Not only were their main spheres of activity different but they were of marked individuality both in their characters and attitudes in life, so that if one compares any two of them, one is immediately struck with certain fundamental differences between them. On closer examination, however, one notices also that contemporary conditions had brought about a whole web of inner mental links of which they themselves were perhaps unaware.

They all sprang from *samurai* families in feudal fiefs whose lords were relative, or in hereditary vassalage, to the Tokugawas: Fukuzawa came from the Nakatsu 中津 domain of Buzen 豊前, Uchimura from the Takasaki 高崎 domain of Jōshū 上州, and Tenshin the Fukui 福井 domain of Echizen 越前. The circumstances where they found themselves were therefore such that, contrary to men from the Satsuma 薩摩 and Chōshū 長州 domains who could triumphantly take the tide of the upheaval, they had to suffer more or less a by-blow from the Rest[o]ration and be tossed about

Masao Maruyama, "Fukuzawa, Uchimura, and Okakura," from *The Developing Economies,* Vol. 4, No. 4, pp. 1–18. Reprinted with permission of the author and the Institute of Developing Economies. Footnotes omitted.

by the waves of the time. In addition, they were all brought up in cities such as Ōsaka 大阪, Edo 江戸, and Yokohama 横濱 where the impact of the "opening of the country" appeared earlier and on a larger scale than elsewhere, and where they were given the opportunity of acquiring excellent ability in foreign languages in their youth. Eventually Uchimura and Tenshin were to make "the Japanese" and "Japanese civilization" known to the West by their equal proficiency in English whereas Fukuzawa transplanted with a surprising skill various categories of western civilization into the context of the Japanese language, all three thereby providing the most excellent cultural bridge between Japan and the West. Again, Fukuzawa made it a principle to remain a non-official civilian all his life, and Uchimura became the most shrewd critic of the Meiji oligarchies following the lèse-majesté affair in which he was involved when he refused to make obeisance before the Imperial Rescript on Education (1891). Tenshin, who stood closest to power among the three, was still to play a role in establishing the first non-official academy of arts in Japan on the occasion of his eviction from office at the Tokyo School of Fine Arts (*Tokyo Bijutsu Gakkō* 東京美術學校). In short, their way of life or thought was attended on by something which had to lead them to swerve from the orthodox pattern of Imperial Japan, and which provided them with the very source of their vitality as thinkers.

Diametrically opposed in their view of religion as they were, Fukuzawa and Uchimura had in their background such important assets in common as the concepts of European civilization of Guizot and Buckle. Further, Tenshin was related to Uchimura in that they both studied in their school days Hegelian philosophy and Darwin's theory of evolution, which were to form a special "compound" deposited in their views of history, though they differed greatly in its practical application. In respect of age, Uchimura was Tenshin's senior by one year, while Fukuzawa was twenty-five or six years older than the two others. The years around 1870 happened to mark a turning point of history on the quickly revolving stage of world affairs, and it was no wonder that that disparity in generation should have caused a substantial difference in the manner in which these three were to comply with "modernity." Nevertheless, both Uchimura and Tenshin grew to maturity by fully absorbing the lively spirit of enlightenment immediately following the Rest[o]ration, and the hoard of nutriment thus built up in their youth was never exhausted even in the close of their days. Not to speak of Fukuzawa, for Uchimura, too, at least in the period when he was most active in intellectual life through the *Yorodzu Chōhō* 萬朝報, "History is the record of progress of mankind," and the progress of civilization was another word for the development of the nation. Even Tenshin, who professed to be a traditionalist, spoke of "the lively individualism of the Meiji era" at the same time, and did not lose sight of a possibility open to civilization when he said, "Japan in the future will not be what she was in the past. The Japan of today, at a strategic point of world affairs, should not be regarded in the same light as during the 300 years of seclusion. In meeting trade demands from abroad, she must be informed of conditions and life in foreign countries, and keep pace with the times." Tenshin's romantic sense of history had not yet broken off its original relations with the enlightened spirit of freedom and progress.

As intellectuals educated in international culture, none of these three thinkers was content to be a mere mediator of enlightenment between East and West. They inseparably united *their* mission in Japan with *Japan's* mission in the world and persistently held fast to that sense of "calling" all their life. A profound feeling of crisis over the inevitable effects of the "opening of the country" and a pathetic aspiration for the independence and security of Japan were both leading motivations behind their expression of views on intellectual problems. Fukuzawa, who was acknowledged both by himself and by others to be one of the bitterest critics of Confucian culture, wrote that "we cannot discuss the matter of civilization before the establishment of a Japanese state and a Japanese people"; preferred patriotism which he took upon himself to call "prejudice" as against the universalist corollary of the concepts of *tenchi no kōdō* 天地の公道 (universal justice) or *benri* 便利 (utility); and found invaluable resources for national independence in *yasegaman no seishin* 痩我慢の精神 (the spirit of grin and bear—an aspect of the traditional samurai ethos—which may seem "almost childish from the point of view of cool calculation." On the other hand, the passionate glorification of Tenshin of Asian identity and tradition was simultaneously supported by his universal idea of mankind. Tenshin said, "Art is a universal possession which has nothing to do with discrimination between East and West. Sectionalism is the source of abuses," and "we can be more human only by becoming more universal." Fukuzawa, a pilot of the western civilization, had written, in 1875, "What is the plight of the countries of the East and of the islands of Oceania? Is there any country within reach of the hands of the Westerners which secures its national rights and interests and maintains real independence? Look at Persia, India, Siam, Luzon, and Java. . . . What does all the talk of 'civilizing these areas' really mean? It means simply that the natives of the islands have come to abstain from cannibalism and have accommodated themselves to slavery in the service of the white men. . . . As I see the future, even the Chinese Empire is likely to become little more than a garden for the Europeans." His voice of deep regret was soon to resound in India and America through Tenshin's agitating cry of "The Awakening of the East" and also through Uchimura's scathing denunciation of Imperialism.

Furthermore, they were unanimous in their criticism of the superficial appearances of enlightenment in the period following the Rest[o]ration. It is true that when they pitted against this "the immanent spirit of civilization" (Fukuzawa) or "realization of the self within" (Tenshin), their central ideas were different from each other. But, to cite one example, Fukuzawa's scathing criticism of "ready credence and ready doubt" peculiar to "reformers" was repeated by the two others almost in the same context. And, in the case of these thinkers, Japan's self-assertion *towards* the world was restrained by their sense of Japan's position *in* the world. What was to be the manner of Japan's *contribution* to the world? This was the question they had to ask in common out of their "sense of mission" and also it was a corollary of the idea of "independence." Needless to say, these thinkers' concern stands out in sharp contrast with the "auto-catalytic" concept of the Japanese Empire's mission as noted among the later expansionists.

Fukuzawa, Tenshin, and Uchimura devoted themselves respectively to the causes of "exhortation" to learning and education, developing art in Japan and "Japanizing" Christianity, all expecting that the future of their fatherland would lie in these directions. However, Fukuzawa was not entirely a "professional scholar," Tenshin not a mere "art critic," nor Uchimura but a "preacher of religion." Rather they were all "critics of civilization" who deliberately rejected the confines of professionalism. In their respective spheres of learning, art, and religion, they brought their themes to a broader scope of cultural correlation and probed deeply into problems of the mental structure of the Japanese people. Furthermore, they were eventually led to attack their common problem of how to fight hard against conventional formalism in their respective fields and push forward the "reformation" of learning, art, and religion. It is well known that in his *Nihon Bunmei no Yurai* 日本文明の由來 (The Origins of Japanese Civilization), Fukuzawa scathingly criticized the convention of learning as a pastime and the exclusionism of scholars under the old régime. Even stronger emphasis may be laid on the point that Fukuzawa never advocated *jitsugaku* 實學 (practical learning) in the sense of rejecting futile studies "of little practical use"—as was noted of Confucian and Shingaku 心學 learning in the Tokugawa period—nor was his *jitsugaku* to be regarded as a mere continuation of the traditional idea of uniting study and life. According to Fukuzawa, the guild-man or craftsman mentality of scholars who "are confined in a cage called government, which they regard as the cosmos for them to live in, and who agonize in that small cosmos" was nothing but another expression of the lack of independence in learning. The crucial idea of his *jitsugaku* was that learning could not have the effect of improving actual life unless it is solely based on "truth" and "principles," thereby freed from the vulgar type of artisan-cult, meaning conformity to the established social relations.

The direction in which Tenshin sought to reform Japanese fine arts is most clearly shown in his lecture given at the Tokyo School of Fine Arts in 1891. Here he rejected the idea of "art for art's sake" when he said, "If on earth the sole aim of art is to give aesthetic pleasure to human minds and not to seek *jitsuyō* 實用 (practical use), then it will be no more than a craft after all. I cannot side with such arguments. Unless a work of art conveys beauty in itself and is simultaneously accompanied by the highest levels of contemporary literature and religion, it cannot be taken as a genuine one." What he meant here by *jitsuyō* is an opposite to the artisan-cult in the name of "art for art's sake." This flow of ideas, in a sense, finds an echo in Uchimura's view of religion, as well as having something in common with his view of literature. This of course does not mean that Uchimura rejected a "religion for religion's sake" in the sense parallel to art for art's sake. But when he pitted the relentless principles of "non-church" against the existing Christian orders, which seemed to rest complacent with the self-sufficiency of their tradition and systems, was it not that what he called the Second Reformation was designed to criticize the "church for the church's sake"? Uchimura repeatedly pointed out that the moment the absolute of religion transforms itself into that of the church, on the one hand, it begins to attain the level of an entrenched religion which eventually takes the course of compromising with and following such secular authorities as power and wealth, and on the other, finds expression in the hypocritical missionary work designed to favour uncivilized heathen countries with the opportunity of benefiting from "civilization." The acceptance of the church as the supreme authority only changes clergymen into craftsmen, whereas the purer the belief in the Gospel is, the more effective is the "practice" of religion in the proper sense of the word —this was the conviction that Uchimura gained under the intellectual influence of Calvinism and through his personal observation of the facts about Japanese and foreign missionaries in Meiji Japan. The foregoing may have brought to light the fact that there was a certain affinity between these thinkers concerning the manner in which they responded to the prevailing trends in their respective spheres of activity and in which they set forth their respective problems.

II

There are, then, between these three men, with their common background as contemporaries, more parallel factors than might be casually imagined. But one cannot shut one's eyes to an immense cleavage which separates them in individuality, thought, and life. Since this occasion does not allow me to compare them inclusively on such differences, I will try below to focus attention, by citing some examples, on a dimension where the lines of their thought met with one another, thereby groping for a few clues towards an understanding of how the initial differences in their mental reactions eventually led to a great divergence of views in the context of intellectual history.

As already stated, they became reformers in their respective spheres through the "exhortation" to learning, art, and religion, and by uniting their own "mission" with that of Japan. The very sense of mission was, in its inner structure, fundamentally conditioned by their innate dispositions and original spheres of activity, a fact which was to leave a particular mark on the nature of the "nationalism" of the three. Fukuzawa's way of thinking was thoroughly pragmatic concerning his sense of mission, too. His decision on which particular problem should be most urgently attacked was determined first and foremost by consideration of current circumstances. In a traditional community or in a status society, the field of human behaviour is fixed, and no need to judge the existing conditions is keenly felt. Depending on what one is—a feudal lord, a peasant, or a city commoner—what one is to do is "automatically" decided. Human relations usually connoted in a few norms such as the Five Human Relations and Five Virtues of Confucianism or the Ten Commandments of Christianity. As civilizations grow, with human relations getting more complicated internally and internationally and with social functions diversified the situational changes intensify and the pattern of behaviour becomes correspondingly versatile. As the old social status ceases to exist and the "innate criteria" for discriminating men and things lose their authority, men must be judged by "works," or by what they do rather than what they are. In the past it could suffice to make distinction between the good and the bad, but now the actual situations are such that "the good with virtues do not always do good: the bad without virtues do not always do bad." In addition, as there emerge more "problems" to solve, there will be the need to establish an order of priority among them and make choices between relative values. Here involved is the problm of how to judge existing conditions. Thus a matter which was once decided easily by customs, "intuition" or traditional norms, is brought to a pass where only intellectual cognition will do. Such was the general trend Fukuzawa himself perceived in civilization. He writes, "At this point, the duty of the Japanese is nothing but to preserve the national polity (Kokutai). What is meant by preserving the national polity is not to lose our sovereignty. If we would not lose our sovereignty, we have to develop the intellect of the people . . . . . In the course of developing the intellect, the most urgent thing is to adopt the *spirit* of civilization originating in the West and defy completely the addiction to old customs." This famous declaration of Fukuzawa, implying both the immediate task for Japan as a nation which had just joined the international community and his own immediate mission in Japan, was itself based on his consideration of existing conditions. Fukuzawa represented in his time a rare case of a mind awakened to his "role." His views and choice were, in many cases, decided, through exceedingly cool judgment as to what aspect of a matter needed to be emphasized in a particular situation. When it was charged that in *Gakumon no Susume,* Part VII, he had equated the loyalty to his master of a petty servant in a merchant house to the devotion of the great 14th century warrior, Kusunoki Masashige 楠木正成, to the Emperor (the well-known Nankō-Gonsuke controversies), Fukuzawa wrote in his vindication contributed to the *Chōya Shimbun* 朝野新聞 under the pen name of Gokurō Semban, "They [i. e., his opponents] confuse one thing with another by making conjectures and suppositions. For they assume that equality of rights for the people derives from republicanism, republicanism from Christianity, and Christianity is a western teaching. Thus they are indignant, presuming that because Fukuzawa is a scholar of western learning his theory of popular rights is certainly tantamount to Christianity and republicanism." In answer to such a dogmatic assumption arising from the habit of "seeing things with one eye closed," he countered with a few lines of allegory which read, "A wine merchant is not always a drinker, a cake dealer does not always go in search of sweets. You should not make hasty judgment on a dealer's taste by what he sells in his shop." This allegory not only gives an adept contrast of the conception of "emanation" and that of "function," but seems to symbolize the basic motive in Fukuzawa's sense of mission more clearly than he was aware. At the same time, there is no more denying that an over-all understanding of Fukuzawa's thought has been made very difficult by the fact that the goods to be produced and sold at his "shop," the products of his literary work, were determined not always by what his "natural" inclination would dictate to him but primarily by current "demand," or by what he judged to be such. In this regard, there may be need to entertain some doubt from the first as to the extent to which even his "Autobiography" may represent his self-expression as opposed to "acting," originating in his sense of a "role" to play. Relevant to his point is the interlocking of rational moments with irrational ones in Fukuzawa's thought. Deep in his heart and blood was the old *samurai* spirit. However, just because he sought his primary mission in playing the role of a preacher of "the spirit of civilization," Fukuzawa generally forbade himself to give an intellectual expression to and make "shipment" of such *samurai* sentiments. Had he been successful in completely excluding his natural likes and dislikes from the expression of his views and in thus controlling every bit of his speech and behaviour in consideration of his "role," something of an insufferable affectation would have pervaded his work. If Fukuzawa is free from such an impression, would not the secret lie in his occasional outbursts of irrationality, as, for example, in his tirades against Katsu 勝海舟 and Enomoto 榎本武揚?

When Uchimura was in the extreme of sorrow and solitude following his dismissal from the teaching post at the First Higher School (*Daiichi Kōtō Chūgakkō* 第一高等中學校) and the almost simultaneous loss of his wife, he wrote to Struthers, an American friend of his, as follows: "Yet I must understand Liberty and freedom of conscience was not ever

bought in any country without some such trials among some of her devoted children, and must I not be thankful that God hath chosen me to
bear such burdens!"

His sense of mission represents a type closest to that of a "rational and
ethical prophet" in the terminology of Max Weber. His ardent love of
the two J's, namely, Jesus and Japan, and the confidence with which he
stood against all kinds of persecution, originated not in any belief in the
oneness of the ego and the ultimate, as in the case of the "exemplary
prophet" or of a romantic pantheist, but exclusively in his awareness of
himself as being a very tiny, faithful servant of God. Compared with
Fukuzawa, whose pragmatism led him to emphasize "working" rather than
"being," Uchimura had to ask himself constantly "what is to be done" just
because he found his mission in serving as a "tool" to realize the absolute
will of God. He was thus to be a "patriotic Christian of the extreme left,"
who was ready to fight against the drift of *denationalizing influences.*"
This "leftmost inclination" has the same inner motivation as that type of
radicalism that inevitably brought the prophets of ancient Israel, who were
breaking down the stereotyped rituals and informing it with a new life,
into sharp opposition to the hierocracy as the day-to-day executors of
feasts and rites and, for that reason, led them to cut off the gradation of
values from established gradation of ranks in society, thus unleashing the
potential energies of the masses of "patriotism," both internal and external,
would be inconceivable without reversing the prevailing concept of patriotism. In the internal sense, it was to shape into populism (*heimin-shugi*
平民主義) and, in the external sense, into the absolute defiance of war
and armament. According to Uchimura, "The Upper Ten Thousand of
Japanese society is perhaps the *lowest* Ten Thousand of Japanese morality," while the commoners were no doubt "the born aristocracy of the
country." Also, war and territorial expansion meant to him the road to
the fall rather than the rise of the country. When he says "skepticism is
needed for faith and destruction for construction" or "the world makes
progress through antagonism and opposition," his conception is quite
similar to that of Fukuzawa, who writes: "There is much falsehood in
the world of faith: much truth in the world of scepticism," or "the spirit
of freedom exists only where there are conflicts and controversies."
Fukuzawa wrote "the authority of the bureaucratic *samurai* has a certain
elastic property just like a rubber ball . . . it is inclined to expand greatly
in the face of the lower [i.e., weaker] orders and to contract with alacrity
before the upper [i.e., stronger]." Thus he formulated the structure of
Japanese society in the expression "preponderance of power" Uchimura,
too, regarded Japanese society as an "inverted pyramid society" where the
center of gravity is at the upper part and where "we are bound upwards,
and free downwards." Both saw individual freedom and spiritual independence as internally related to national independence. Here noticeable is

the influence of their common mental furniture already mentioned, provided by Buckle and Guizot. Concerning, however, their relationship to the "world" within which they found themselves, what mattered to Fukuzawa was his pragmatic adaptation to it; while for Uchimura who "stood only with God," the relationship implied an absolute dichotomy in terms of what was "alltäglich" and what was "ausseralltäglich." It was on this point that Uchimura was to diverge from Fukuzawa, and the difference between the two was bound to center on the problem of how to deal with the "preponderance of power,"; Fukuzawa sought an equilibrium of values, while Uchimura a reversal of them. It was a contrast between Fukuzawa's idea of populism with the "middle classes" as its nucleus and Uchimura's which was to be supported by the "lower-class (*karyū* 下流) Japanese"; and between the former's hopes of the continuous progress of Japan and the latter's expectations of a discontinuous or rather eschatological "rise of the nation." When in the face of an imminent partition of Asia by European imperialist powers Japan's defense could hardly be told from her expansion, Fukuzawa's conception of preferentially choosing the most urgent task under existing conditions led him to the same conclusion that Tenshin reached, that "if we do not wish to be crushed under the wheels of the Juggernaut, we have to get on it." Uchimura's sense of mission was so categorical that he was not affected by situational thinking and continued to predict and warn against a catastrophe which would fall on Japan if she should "get on the Juggernaut." It must be remembered, however, that his denunciation of authorities and the ruling groups, even in the first decade of this century when it was most violent, remained "extreme leftist" from an entirely transcendental point of view, so that his radicalism was derived from an *anti*-political standpoint. There is no wonder in this connexion that as the historical course of Japan and the world got far away from his wishes and expectations, the view of history based on civilization and progress which he entertained in his youth receded, and instead the moment of religious eschatology came further to the fore.

In 1892 when he wrote on "Nihon-koku no Tenshoku 日本國の天職 (The Mission of Japan)" for the *Rikugō Zasshi* 六合雜誌, Uchimura could be so optimistic as to expect Japan to play the role of a mediator who would make "mechanistic Europe" known to "idealistic Asia" and open up the doors of the conservative East by way of the progressive West. In 1924, when he wrote once again on the same theme, however, he sought Japan's future solely in rehabilitating Christianity which had been deserted by and lost from the whole world. Japan would not accomplish this mission and thus rise as a nation in the true sense until she "discards her position as a first-class power, even if she does not cease to exist as an empire." Here the spiritual renovation of Christianity and the reversed meaning of the "rise as a nation" remained as firmly combined as they were in the third decade of Meiji. Nevertheless, it cannot be denied that the politico-social aspect of Uchimura's patriotism had become remarkably colourless. In other words, Uchimura's sense of mission disclosed its nature where it shifted from *anti*-political activity to *non*-political resignation, leaving his *religious* "radicalism" alone to get steadily accelerated.

If it can be said that Fukuzawa was an all-out prose-writing mind, and Uchimura a poet in spite of himself, Tenshin was certainly a poet to the bottom of his heart both in attitude to life and mode of thinking. Still retaining some of the spirit of enlightenment, his nationalism was deeply permeated with romantic sentiments. Furthermore, it clearly shows a pitfall peculiar to the theory of political romanticism.

Underlying his sense of mission and Asianism was an aesthetic and hence contemplative character. Like his contemporary, Uchimura, Tenshin, too, contrasted the "idealistic" East with the "mechanistic" West. While Uchimura's "ideals of the East" meant, more than anything else, religious values including Christianity itself, Tenshin's "ideals" had in their core the aesthetic. Of course he did not talk about oriental art in a sense opposed to religion. Rather Tenshin laid emphasis on the religious nature of art in the East. Important here, however, is the fact that his very concept of religion is permeated with aesthetic values. When he characterized the East by "love for the ultimate and universal," the ultimate really meant *advaita* (state of undividedness) where a fundamental breach of ego from non-ego was not known.

Contrary to the ethics of the prophets and Calvinists who seek to "resist the world" by taking an active part 'in the world" to realize the divine will therein, ideals here mean a state where one, remaining in the world, transcends it by uniting oneself with the cosmos through meditation and ecstasy. There is, in this sense, only a hairbreadth between mysticism and aestheticism. This difference in world-views was destined to find expression in the diametrically opposed ways in which Uchimura and Tenshin interpreted "the modern scientific method." It implies much more than the apparent fact that the former was a fishery scientist by training, while the latter was an artist.

Originally, romanticism was born where minds awakened to the ego by the French Revolution but disillusioned at what it actually accomplished sought a flight into the arena of history and recovered from the —actual or imaginal—loss of ego-consciousness through idealizing past times or figures. If such a recovery is sought in a flight of mind into the world of history, then history must be something that gives, among other things, a sense of security to the ego. This could be given by great personalities of the past, on the one hand, and by some "spirit" continuing throughout the changing phases of history, on the other. The romanticist *chooses* such personalities or spirit out of history. It is *by* his present self and *from* his present position that the choice is made. In so far as this is the case, it can

be said that the "spirit" of romanticism has two vehement drives contradicting each other, one seeking to be emancipated from historical conditions
and the other aspiring to become one with the historical past through
personal experience. Such a passionate champion of the history and tradition of the East and Asia as he was, Tenshin was at one vigilant against
allowing "our historical sympathy to override our aesthetic discrimination,"
and maintained "art is of value to the extent that it speaks to us" and "it
is indeed a shame that despite all our rhapsodies about the ancients we
pay so little attention to our own possibilities." The intellectual structure of
a romanticist, however, has another aspect: two such drives in his self are
not felt in a clear-cut contradiction or opposition but left to fuse into an
indistinct and unqualified sense of freedom. This is because the romanticist
idealizes history above all through rediscovery of "beauty" in the past.
Aesthetic evaluation is bound to depend more on direct sensibility than on
rational and ethical judgments. Therefore, the "choice" from history depends all the more on subjective likes and dislikes. Such tendencies exactly
fit the romantic spirit which enjoys the "unshackled" self in defiance of
rational or ethical norms. So respect for the givenness of history and an
arbitrary choice *from* history would seem to fuse without contradicting
each other. Herein originated the irony that, while attacking the non-
historicity of the spirit of the Enlightenment, romanticists often coined
from historical data conceptions of a "national spirit" or "national character,"—by far less historical than the frameworks employed by the Enlightenment thinkers.

   How did Tenshin unite his individualistic idea of freedom with his
nationalism? It has already been mentioned that he found the driving
force of progress in the "realization of the self within" and pitted it against
the external influence of westernization. Fukuzawa, Uchimura and, as is
well known, Natsume Sōseki 夏目漱石, too, presented this question in
the same manner. But Tenshin diverged from them where his assertion
of emanation from within is connected with the organistic conception common to romantic thinking as apparent in his words, "No tree can be
greater than the energy that is in the seed." For since spontaneity and
creativity are presented here as the revelation of what has been originally
immanent, not as dynamic interaction with the environment, the "Ideals
of the East" have to be sought for exclusively in the historical past *prior*
to "the impact of modern times." Thus, while willingly admitting that
modern times for the first time brought about the concept of individual
freedom, Tenshin praises the Eastern freedom of living under the roof of
clouds and sleeping on the bed of mountains as representing a higher level
of values than the European based on "that crude notion of personal
rights." The freedom of self-realization is channelled into the Eastern
"spirit" of becoming one with the Universal, losing almost all its historical
character. Furthermore, when he sees the glory of Asia in "that harmony

that brings together emperor and peasant" and "that sublime intuition of oneness," and also when he praises the Meiji Restoration solely from the viewpoint that "high and low became one in the great new energy," it is undispuatble that the joint current of organistic thinking and the aesthetic view of history should have overflown into the realm of politics only to conceal the cleavage between social classes and to beautify the stagnant polity. Is it simply due to the non-political mind of an artist that Tenshin's nationalism, compared with Fukuzawa's and Uchimura's, was noticeably lacking in criticism of the dominant state system? In fact, a passage from "The Ideals of the East" reads, "In spite of political squabbles—natural-unnatural children of a constitutional system such as was freely bestowed by the monarch in 1892—a word from the throne will still conciliate the Government and Opposition." What a contrast is this to Uchimura, who writes, "Rightly understood, the Japanese parliament can be no more than a body of advisers. It can scarcely be called a parliament, therefore—a parliament that expresses the will of the people, *against* the will of the sovereign if need be." (emphasis as in original). If underlying Fukuzawa's thinking was pluralistic equilibrium and Uchimura's were opposition and tenson, Tenshin's catch phrases were always harmony, oneness, and "*advaita.*" "The true infinity is the circle, not the extended line. Every organism implies a subordination of parts to a whole. Real equality lies in the due fulfilment of the respective function of each part." Tenshin understood Hegelian dialectics simply in terms of the organic theory. Nevertheless, there was a factor of consistent conflict in Tenshin's thought, too. That is, a conflict between European "science" and Asian "ideals" or art. The crucial problem in his view of "Western encroachment" was that the beautiful was sacrificed to "system," "division," and "classification." When he pointed out vulgarism in taste and standardization of individuality as resultant from industrialization and mass democracy and also a strange alliance of Christianity and torpedoes, his criticism of modern times was certainly penetrating. Such criticism was emotionally exalted through the "disintegration of concepts" particular to romanticism. Consequently Asia or Japan was, on the one hand, to be denied any sign of internal split because of such ideals as "harmony" and "non-duality," and, on the other, to be driven into a categorical opposition to the external, i.e., the Western world. The latter aspect is symbolized by putting "art" and "science" in an antithetical relationship. Needless to say, Tenshin should be "rehabilitated" from the pulpit where he was thrust up by fascists in later years as "the prophet of the New Order in Greater East Asia," and it is not difficult to do so. Nevertheless, the moment the conception of development "emanating from within Asia" became connected with the formula of confrontation with modern Europe, Tenshin's view of his mission, whether or not he was aware, had crossed the Rubicon at a fatal point.

III

Although the structures of thought in these three thinkers' sense of mission show patterns typically different from each other, invariably underlying them was an infinite confidence in the future of Japan and the Japanese, based on the energies unleashed in the early Meiji years. This was the case even with Uchimura, a prophet of national collapse. Such confidence, constantly mixed with their grave worries about existing conditions and their sense of almost hopeless difficulty in solving the "problems" facing them, always made their patriotic appeals resound simultaneously in major and minor modes and thus, along with their unique styles of writing, would captivate the audience with fascinating allurements. Probably relevant to this may be the strange unanimity in paradoxes or ironic expressions which everywhere attend on their voice in society. Yet the three are divided again on the internal structure of paradoxes or ironies. For instance, Fukuzawa wrote that in terms of checks and balances between such values as power, wealth and respect, the Tokugawa period enjoyed greater freedom than the Meiji period, or that "priests, having emerged from the secular, are often more secular than the secular." Underlying these propositions was his own judgment on the situation of contemporary Japan, that "the people's minds in Japan are liable to be one-sided. . . . They are too much prejudiced towards their likes and opposed to their dislikes. . . . They seem to run in one direction along a straight road which abruptly discontinues without leaving them even a little room for a nimble adaptation." Thus he sought to apply his "tactical" consideration for the purpose of undoing such a "stiff pattern of thinking" (*wakudeki* 惑溺) as seen above. In contrast, the paradoxes in Uchimura's writings sound like something in the nature of the groans a prophet would heave at the climax of despair and indignation, and therefore involve virtually no factor of "play" seeking. For instance, he writes: "I dislike superstitions. Superstitions are, however, by far more amiable than the Christianity of modern men. The superstitions are at least sincere and serious, and differ fundamentally from the religion of modern men, which is a kind of hobby."

Compared with this, Tenshin's remarks are more of an irony than a paradox, when he writes:

"He [the average Westerner] was wont to regard Japan as barbarous while she indulged in the gentle arts of peace: he calls her civilised since she began to commit wholesale slaughter on Manchurian battlefields."

The irony here is typical of a romanticist who remains betwixt decadence and strain. The differences in "philosophy" between the three are also revealed in this respect, and yet it remains worth noticing that each of them, out of the profound sense of crisis, irresistibly turned to paradoxes and ironies for a remedy. Needless to say, they come under the category of men different from that of mere "paradox-lovers" who proudly sport their talent.

Fukuzawa's motto of "independence and self-respect" represented the creed or attitude in real life that in a sense applied also to Tenshin and Uchimura. At the same time, the three had a savour of the frankness and innocence of children in their manner: instead of adopting a dignified pose, they were unreserved in disclosing their weaknesses to others. This aspect of character of Fukuzawa and Tenshin is relatively well known. But the same can be noted of Uchimura who lived with the unshakable confidence that reminds one of a phrase of Mencius: "I dare to go my way even in spite of an enemy of tens of thousands of men" and who boasted of "being a son of a *samurai*." For instance, learning that Nakae Chōmin 中江兆民 had started writing his *Ichinen Yūhàn* 一年有半 (One Year and a Half) on hearing the doctor's pronouncement of the time of his death, Uchimura is said to have told Narusawa Reisen 成澤玲川 "I could stand that by no means. If my doom were pronounced like that by the doctor, I would weep the whole night away and pray." How Fukuzawa was uncritically pleased at the victory in the Sino-Japanese War has been described in his "Autobiography" (*Fukuō Jiden* 福翁自傳), and this is not exactly surprising. One should certainly have been surprised at the contrast in the behaviour of Uchimura who had been so passionately crying against war before and just after the Russo-Japanese War broke out but who, on hearing the news of the great naval victory at Port Arthur, expressed his delight in a letter to Yamagata Isoo 山縣五十雄 saying: "I gave three loud 'Teikoku banzai' (Three cheers for the Empire!) which could be heard throughout all my whole neighbourhood." To say that he, too, was after all a Meiji personality does not explain everything. Towards the end of his life, Uchimura wrote in an article "Self-Contradictions":

"Said Walt Whitman: 'I have self-contradictions, because I am large,' and God the Largest is the most self-contradictory of all beings. He loves, He hates. He is love itself, and a consuming fire at the same time. And His true children are always like Him. Paul, Luther, Cromwell,—what combinations of self-contradictions, of mother-loves and father-angers."

These words may be taken as an unrequested self-revelation. If such was the case even with Uchimura, it is no doubt easy to pick out a good many contradictory propositions from Fukuzawa who always spoke in consideration of particular circumstances and from Tenshin, a romantic poet. However, as a man has little personal attraction if he is completely guarded against getting out of himself, a system of thought which is constructed in perfect order like a textbook of formal logic is not always high in value as *thought*. On the other hand, a mere promiscuous collection of casual ideas, no matter how novel these may be, will not produce an original thinker. The views and behavior of these three have some basic tone which resounds persistently throughout their writing, despite all their contradictions. Or rather, something that is basic in them gives those contradictions a refreshing vitality and dynamism. Is this not the hallmark of a thinker of marked individuality? The thought that is most unique to the point of including in it the most universal is indeed worth studying. It is, at the same time, a form of thought not easy to "learn." No wonder it is often from among epigones of the thinker who really deserves the name that a thought-peddler who has the greatest smack of a thinker comes.

"*Spricht* die Seele, ach, spricht die *Seele* nicht mehr," said Friedrich Schiller. The moment thought leaves the flesh and blood of the thinker to become an "objective figure," it begins to go all by itself. When it gets into the hands of an epigone to be praised and even "worshipped," its original, internal tension is relaxed, diversity is polished into smoothness and lively contradictions are unified or inherited only partially with the dynamism therein replaced by coagulation. Like Uchimura, who said in his posthumous manuscripts, "I am not the non-churchmen now in fashion." Fukuzawa or Tenshin, had they been alive during and after the Second World War, would have entertained the same emotion, with indignation and also with a tincture of resignation, about the Fukuzawa-ism or Tenshin-ism "now in fashion." The well known lamentation of Karl Marx—"*je ne suis pas Marxist*"—may therefore be a murmur eminently adaptable to the lips of any thinker who has witnessed his thought irresistably borne off on the great sea of history.

20

The Japanese have often tried to use terms such as fate and destiny to explain social and human affairs. Are the Japanese merely fatalistic? If so, how have they so successfully dealt with sudden change? In the following essay David Plath shows that the Japanese belief in fate is not at all incompatible with careful planning, responsibility, and optimism.

Japan and the Ethics of Fatalism

DAVID W. PLATH

JAPAN IS DIFFERENT

WHEN he pronounces on Asia the cautious scholar adds, "But Japan is different." Even the earliest observers from the West, who reached Japan in the sixteenth and seventeenth centuries, often found that the Japanese were unlike other Asians they had encountered *en route*. And I have overheard colleagues say that Japan is not really even 'Asian' except for obvious but trivial matters of geography. The pattern of Japanese history sometimes is claimed to be more European than Asian. And Wittfogel as chief architect of the theory of Oriental Despotism agrees that although "traditional Japan was more than Western feudalism with wet feet," nevertheless its "quasi-Oriental trends" did not result in a hydro-despotic state.

The same applies to Asian Fatalism. If it means some oriental despotism of the mental canals, that can always regenerate but never outgrow itself and become modern, then Japan seems different. This was recognized recently by participants in the 1963 Conference on Cultural Motivations to Progress in South and Southeast Asia. A "fate-dominated mentality," says the conference report, is part of an Asian heritage that may hinder "modernization of the soul" in Filipinos, Indians, or Muslims—but not in Japanese.

Negatively, then, the Japanese case may help curb our propensities to overgeneralize. Positively, it may spur us to pose the problem in a more productive form. Let us take each of these aspects in turn.

David W. Plath, "Japan and the Ethics of Fatalism," *Anthropological Quarterly*, Vol. 39 (July 1966). Reprinted with permission of the publisher. Footnotes omitted.

Our popular song writers define fatalism succinctly for us as *que sera, sera*: "what will be, will be . . . the future's not ours to see." Our encyclopedists are more prolix. Fatalism, writes one, is "the belief that underlying the events of nature and human life there is an inscrutable and relentless necessity." Others add that this means events occur "independently of the wills and acts of individual men," so that "human efforts cannot alter them."

The rationalist quickly discounts the view because it allows no empirical proof. "There is no test of the basic fatalist hypothesis, that our ends are fated, but only of whether or not we know what is fated," writes one; therefore, "fatalism is either obviously false or else tautological."

And the moralist fears that fatalism is the opiate of the people. At best it tends to "yield a cosy quietism," and at worst it becomes a "doctrine of despair and saps individual responsibility." The Western moralist may claim that such a view of blind cosmic process "has no place in Christianity, but is commonly encountered in Oriental religions." But in any event he will opt for some lesser kind of determinism that can be reconciled with free will, reflective choice, effort-optimism, or ethical responsibility. Let there be some divinity that shapes our ends, he may concede, so long as we have a mandate to do the rough-hewing.

The Japanese have usually sided with the moralists. In Japanese tradition we can readily find terms that can be glossed as fate or destiny, luck or fortune. Most of them have Sino-Buddhist parents, although one is an adoptee from the modern West: *chiyansu* ("chance"). Some of them have been adumbrated in one or another strand of Japan's complex web of great and little traditions. And all of them occur widely in Japanese vocabularies today. But the extent to which they serve as dominant guides to action is debatable.

Perhaps the most prominent of them is the notion of karma (*innen, inga*). In earlier centuries it was woven into many parts of the religious and artistic fabric. The greatest of Japanese novels, the eleventh century *Tale of Genji*, is said to have been written principally to illustrate the workings of karma. And the theme threads through a thousand years of subsequent stories of love and death. To give just one example: In the medieval ballad-drama *Atsumori* the young samurai Atsumori has been thrown down in battle by the veteran foeman Kumagae. Kumagae wants to know whose head it is he is to remove, and pleads:

How well you know the code of the samurai's daring, courtier. We are the sorrowful ones of this world. When we comply with our lord's wishes and endeavor to advance ourselves, we dispute with our parents, war against our sons, and only create wrongs that we did not foresee. This is the custom among the samurai. [The pleasure of entertaining] a guest for a half day under the blossoms, or a friend for an evening while viewing the moon; the enjoyment of a clear wind, of the moon viewed from a tower, of the scattering of blossoms, the falling of leaves—all are decreed, they say, by a marvelous fate that is not an effect of our present life. Although there were many men in this battle, it was I, Kumagae, whom you encountered. Accept this as a fate ordained in a previous life and speak your name. Though I shall take your head, I will pray for your soul in the afterworld.

Lafcadio Hearn, spooking about in his "ghostly Japan," was intrigued by the notion of karma. And he once translated samples of romantic karma tales together with sayings and commentaries on the concept, including one attempt to explain by karma the relatively equal proportions of male and female births in human populations.

Buddhist priests of course helped diffuse the notion, especially after the emergence of popularizing sects in the twelfth century. And in modern times we find versions of karma in the doctrines of several of the revitalizing "new religions," including the powerful and energetic Tenri church. But if the efforts of the priests and poets have brought the idea of karma well inside the mental horizon of most if not all Japanese today, its cognitive salience does not seem strong. I have heard the word uttered numerous times, but almost always in a skeptical or light-hearted way translatable as "well, that's life." And when Dore's interviewers raised the topic with a sample of 100 persons in a Tokyo ward:

A question to the effect, "When people come into this world do you think their future is already fixed, or do you think that depending on a man's will and ability and effort, there's no limit to what he can become?" produced only thirteen responses which spoke of the power of fate, and of these only one used the Buddhist word *innen;* the others, apart from a few sophisticated determinists, used a word (*ummei*) which has become common as a translation of "Fate" in Western romantic literature.

Karma as an ineluctable chain of deeds and their dispositions might easily be used to justify suffering. Extended over many situations, it might yield a cosy quietism, since one's past deeds would already have programmed one's future. But Japanese interpretations of karma have tended to take a different tack. The original Indian vision of continuity through multiple existences is dropped or muted so that karmic results are likely to appear already in this life. And since one can influence karma by right action, one should, energetically. As Anesaki puts it:

Belief in karma is not a blind submission to fate, but a step towards a strenuous effort to overcome selfish motives and to emerge from the vicious narrowness of individual life. . . . Buddhist fatalism, as it is often called, teaches how to renounce self for broader selfhood and a higher cause.

Shinto and Neo-Confucian traditions, as they waxed prominent after the seventeenth century, lent further impetus, and this influence was not limited to the literate elite. For example, the famed Tokugawa "peasant sage" Ninomiya did indeed acknowledge a natural order in the world (borrowing the Confucian *t'ienming*). Some matters, he said, must be left to this "heavenly law." But the burden of his teaching was that "Heaven's will may be influenced by man's industry or indolence." Ninomiya's teachings were widely taken up by Tokugawa farmers, and Bellah has described the emergence of a similar sort of inner-worldly asceticism among Tokugawa townsmen. A high capacity for striving to repay obligations is a core feature of the modern Japanese ethic, as Ruth Benedict made plain in her famous discussion of *on*. Bellah, following Weberian reasoning, points to ethical demands for duty and diligence as having been a major propellant behind Japan's industrial success story. And Caudill and DeVos have shown how these motives are grounded in Japanese family relationships and personality patterns.

Furthermore, this plenitude of *n* Achievement does not seem to have been trammelled by a cognitive Image of Limited Good of the sort Foster ascribes to peasant societies. Confucian and Shinto teachers might not have claimed that goods were unlimited; but they did say that if men were pure and proper, goods probably would be adequate. And Confucianism did offer an image of almost unlimited *moral* good. Right conduct on the part of any man—especially a leader—could elicit right conduct from others in an ever-expanding circle of interactions.

To this earlier sense of moral possibilism the twentieth century Japanese have added ideas of technological, material, medical, and scientific progress. My Japansese friends are as prone as are my American ones to imagine how their grandchildren will look back upon today's vehicles and vaccines as having been ridiculously primitive. The editor of almost any mass-circulation magazine is likely to fill his new year's issue with forecasts of scientific miracles in the offing. And in 1960, I watched Nagano villagers rummage in their attics for old oil lamps and farm tools to put into permanent displays in the local primary school, as homely testimony of how the world has grown better.

Concepts of luck and fortune probably are even more plentiful than those of karma and heaven's will, and they are more visibly in use today. But their history defies summarizing. At any rate, one can certify that Japanese tradition has provided a profusion of luck charms, gods of fortune, forms of divination, systems of geomancy and chronomancy and other mantic techniques. Collectively they are known as Popular Shinto, a residual category set apart from Sectarian Shinto and the now-defunct State Shinto. But popular Shinto never has been synthesized (or "rationalized") into a coherent system on a par with other ideologies of the Japanese great tradition. Many of these ideas and practices have long been shunned as mere superstition, first on Confucian and now on scientific grounds. But they remain widespread (as do, for that matter, their counterparts in the West). Even a Japanese scientist is likely at times to be circumspect about choosing auspicious times or directions, or personal names for his children. Japanese scholars have compiled a mass of material on these topics, but not much of it has been rendered into English. Western observers from Hearn to contemporary ethnographers usually report on some of these practices, but detailed studies such as Norbeck's one on "calamitous years" (*yakudoshi*) still are few.

Shall we consider these fatalistic? I do not see what can be gained by doing so. Popular Shinto provides a magical world view that does assume the existence of beings and forces able to influence human affairs. But man is in a dialog or dialectic with them: he can influence them in turn, or forecast their workings and so attempt to allow for them. This is a form of determinism but it seems no more narrowly fatalistic than does a recognition of the laws of thermodynamics. Both are compatible with planning, optimism, and moral responsibility.

In his *Psychology of the Japanese,* social psychologist Minami Hiroshi twits his countrymen that, "There don't seem to be many civilized peoples who try to explain social and human affairs by words like fate and destiny as much as the Japanese do even today." But after examining in much greater detail an array of evidence of the sorts I have been citing, Minami too recognizes that karma and luck are counterweighed by demands for personal striving. Indeed, any attempt to claim that modern Japan is riddled by fatalism would somehow have to explain away (1) Japan's feat in becoming the first industrialized world power in Afro-Asia; (2) current Japanese effort-optimism and rational planning about birth control at a time when other modern nations still tend to be fatalistic about it; and (3) the fact that while Japanese may not echo *Invictus* and claim captaincy of their souls, the most universal Japanese symbol of manly virtue is the *koi-nobori*, the carp-steamer flown for every boy on Boys' Day, portraying a fish that swims tirelessly—against the current.

FATE AND FORGIVENESS

Concepts of fate and fortune, then, have not prevented progress in at least one Asian nation. For that matter, they apparently have not in other Asian nations either, if I understand rightly what my colleagues in this symposium are saying, contrary to the image of an Asian fate-dominated mentality propounded by the 1963 conference. So in this respect, then, Japan is not so un-Asian after all. Japan's success at modernizing will have to be explained on other grounds. Looking more widely, Niehoff concludes from a survey of fatalism in peasant societies that it is "one of the most insignificant problems that exists in inducing change."

A useful finding, especially for the innovator. I am tempted to press it further and argue that fatalism probably never has been a major problem for mankind. Because, fatalism taken as a dominant and wide-ranging "superordinate meaning system" by a group of people would lead logically to some sort of catalepsy. And that, so far as I know, has never been the usual condition for the majority of any population. Reading Niehoff's essay, one begins to wonder whether fatalism is even in the mind of the peasant as much as in the eye of the frustrated "change-agent." That may sound flippant or ungracious, but it points the way to a restatement of the problem.

Ideas of fate and fortune occur in even the most sophisticated of human actors. It is that most rationalistic of our change-agent subcultures, engineering, that has created Murphy's Law—If anything can go wrong, it will. And Americans in general are prone to label undesired events in industry, or involving their pet item of material culture, the automobile, as "accident." If I am the victim of an accident, I am not to be blamed. If I design a machine that fails to operate as hoped, Murphy's Law excuses this because error is unpredictable.

Accident, destiny, luck and such are called "explanatory devices." But our intellectual bias leads us to concentrate on the cognitive content of the explanation when we should be attending to the process of devising. This process can be seen as part of the more general system of action by which men in any culture allow themselves to be held somehow accountable for the results of their actions, yet fend off a crippling burden of blame for all of life's vicissitudes. As Kumagae puts it to Atsumori: we try our best, but what happens? We "only create wrongs that we did not forsee." If karma is at fault, both Atsumori's failure and Kumagae's transgression can be forgiven.

Fate and fortune need to be seen as part of what Everett Hughes calls the *moral* division of labor: "the processes by which differing moral functions are distributed among the members of society, both as individuals and as kinds or categories of individuals." It involves "both the setting of the boundaries of realms of social behavior and the allocation of responsibility and power over them." Fate and fortune, seen only as abstracted superstition, might seem to be utterly amoral "explanatory devices" that yield to quietism and irresponsibility. The Japanese case suggests instead that these wild-seeming devices are in fact caught and domesticated by a network of ethical demands. And Meyer Fortes has demonstrated in a more limited way how this occurs among the Tallensi, in his remarkable essay on "Oedipus and Job in West African Religion."

Claims of fate or luck, then, are not just specimens of some curious form of belief. They are an essential form of forgiveness, which is an essential attribute of social action. Hannah Arendt has put it this way:

Trespassing is an everyday occurrence which is in the very nature of action's constant establishment of new relationships within a web of relations, and it needs forgiving, dismissing, in order to make it possible for life to go on by constantly releasing men from what they have done unknowingly. Only through this constant mutual release from what they do can men remain free agents. . . . The alternative to forgiveness, but by no means its opposite, is punishment, and both have in common that they attempt to put an end to something that without interference could go on endlessly.

To say that forgiveness is necessary if life is to go on is not to succumb to a quiet functionalism. Claims to fate or luck, like claims to tangible property, must be ratified. Blame, as Hughes puts it, is subject to "jurisdictional disputes." And every culture seems to have its regular procedures for adjudicating such blame and forgiveness, even though many of these are not so highly formalized as are, say, the inquiry commissions of Japan or the U.S. Nor are fate or forgiveness always claimed after the fact. Kumagae pleads in advance, and so do politicians clutching for the robe of Manifest Destiny.

Seen in this way, the question of Asian Fatalism is tied to pan-human questions of how to allocate blame and forgiveness. It also puts the acts of the change-agent into the picture, when he seeks to ascribe his own thwarted hopes to fatalism on the part of others. My colleagues in this symposium argue that Asian Fatalism is no bar to progress. I am suggesting that if we can begin to link concepts of fate to processes of moral allocation, we may begin to be able to show *how* fatalism fails to be a barrier.

21 *Yukio Mishima believed that the future offered no hope. Why, in the face of such extraordinary postwar economic and social achievements, did Mishima become "fed up" with Japan and sacrifice his life in order to wake up his countrymen? In the following selections he explains his disgust with Japan and his belief that Japan could never come to terms with the demands of a truly Japanese revolution and a true Japanese future.*

Tate No Kai and Selected Writings

YUKIO MISHIMA

WHEN I say I am fed up with Japan's postwar hypocrisy I do not mean to equate hypocrisy with pacifism. I simply wonder whether there can be another country in the world where due to the political machinations of both the right and the left, the two words have come to be synonymous. In this country, the way of life that is least dangerous and which gains people's respects is to be slightly to the left, pacifist, some one who rejects violence. That in itself is no cause for rebuke. However, I, myself, feel that intellectuals should not all seek to conform to the above ideal as they have done in the past, rather, their roles as intellectuals are best fulfilled when they entertain doubts about every conformity, and that in itself should imply a more dangerous existence. In the meantime the influence of coffee house revolutionaries has become all pervasive, and has been carried to extremes. Mothers warn of the dangers of giving war toys to children. At school teachers claim giving numbers to children and making them line up in single file is tantamount to military indoctrination, so children loiter about aimlessly like Diet representatives.

Some will say, "If that's the way you feel, since you're an intellectual, shouldn't you fight your battle with words." As a writer, however, I am appalled by the cheapness of words in this country. Words have become as cloudy as imitation marble; they have come to be used to hide arguments behind arguments. They are clever alibis to cover any and all points of view. Just as every pickle in a jar is tinged with the flavor of vinegar, so words have come to be tinged with hypocrisy. The words I

Yukio Mishima, "Tate No Kai and Selected Writings," *The Japan Interpreter,* Vol. 7 (1971), pp. 77–78, 84–85, 85–87. Reprinted with permission of the publisher. Footnotes omitted.

trust as an author are only those words which exist in the perfectly fictional realm of literature, but, as I have said before, I believe that literature is absolutely unrelated to the secular world of conflicts and responsibilities. If this were not so I could not love Japanese literature for all its tradition of magnificence. But if the words of action have all become defiled, then we shall have to rely on a different tradition of Japan. We must revive the warlike spirit of the samurai and take action even in the face of misunderstanding, silently, without words. Deep within me, I've always had the samurai's disdain for self-justification.

It is interesting to note that the concept of an irregular army has completely disappeared in Japan. Since the beginning of our period of modernization in the last century, Japanese armies have in the main been composed of regular troops, and this has not changed with the present Self-Defense Forces. As a result Japan has not seen a militia in over a hundred years. Even during World War II, it was not until two months prior to defeat that the Diet passed the law establishing people's militias (*Kokumin giyūhei hōan*). The Japanese possess no other fighting skills except those learned in a regular army. They are unprepared in the face of the 20th Century's latest form of warfare, namely, guerilla combat.

Nevertheless, everyone I talked to laughed at my ideas of a popular militia, arguing that one just cannot form such groups in Japan. So I declared my determination to set up such an organization. And that is how the "*Tate no kai*" came into being.

In Japan, with the exception of Self-Defense Force veterans, there are no civilian youth outside the *Tate no kai* who have undergone even one month's military training. A similar situation might be unimaginable in European countries. Though we have only 100 members the military value of each is high. Should the necessity arise, each of these men could lead fifty. They are competent in rear guard operations and could engage in guerilla and intelligence activities.

Inferior as I am to the task, I am simply rekindling the dying embers of Japan's warrior spirit.

YANG-MING MYSTIQUE IN JAPANESE POLITICAL ACTION

I think that Yang-ming Thought probably disappeared as a tangible factor in Japan's modern history with the death of General Nogi. After that, action principles of the Yang-ming Thought variety were no longer current among academics but took shape as the basis of the behavioral and attitudinal patterns of the Japanese people and began quietly to run beneath the surface. From the time of the early Shōwa disorders up to the present, deliberate actions of the Japanese have included various important mysterious elements which westerners could not have attempted or even imagined. And in those political actions of the Japanese there can be seen many striking examples completely contrary to reason and intellect, of unaccountable explosions and behavior resorted to with full acknowledgment of its ineffectiveness.

Why do Japanese undertake political action which they know to be futile? Yet if an act has really passed the test of nihilism, then even though totally ineffective, it should surprise no one. I can even predict that from now on, to the extent that the action principles of Yang-ming Thought are imbedded in the Japanese spirit, perplexing political phenomena which are incomprehensible to foreigners will continue to crop up in Japan.

THE JAPANIZATION OF REVOLUTIONARY THOUGHT

The revolutionary movement in Japan has long neglected the question of what a really Japanese revolution is. Revolutionary theories have all been imported and Marxism is an idea which entered Japan on one flank of western modernization. When the backward Asian country called Japan began to modernize through material progress, it was inevitable that an antithetical idea accompanying that modernization would be brought in. Then, to make Marxism Japanese, a painful and bloody effort was needed.

The problem of *tenkō*, once it had filtered foreign ideas through the human body and spirit, brought an important turning point to Japanese intellectuals by asking, in the innermost recesses of their spirit, "What *are* ideas?" I think that if the ideological experience of that *tenkō* had properly penetrated postwar revolutionary thought, the issue of "What is a really Japanese revolution?" truly would have been elucidated.

However, the question of the Japanese incarnation of revolutionary thought was for the time being left behind by the sudden postwar liberation by American democracy. That is, in the return again to ideas of enlightenment and to modernism, a second effort was made to become new apostles of modernization and westernization, which meant starting everything all over again. It was a matter of course that this kind of modernism soon became bankrupt in the postwar period.

The rise of the New Left which followed was the antithesis of orthodox Communist revolutionary thought, which, experiencing such confusion and inconsistency, had become obsolete; but later, in respect to the embodiment of their own ideals, the New Left found themselves in a temporal context where they could not help but depart from the question of Japanization. In Japan, where the bourgeois revolution was completed with the rural land reform, transformation to mass society accompanied the extremely rapid industrialization, and the development of industrialization and urbanization brought a reduction in the rural population. As a result, the indigenous traditional quality of Japanese thought found itself without roots to which it could revert. For the most part, the student movement grew out of the cities, and it was only in the emptiness at the climax of urbanization that it related to the spiritual void of the general masses. But at that point, revolutionary thought had already lost the connection it needed to be restored as something Japanese and indigenous. In the urban emptiness, in internationalism, everything was aimed at standardized freedom of spirit and destruction of taboos in the same way that characterized the student movements in other countries.

In spiritual conditions of this kind, nationalism has always had to wear a deceptive and unwonted mask. The old nationalists, having lost their base, raised cries of empty nationalism, and the new nationalists only used them as a weapon for their own purposes. Revolutionary thought and nationalistic thought, knitted together but mutually in conflict and estranged, never developed sufficient amplitude of action based on real spiritual values to move people's souls.

I am here advocating Yang-ming Thought under just these conditions. While it has not evinced disorders as anticipated, 1970 has been useful in reactivating the same kind of logic that existed under the occupation system. The Liberal Democratic Party and the Communist Party have degenerated into parliamentary parties of the same order, and both of them, knowing the final impossibility of achieving their political aims, devote themselves to tactics calculated to attract the most support from mass society by dealing with immediate problems. This kind of political activity is measured by its mercenary effectiveness in every area, and judgement of results has become the sole standard of political merit. Like the Liberal Democratic Party which was already that way, the Communist Party judges all its day to day political activities by their effectiveness measured by the degree of their penetration into the daily life of the people and by the increase in numbers of votes which it needs to gain political power.

YANG-MING THOUGHT VERSUS WESTERNIZATION

Our modern history has buried many frustrated and tragic aspirations beneath immense waves of modernization. We never really understood the moral basis of the battle when we fought against the west. And only those who adjusted fully to westernization became the leaders of Japan during the modern period. When the Meiji government itself promoted the idea that victory against the west should be gained through westernization, the final vindication in practice was the Russo-Japanese war, and so Japan subsequently proceeded with the fixed notion of overcoming the west by fighting a western war and met with the catastrophe of World War II. But elsewhere, an awakened Asia organized unremitting resistance against westernization in Vietnam and Communist China with characteristically Asian methods. It is of course true that that was facilitated by various advantageous geographical and other regional factors, and if

Japan is to attempt a last resistance against westernization by identifying herself as an integral part of Asia in spite of her insular character which requires that she live by international trade, it shall have to be a spiritual resistance.

Regardless of whether that spiritual resistance will be antiestablishment or not, its ultimate success will depend on eliminating the evils of the westernization which has permeated Japan. Postwar history has tragically demonstrated that the existing forces of reform will be dragged endlessly in the direction of political expediency if they make the wrong compromises with westernization. Must we not rather profoundly revise our quest for a spiritual fighting technique in this conflict between spirit and politics by returning to the forgotten action philosophy of Yang-ming Thought?

In the following essay Professor Yoshiyuki Hagiwara takes a peek at Japan's economic past in order to review the promise of the future. After considering the past, looking at Japan's energetic pursuit of the dream of a "wealthy country and strong defence," seeing its prewar impact upon Asia, Hagiwara attempts to assess the role that Japan will play in the future in Asia and in the world. While not optimistic, he concludes that Japan can both reform itself and prepare to take a cooperative role in the new world of Asia. His belief in a new Japan which will build a new society may be profitably contrasted with Mishima's vision of a Japan turned rotten and decadent by a too obsessive concern with prosperity.

"'Economic Animal' Reconsidered"

YOSHIYUKI HAGIWARA

JAPAN AND ASIA BEFORE THE WAR

THE Meiji Restoration produced the first Asian country to take capitalism for its course of development. Modernization was to be carried out under the banner of *"wakon yōsai"* or "Japanese spirit, Western science." "Japanese spirit" served as the unifying ideology of the so-called familial state, at whose apex was the emperor, while "Western science" became the force behind our rapid industrialization. The two concepts in that slogan, placed side by side, were responsible for attitudes which permitted importation of Western technology *sans* the essence of Western modernity—social relationships based on the idea of individual freedom. For modern Japan, the result was twofold: on the one hand, there developed a too-easy, almost casual, attitude towards technology, while on the other, satisfaction with superficial imitation frustrated the indigenization of Western values. This tendency became a tradition, one which was revitalized in the postwar period. It was used to push economic growth, which, in turn, meant importing advanced technology, and hence it became a serious barrier to technological self-reliance.

The Popular Rights Movement (*Jiyūminken undō*) of the 1880s aimed at modernization based on the philosophy of freedom of the in-

Yoshiyuki Hagiwara, "'Economic Animal' Reconsidered," *The Japan Interpreter*, Vol. 7 (Spring 1971), pp. 138–149. Reprinted with permission of the publisher.

dividual, but the movement could not break down the strength of *wakon yōsai*—the Meiji oligarchy's official ideology that encouraged respect for group and State loyalty rather than individual freedom. The *wakon yōsai* principle was thus allowed to survive throughout Japan's modern century to guide the behavior of the nation. It gave rise to the fixed notion that Japan, the bearer of a unique sense of value called the "Japanese spirit," had only to learn technology from the West, while Asia, which had nothing to offer in the way of technology, should let our nation assume regional leadership.

Thus, our feelings of inferiority towards the countries of the advanced West, compensated by the elevating "Japanese spirit" and concomitant superiority towards the rest of Asia, find their origins in the double-edged concept of *wakon yōsai*. The humiliating awareness that their country lagged far behind in technical and material development, particularly apparent in a weak economy and military establishment, stirred the Meiji leaders to fix a course of rapid economic development with yet another slogan to rally the people: *"fukoku kyōhei"* or "Rich country, strong army." It became the symbol of a successful program carried out through what Professor Ishida Takeshi calls a "loyalty race"; in the name of "Japanese spirit" individual freedom and dignity were minimized, and remained so until World War II. The slogan symbolized Japan's direction until the war, which, in altered form, has continued into the present day.

It is true that history is irrevocable. It is also true that we owe our country's phenomenal progress to the policies designed by the Meiji oligarchs, which we have been discussing. However, if we are willing to acknowledge the negative effects of our rapid development, one of which is our reputation in Asia today as an "economic animal," it is not too late to find a better way to handle ourselves in the future. The fatalistic point of view contends that our country could not have developed without negative aspects. Such an assumption either leads to an affirmation of the status quo, or it gives rise to a demand for revolutionary change. I am of the opinion that we should avoid either extreme, and try to build the future through gradual, steady improvement.

The Meiji leaders in 1871 signed a treaty of commerce with China in accord with its *fukoku kyōhei* policy, thereby taking the first step towards intervention in China. In 1874, the government launched a punitive expedition to Taiwan. Two years later it signed a treaty of commerce with Korea and in 1884 intervened in Korea's internal affairs with the less than skillful assistance of Kim Ok Kyun and his pro-Japanese faction. As a result of the Sino-Japanese War of 1894–1895, victorious Japan gained control of Taiwan. Economic progress was a goal that demanded sacrifices of Japan's farming population, including highly unfavorable market conditions. These could only be compensated for by entering the markets of neighboring Korea and China. While such incursions, invariably military, placed Japan side by side with Europe as an Asian invader, they contributed a great deal to the negative image of Japan building up among other Asian peoples.

Japan's victory over Russia in 1904–1905, seen as Asian Japan defeating European Russia, did much to dispel the illusions of European superiority held by Asians. However, the annexation of Korea in 1910, and the presentation of the Twenty-One Demands to China in 1915 only invited nationalistic reactions against Japan, the "aggressor," in the form of the famous 1919 Independence Day demonstrations in Seoul and the May Fourth Movement in Peking. Japan had sided with the victorious Allies in World War I, and although her activities were confined to the Far East, that war brought her into the ranks of the five great powers. Thàt accomplishment was seen as yet another success of *fukoku kyōhei,* and it gave the ideology even greater strength.

Such clear-cut victories became justification for the rising militarism at home that led to such disasters abroad: the 1928 landing of troops in Shantung; the assassination of Chang Tso-lin in the same year; the Manchurian Incident in 1931; full-scale war with China starting in 1937, and finally, entry into World War II. Thus, we find Japan, beginning in the Meiji period, moving steadily down the road to become a militarily powerful and economically wealthy nation. There grew up various movements along the way to protect the Constitution from rising militarism, and the activities of reform parties to counter the *fukoku kyōhei* policy increased. But in the end, Japan rushed headlong into a major war to conquer the Asian continent and to replace Western colonial power, in order to gain complete control over her economic lifeline.

As one reflects on the seventy or so years between the Restoration and 1945, the slogan, "Catch up with the West, surpass the West!" stands out as an important element in the drive behind Japan's development. How, then, does the development relate to the *dénouement* in her foreign policy—the attempt to place the rest of Asia into the Greater East Asia Co-prosperity Sphere? The answer is simply that Asia had become indispensable as a source of raw materials and a market for domestic manufactured goods; logically, it was necessary to replace the European colonial powers with "allies" clustered about Japan. Because her modernization had been oriented toward westernization and a rejection of solidarity with Asia, it became necessary to restructure relationships within the region in the name of Asian "co-prosperity." How these countries reacted to the projected Co-prosperity Sphere was of course a different matter altogether, especially since all Asia had witnessed the treatment already meted out to China and Korea. There was no difference between Japan's behavior in those countries and the behavior of the other great powers. In most cases, the people probably met the Japanese advances with an ambivalent mixture of love and hate.

JAPAN AND ASIA IN WAR

In 1940 the Japanese army entered northern Indochina. By the end of 1941 it was engaged in battle with U.S. forces in the Pacific, and by 1942, had advanced upon Indonesia, the Philippines, Malaya and Burma. In each country, the Japanese army toppled the Western colonial government and replaced it with its own military rule. In 1945 Japan's plans to dominate Asia ended in defeat. The results of the war were twofold. On the one hand, it terminated European colonialism in Asia, paving the way for independence in these countries. On the other hand, the extremely cruel and oppressive treatment at the hands of the Japanese army whipped up popular outrage and strong anti-Japanese movements. In each case there grew up a center of resistance to Japanese military rule which remained to become the nucleus of one of the many independence movements after the war. In the Philippines, it was formed around the Hukbalahaps; in Burma, around the Anti-Fascist People's Liberation League; in Indonesia, the Anti-Japanese Battalion of Youth and the Anti-Japanese Army of Volunteers; in Malaya, the Communist Party, and in Indochina, around the Labor Party.

As Professor Koentjaraningrat stated, it was the oppressive military police that warped Japan's image. Her troops were especially cruel in their treatment of Overseas Chinese, extending to them sentiments stemming from the ongoing war with China. It was that history that caused Malaysia and Singapore to demand reparations after the war for those who lost their lives in labor battalions. Noma Hiroshi described the Japanese army in his novel, *Zone of Emptiness*, as an organization built upon the repression of human desires. Thus, when the troops were placed in the extreme conditions of war, they reacted by transferring repression to the conquered peoples. If, indeed, the strength of the Japanese army derived from the rechanneled energies of peasants and laborers, impoverished by sacrifices made for the economic power and military might of the nation, the army was in reality a microcosm of contemporary Japanese society. The very fact that the kind and sympathetic Japanese whom Professor Koentjaraningrat described could, in his capacity as *kempei*, become arrogant and cruel reveals a deep contradiction within our society. This problem lies imbedded in the "group-first" principle that underlay *fukoku kyōhei* and it touches on the basic question of what the individual is in Japanese society.

JAPAN AND ASIA IN THE POSTWAR PERIOD

After the defeat, Japan was occupied by the Allied Powers. There followed a period of transition from the old order to the new constitutional system; that interlude saw some far-reaching changes take place, among them the land reform, dissolution of the *zaibatsu,* recognition of labor's right to organize, and the introduction of a democratic form of government. Reforms were carried out on orders of the Occupation authorities, however, and what would otherwise have been truly revolutionary changes were undermined by the lack of any basic change in Japanese values. It is relevant to note that the question of war responsibility was not pursued very far by the people themselves. Prime Minister Prince Higashikuni's urging that *all* Japanese should share that responsibility was not challenged by any of them. Such a process of democratization, like national development under the superficial duality of "Japanese spirit, Western science" of Meiji times, avoided the necessity of understanding or even confronting the values of democracy; it was rather an attempt to build democracy only as a ready system of institutions. Thus, it became quite simple for yesterday's militarist to be today's democrat.

On the international level, as a result of the Truman Doctrine and the Marshall Plan on one side, and the formation of the Cominform on the other, the United States and the Soviet Union found themselves bitterly opposed in the ensuing cold war lineup, and Japan became aligned with the American side. There was, at that point in Japan's history, perhaps no other choice for her democracy than to become patterned almost exclusively on the American model. The U.S. in return, began taking active measures to promote Japan's economic development and recovery. The Japanese government, having lost both political and economic autonomy, placed top priority on economic development, ignoring the need for change from totalitarian to democratic values. Instead, all resources were concentrated on the cause of economic prosperity. Popular concern for responsibility for the past war diminished. There arose a tendency to emphasize Japan's positive contribution to the eventual independence of the Asian countries, while simultaneously accepting defeat with a kind of fatalism.

In 1949 the Chinese Revolution entered a new phase, control of the mainland having been gained by the Communists. The special procurements for the Korean War, the concomitant peace treaty with the Western bloc, and the subsequent Mutual Security Treaty with the United States all served to establish a well-reinforced system of Japanese-American cooperation in both economic and political realms. Japan became politically dependent on the U.S., and her energies—liberated by the postwar reforms—were funneled exclusively into the task of building economic prosperity.

America gradually began to pressure Japan into becoming a stabilizer in Asia, while paying less attention to her democratization. Reverberations to this tendency were felt in Japan when the government proclaimed in the middle of the fifties that the postwar period was over, and that proclamation was echoed by immediate moves to undo many of the postwar reforms. This "reverse-course" policy was greatly facilitated by improved economic conditions. As Professor Miyata Mitsuo emphasized in his book, *Gendai no minshushugi—seido o tsukuru seishin* [The Intellectual Basis of Modern Democracy], not until people understand democracy in terms of its basic spirit can it become a living system. Japanese society will only move further away from the basis of democracy—the principle of individual dignity—as long as the government continues to use majority rule as a tool to restore group superiority over individual, and with it, the prewar order.

In postwar Japan, democracy and economic progress have been considered almost synonymous, and economic progress has been the sole purpose of government. This kind of government owes its success to a strong popular conviction that economic progress alone is a sufficient goal; as long as the economy is growing, there is the feeling of security. Government, however, should have its own set of goals. The new Constitution guarantees that basic human rights will be protected, that Japan will not rearm, and that she will follow a peaceful course. If these are representative of the most significant change in values from the prewar to the postwar periods, then is it not the essential function of government to constantly question whether the country is in fact pursuing these goals? Such a task goes beyond the typical concerns of the technocrat, and it goes beyond simply deciding the appropriate rate of growth.

From 1955 to 1965 our annual growth rate was above ten percent; our trade balance turned from unfavorable to favorable; in those years our gross national product increased threefold, and now we can boast of having the third largest GNP in the world. We have become an advanced industrial state. Our progress was achieved by advancing full speed ahead toward the old goal of "catching up with and surpassing the West"; this time the slogan was "*fukoku kyōkigyō*" or "Rich country, strong *enterprise*" instead of "strong army." But, just as before the war there lurked in the background poverty-stricken farmers and laborers, today industrial pollution, inadequate welfare facilities, and growing alienation among the people spoil the picture. Japan may be creating a new zone of emptiness.

During the course of making such rapid progress, one-third of Japan's exports have been aimed at Asian markets. Her imports from these countries have always been less, with the result that, excepting Malaysia, Indonesia, and India, Asian countries face an unfavorable trade balance with Japan.

Our country has extended aid, at first in the form of reparations, to the Philippines, Indonesia, Burma and South Vietnam. As compensation for World War II, it is doubtful whether such payments actually constitute aid. Furthermore, although Japan has given outright gifts, technical aid, direct governmental loans and export credit, as well as engaging in private investments, Japanese aid often has strings attached. Much like the aid policies of West Germany, the purpose of the "strings" is to promote the exports of the donor country, Japan.

Most private investments have been directed toward increasing sales, procuring sources of raw materials, gaining access to cheap labor or a combination of these. Obviously our methods of trading and the way we handle investments and aid—there has been a marked increase in all these since 1965—have done much to arouse suspicion in the rest of Asia. As mentioned above, Asians look upon Japan as an advanced country, and as such, a source of aid which will contribute to their own economic development. But, because our aid policy reflects a strong inclination to pursue only our national interest, the recipient countries naturally become suspicious and antagonistic.

GOVERNMENT AND INDIVIDUAL DIGNITY

The prewar and wartime image of Japan's energetic pursuit of *fukoku kyōhei* is still around, and with it, fear that Japan might once more militarily interfere in Asia to protect her economic lifeline. It is with that in mind that the people of Asia are wary of the encroaching "economic animal," and it is to protect themselves that they are determined to establish economic ties with Japan on a more equal basis. To allay these fears, we should immediately make clear that, as written in the Constitution, Japanese troops will never again be sent overseas. We should also prove that we can readjust our economic relations, by showing more active concern for their interests and benefit.

If we view our wartime invasion of these countries as an inevitable result of our prewar economic development, and if we then conclude that our present economic advance into Asia is inevitable because of our need for raw materials and markets, we are making the same disastrous mistake all over again. As Professor Miyata stated, "In order to make our history really meaningful, we must identify the root of the basic evil which drove us on through catastrophic defeat, and which hovers in the background of what once seemed to be the crowning glory of modern Japanese history, and then we must strive to eliminate it completely." Needless to say, I am in complete agreement with Professor Miyata.

This simply means that we must reconsider Japan's national goal apart from *fukoku kyōkigyō,* the postwar version of *fukoku kyōhei,* and direct all our energies towards building a nation in which a rich, full life for all is guaranteed. It is this sort of unpretentious goal that will guard us from another catastrophe. There is no doubt that our pursuit of *"fukoku"* has produced higher individual incomes. If we hope for any improvement in our relationships with the countries of Asia, however, we must create a government that will safeguard the dignity and freedom of each of its citizens, and we must shift the emphasis from economic growth to improvement of the social environment and individual livelihood. On the other hand, if we continue to pour all our energies into *fukoku kyōkigyō* and if our people try to better only their lot, and theirs alone, in the manner of a "loyalty race," our relationships in Asia will inevitably deteriorate.

ASIAN TRENDS AND THE INTERNATIONAL SCENE

The Japanese-American joint statement in the fall of 1969 concerning the reversion of Okinawa to Japan expressed the notion that this country, South Korea and Taiwan share a "common destiny"; the defense of the latter two is of vital interest to Japan's security. It is certain that a statement like this will make things even more difficult for Japan in her dealings with China. Moreover, although Taiwan and South Korea may wish to see an increase in Japan's defense capability (especially in light of the anticipated post-Vietnam withdrawals of U.S. troops from Asia), greater military preparedness would mean troublesome times ahead in Japan's relationship with the Southeast Asian countries. In the final analysis, the so-called common destiny "shared" by Japan, Taiwan and South Korea boils down to a mutual antagonism towards China and North Korea. In commerce and in other respects these partners are rivals, and it should not be forgotten, moreover, that both Taiwan and South Korea view Japan's economic advance with growing suspicion.

How do the five member nations of the Association of Southeast Asian Nations (Thailand, Indonesia, Malaysia, the Philippines and Singapore) view the post-Vietnam Asian scene? Beset internally with the frictions between their Overseas Chinese populations and other groups, as well as the grating presence of antigovernment movements, these countries seem to prefer not to depend too closely on any one great power, but rather on several. At the same time, they will probably seek to strengthen regional cooperation among member states. The "economic animal" variety of anti-Japanese criticism emanates mostly from these five countries, for the following reasons: First, they wish to check the overwhelming flow of Japanese capital into their countries, and secondly, the problem of handling their relationship with an anti-Chinese Japan, in view of the urgency of improving their relations with China, will only become more difficult as Japan moves in. Cambodia and Burma are also working hard to maintain neutrality.

In his book, *War and Peace in South East Asia*, Professor P. Leon writes that while nonalignment does not extend to all parts of Southeast Asia, one can encounter neutralism in almost every country. He believes that neutralism is simply a modified version of nationalism. Seen in the context of an Asia from which the American and British military establishments are retreating while the influence of the Soviet Union, China and Japan is steadily growing, the countries of Southeast Asia will probably be more inclined towards a pluralistic, neutral foreign policy that will guarantee their political independence. Such a trend can be interpreted partly as overt criticism of the pro-American orientation of Japan's foreign policy, and partly as a step towards preventing Japan from exercising monopolistic control over their economies. As has already been mentioned, an upsurge of popular pressure to revise trade, investment and aid relations with Japan is inevitable—it has, in fact, already begun with the cry of "economic animal."

Japan's links with the South Asian countries, as opposed to the Southeast Asian countries, have been growing weaker since the early 1960s when the area became a bone of contention among the U.S.A., the U.S.S.R. and China. One does not, therefore, find the same degree of criticism of Japan in the attitudes of the South Asians as one clearly does among Southeast Asians.

The above observations lead to the conclusion that Taiwan and South Korea probably cannot help but strengthen their political ties with Japan even as they view her economic advance into their territories with suspicion. The countries of Southeast Asia, on the other hand, will attempt to adjust their relations with Japan to accomodate the building of a pluralistic policy towards the big powers. Prince Sihanouk has been quoted as saying that the countries of the West will eventually depart from Asia but China remains there forever. Japan, also, will have to recognize this and understand the feelings and anxieties of the Southeast Asian peoples in order to continue fruitful economic relations with their countries.

To go back to the starting point, my investigation of the sources of the unfriendly nickname, "economic animal," convinced me that, even though the immediate source of the name may be found in the questionable behavior of Japanese businessmen working in these countries, its basic, primary source is in the very manner in which our country achieved economic growth. It is the logic and tradition of a long history that has encouraged these businessmen to behave in a way that is sharply criticized. For that reason I have reviewed the past one hundred years of Japan's development and tried to analyze the ideology that sustained it.

Today, twenty-five years after the war, nothing would be more foolish than to try and deal with Asia from a position of superiority if Japan wants to maintain the trust of those countries which, as Professors Koentjaraningrat and Somsakdi Xuto pointed out, suffered bitterly through the war at the hands of the Japanese military. It is undeniable that the Asian peoples with whom we come in contact are both materially and intellectually behind, thanks to a long period of colonial rule. But rather than exploiting them further for our own economic interests, it would seem both wiser and more logical to try and assist, cooperating with their efforts to transcend and grow out of the legacies of colonialism. I am aware that such thinking immediately draws the criticism that Japan cannot possibly stand up under today's fierce international competition if she engages in this kind of assistance. Be that as it may, I would like to emphasize, as is clear from this review of the past one hundred years of our history, that both the prewar *fukoku kyōhei* and postwar *fukoku kyōkigyō* demand serious reconsideration as to their bearing on Japan's image and future in Asia.

In *Nihonjin no keizai kōdō* (The Economic Behavior of Japanese) edited by Sumiya Mikio, Professor Hirschmeyer of Nanzan University delineates modern Japanese with the following three characterizations:

1. Japan is the first country in the world to have given modernization of the economy the status of a national policy. Leadership under the power élite was strong, using ideology to push development; power became extremely centralized.

2. Aided by high standards of education, the Japanese pursued economic development along lines symbolized by *"wakon yōsai,"* assuming that they need learn only the technical layer of Western knowledge. In the field of ethics, Japan already had a full, ancient system of religion and morals which was considered adequate and appropriate. Rote learning of foreign technology was emphasized with no stress on the implications it held for society, or on the values it embodied.

3. People exhibit a tendency which can be called "society-centeredness" where the individual too easily succumbs to the demands of his group or group leaders, changing his opinion and course of action accordingly. As a result, the whole nation can be easily manipulated by the government.

In the same volume, Professor Ōno Morio states: "Perhaps a special characteristic of Japanese culture is that it does not have another cultural element that is powerful enough to challenge the domination of 'economics.'" Professor Kōno Kenji suggests in the same book, "Japanese are now in a position where they must have recourse to their own internalized system of values, generated from the inside, if they are to face the future successfully." P. Leon, who was quoted earlier, has pointed out the contrast between the deep cultural influences that both China and India impressed upon Asia, and Japanese influence, which has been almost entirely commercial or military. Superficially, this statement indicates the need for a wide variety of cultural exchanges, but more significantly, it is stating in another way the basic need for a new ethical approach to trade and to our economic behavior in Southeast Asia. That, in short, is the reason that economic development undertaken by Japan over the last century must be thoroughly reappraised and more deeply understood.

Japan's alternatives are to continue in the tradition of *fukoku kyōhei* as an "economic animal," or to discover a new course for the future through a reexamination of history from the Meiji Restoration and a renewed effort to understand the interests of other Asian nations. The former would have the logical outcome of Japanese control over the other

Asian economies with Japanese detachment from the values and ethics of Asia. The latter would place Japan *within* Asia, both economically and spiritually; and it would mean exerting every effort to cooperate as a member of the Asian community of nations.

I hope that the discussion on "economic animal" will continue and deepen, and that with it, our country will see the beginning of real effort directed towards building a society based on human dignity and happiness. I hope that we may rise above the label "economic animal" to become a more human part of world society.